THE
ILLUSTRATED
NETWORK BOOK

TRADEMARKS

To the only person who is able to combine intelligence, patience, and beauty into one.
This book is dedicated to my wife, Regina.

TABLE OF CONTENTS

FOREWORD

This book represents a new form for my technical books. Although technical books do a great job of translating network standards into human terms, the fact remains that most technical books are very dry to read (yes, Jack, even my previous two). Most people in technical fields today do many jobs and do not have the time to sit down and read a book from cover to cover. They tend to pick up a book, read it for ten minutes, then put it down. I believe that a technical book should flow like a textbook, but be formatted to fit the realities of the workplace.

In this book, each topic is covered in two pages. The left page contains text and the right page contains a graphical representation of that text page. Below the illustration is a bullet list of the key points from the text. This allows you to read the book in many different ways. If you are familiar with a subject, the right page will suffice. If you are not, the left page will detail the right page (the slide page). The book reads as a textbook, but it is formatted like a reference.

Packaged in the back of the book is a disk that contains all the illustrations. Making the illustrations available provides you with the capability of custom tailoring the illustrations to meet your needs. The illustrations can be formatted to produce slides for seminars, training classes, etc. The illustrations can be used to produce an automatic slide show. The illustrations on the disk are produced in black and white. Color can be easily added to the illustrations.

The illustrations were produced using Microsoft PowerPoint 3.0 for Windows 3.1. There are a lot of presentation programs available today but PowerPoint is an easy to use presentation package. If you do not have PowerPoint the files should be able to be converted to another presentation package. There is a Readme file on the diskette to assist you in using my illustrations with Microsoft PowerPoint. A disk containing all the illustrations is available for the Macintosh version of PowerPoint for a small administrative charge. Simply fill out the card in the back of this book and I will send the disk to you via regular mail. Also, it should be noted that the software licensing of the disk allows only the purchaser of this book to utilize the files that are on it.

The main purpose of this book is to provide easy to read detailed information about networks. The information in this book was compiled from the specifications and books listed in the bibliography. Networks are complex, but learning about them is not difficult if the information is presented in a user-friendly format.

Finally, I gratefully acknowledge the assistance of three people in putting this book together:

Jack Maxfield, senior systems engineer for Wellfleet Communications in Atlanta, GA
Brad Black, director of the internet for Duke Power in Charlotte, NC
Chuck Robbins (that's R-O-BB-INS), account manager for Wellfleet Communications in Greensboro, NC

I know that it is hard to review an unfinished manuscript and I appreciate the work that they did. Many of the edits that they provided are incorporated into this book. Nice job, guys.

I would also like to thank my editor, at Van Nostrand Reinhold, Neil Levine. Neil was very patient as I struggled to get this book done. He always offered positive advice and kept telling me to hang in there. Thanks, buddy!

It is my hope that every reader enjoys the book. It was a lot of fun to write and should provide useful information to the reader.

MATTHEW G. NAUGLE

THE PHYSICAL LAYER FOR ETHERNET, TOKEN RING, AND FDDI

DEFINITION

There are many ways to define networks. They serve an important function for nearly every aspect of business. They allow devices to exchange data. They allow different types of computers to communicate with one another even if the communicating devices are geographically separated. They allow users to log in to hosts even if there is not a direct connection between every terminal and every host. They allow effortless user-to-user communication locally and by remote.

Networks allow multiple users to share one or more devices. For example, a single physical attachment to the LAN allows multiple users access to one host. Peripheral devices such as hard disks, modems, terminals, and printers can be shared on a network. File servers can allow many users to share one or more hard disks; this can save individual hard disk space as application software can be loaded on one shared disk rather than on every user's workstation. Information between users can be shared in seconds, whereas it used to take days or even weeks to retrieve data information from remote sources. Although the price of modems has decreased dramatically, they are still relatively expensive when you buy one for each user. Individual-user modems are rarely utilized more than 10% of a business day. Networks allow modems to be shared thus allowing better efficiency of a modem.

Though networks do many things, perhaps the best definition is that they permit information and peripherals to be shared efficiently and economically.

Definition

Through a combination of hardware and software, networks
permit information and peripherals to be shared efficiently and economically.

• Networks allow geographically distant computing devices to communicate with one another.

• They allow effortless user-to-user communication locally or remotely.

• They allow multiple users to share one or more devices.

• They allow users to share peripheral devices such as hard drives.

History

During the early years, computers had a centralized type of configuration. Mainframe or mini computers were located in a central location and operated by specially trained individuals in an environmentally controlled room. All peripheral devices were also located in this room and users were at the mercy of the operators for modem access, printouts, hard disk storage, backup, and tape retrieval. All access to the computer was by individual lines that were run, one per attachment, directly to the host computer.

Around 1981, personal computers arrived in the commercial marketplace. These machines were simple devices by today's standards. They had low-density floppy disk drives (160 kb[1], single-sided floppies), ran on a 4.77 MHz 8088 (although Compaq computers used 8086 CPUs), 640 kb of RAM, monochrome monitors, and so forth. Even though these machines were limited, they had many advantages. They brought the application power of a mainframe to the user's desktop. Applications could be run individually and the user's data was controlled by the user, not by a computer operator. Access to the mainframe was provided by terminal emulation applications that ran on the personal computer. However, users could not easily share data between users. Peripheral devices were not shared, and users could not send electronic messages to one another.

Luckily, about the time that personal computers were introduced, the network arrived in the commercial marketplace. The first standardized, commercially available network is known as Ethernet, and this type of network allows users to connect their PCs or terminals to one cable plant; with special hardware and software other peripheral devices were able to be shared as well.

This allowed electronic mail, shared data, file transfers, and more. The personal computer combined with the network allowed users to regain the advantages of a mainframe, and maintain the advantages of a PC. This was only the beginning of bigger and better things to come.

---

[1] kilobyte or 1000 bytes.

History

- Early years of computing:
  - provided electronic mail (e-mail), word processing, database, and simple messaging.
  - allowed users to share data.
- Personal Computers (PCs):
  - brought mainframe applications to the desktop.
  - gained terminal emulation, word processing, and database applications.
  - could not share data, or send and receive e-mail.
  - one printer, modem per PC (very expensive).
- Networks:
  - have the capabilities of the mainframe distributed among PCs.

• Early computers had centralized configurations, with computers and peripheral devices located in one room.

• Terminal-to-host connection was point-to-point.

• Around 1981, the personal computer arrived in the commercial marketplace, bringing the application power of the mainframe to the desktop.

• The network was also introduced commercially around 1981.

• The first commercial network was known as Ethernet; it allowed the interconnection of PCs and hosts.

• Users regained the advantages of mainframe computing.

HOST-TO-TERMINAL CONNECTIONS

Early computers had many advantages as well as disadvantages. Multiple users on one computer allowed for shared file access, electronic messaging (E-mail), and equal access to the associated peripheral devices. The computer itself was managed in one or more rooms and all external access to this machine could be controlled from there.

However, the cost of running individual cables between the user terminals and the computer room equipment was high. Also, the cost of maintaining a centralized computer was high and beyond the reach of many businesses. Also, if the mainframe went down, all attached users and devices went down with it.

User interfaces to the computer were dumb terminals; that is, they possessed only enough intelligence for minor word processing functions such as bold, underline, blinking, and so on. If the user wanted multiple host connections, there was very little choice. A new connection (cable) could be run or a modem could be used. Those businesses that had the money and resources could purchase a special switch that would allow access to multiple mainframes with complete user control. This device was not inexpensive.

The centralized computing environment was effective for its time, but user demands were growing and the only alternative was to build faster and larger mainframes.

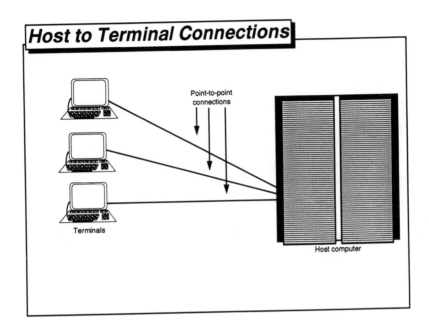

- Advantages included multiple users on one computer who could share data and peripheral equipment.

- The cost of running individual cables between user terminals and the mainframe was very high.

- The mainframe was a single point of failure and the users' terminals were simplistic.

- Multi-host connectivity was limited.

- User demands were growing and the only alternative was to build larger and more expensive mainframes.

THE PERSONAL COMPUTER

Although it was not the first personal computer developed, in 1981, IBM introduced its version of the personal computer. Developed in one year and not expected to expand beyond limited business use, the IBM PC hit the business marketplace like a typhoon. IBM enlisted a small unknown company called Microsoft to port a version of an operating system that was written for the Intel 8088 processor to the IBM PC. During its introduction it did not enter the typical home marketplace. There were very few applications written for it and one of the first was terminal emulation for connectivity back to the mainframe. For IBM mainframe connectivity, IBM introduced a special version of the PC known as the 3270 PC which allowed 3270 terminal emulation for connection back to the IBM mainframe

The first electronic spreadsheet ported to the IBM PC was called VisiCalc; it later became Lotus 1-2-3. Eventually, more business applications were written and the IBM PC became entrenched in the business world. IBM even built this PC as an open architecture complete with hardware schematics and software firmware listings.

The personal computer gave the user a lot of freedom. In effect, a PC brought the mainframe applications to the user's desktop. It eliminated some of the major disadvantages of the centralized computer. The IBM PC was able to operate at room temperature allowing them to be placed throughout the office, thereby alleviating the need for the expensive computer rooms, high cable costs, and so forth.

PCs allowed users control over their computer environment, but stand–alone computers brought many disadvantages. A user could not share files simultaneously with another user. Printers and other shared devices were no longer available.

Some terminal emulation programs had file transfer capabilities with their mainframes. But this was still not the peer–to–peer connectivity that the users used to have with mainframes and mini computers. One of the more popular programs was called KERMIT used on Digital Equipment Corporation mini computers. KERMIT ran on the personal computer and allowed for VT emulation along with file transfer capabilities between the mini computer and the PC.

For PC-to-PC file transfer, users had to copy their work onto diskettes. The diskettes would then be walked over to others for use in their PCs. For distant sites, the diskettes would be mailed. This was affectionately known as "sneakernet."

The Personal Computer

• Advantages

    PCs bring mainframe applications to the desktop.

    Programs provide for terminal emulation to connect back to the mainframe.

    PCs are able to operate without the environmentally controlled computer rooms.

    Users control their own computers and choose their own software programs.

• Disadvantages

    No electronic mail.

    No multi-user capabilities.

    Limited peripheral access.

    Very expensive single entity solution.

    Data interchange known as sneakernet.

PC LAN with Host Connection

The following illustration shows the advantages of personal computers, host computers and LANs. It shows that PCs can access other PCs or they may access the host computer all through the LAN. A workstation can communicate with a file server while another can communicate back to the main-frame. In any case, any computer may communicate with any other computer on the LAN.

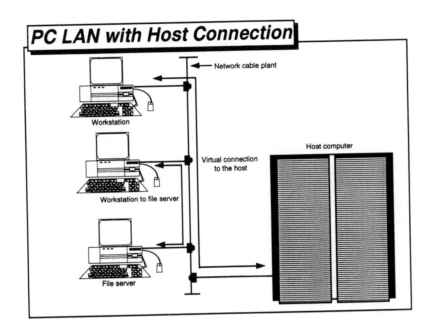

- The advantages of a PC LAN with a host connection are:

    Connectivity back to the mainframe or mini computers.

    In the beginning most devices were attached using terminal servers that allow existing terminals access to the LAN.

    Lower cable costs.

    — Individual cable runs for each terminal were eliminated.

    — The LAN incorporates the use of a cable plant, which allows for use of smaller cable runs between the network device and the main LAN.

    Multi-user communities are easily formed.

    Allows for direct communication to exist between any two devices attached to the LAN cable plant.

THE INTERNATIONAL ORGANIZATION FOR STANDARDIZATION (ISO) AND THE OPEN SYSTEMS INTERCONNECTION MODEL (OSI)

Based in Geneva, Switzerland, the International Organization for Standardization (ISO) is an independent organization that is involved in the generation of worldwide standards. The ISO operates by coordinating the efforts of other standards bodies such as the American National Standards Institute (ANSI) and the British Standards Institution (BSI).

The recommendations by ISO on Open Systems Interconnection (OSI) have a tremendous impact in the information marketplace. The goal of OSI standards is to enable sharing and exchange of information in a multivendor computer and networking environment.

The OSI model is a seven-layer model that was published in 1974. Each layer performs a different function. When applied to networks, all the layers taken as a whole constitute the individual pieces needed to construct a network, whether it is a Local Area Network (LAN) or a Wide Area Network (WAN) or any combination of the two. This model defines the international standard by which an open system should be able to communicate with another open system and also sets the rules for how the standards are to be implemented.

The model will be shown in a moment, but it should be noted that each of the layers are completely independent of one another, yet each of the OSI's layers provide services to the layers adjacent to it. For example, the data link layer provides services to the physical and network layers yet operates independent of them. The layers are independent in the sense that a change in one of the layers does not directly affect the operation of a layer directly adjacent to it. For the layer that is changed, the replacement for that layer must still follow the rules provided for it in that layer. For example, if the data link layer is changed, this should have no regard to the functions of the network or physical layers.

OSI Model

- Developed by the International Organization for Standardization in 1974 as a model for data communications system.

- It consists of seven layers.

- Each layer has a different but specific processing function.

- The whole model constitutes the individual pieces needed to construct a network.

- Each layer provides functions for the layer directly adjacent to it.

- Modules (layers) may be replaced with one of equal type (that is, transport layer may not be replaced with the network layer).

- Being familiar with the OSI model allows for a more complete understanding of a network.

OSI MODEL LAYERS

Application Layer   This layer allows applications to reside as network applications. These applications must be written specifically as network applications such as a file transfer program or a remote terminal emulation program. A stand-alone application that runs on a network is not considered part of the application layer

Presentation Layer   This layer provides for data formatting into the standard codes of American Standard Code for Information Interchange (ASCII) or EBCDIC (Extended Binary Coded Decimal Interchange Code). This layer also allows for data encryption techniques to be employed

Session Layer   This layer allows sessions to be established between two communicating stations. This layer also controls the dialogue between two communicating stations and can end sessions. Network name to network address translation techniques are performed at this layer. When a connection is set up with another network station, human usable names are often used for establishment of that session. These names are never used by the network. Instead, a name will be translated to a network address and then a connection will be attempted. Once a connection is established, the network address will always be used.

Transport Layer   This layer provides for end-to-end reliable or unreliable transmission of data between two communicating stations. It allows data to be reliably transferred between the source and destination station by a sequence mechanism that guarantees data to be delivered by tagging the data with a number that must be acknowledged by the receiver of the data. On the other hand, this layer can also act as transport for those applications that do not need a reliable transport, such as messaging and network management.

Network Layer   This layer allows for data to traverse the same or different networks through a mechanism known as *routing*. Network addresses are assigned similar to the way area codes are assigned in the phone system, indicating a grouping of network stations. There will be different "area codes" for different regions of the network and devices known as *routers* enable data to be transferred to these regions

Data Link Layer   This layer allows for the transfer of units of information known as *packets*. This layer also provides for data framing and error detection in the packets.

Physical Layer   This layer allows the transfer of raw data known as the binary transmission of data across a medium. Included in this layer are the wiring schemes and connectors used.

OSI Model Layers

OSI layer	Function provided
Application	Network applications such as file transfer and terminal emulation
Presentation	Data formatting and encryption
Session	Establishment and maintenance of sessions
Transport	Provision for end-to-end reliable and unreliable delivery
Network	Delivery of packets of information, which includes routing
Data Link	Transfer of units of information, framing, and error checking
Physical	Transmission of binary data of a medium

TOPOLOGIES

Topology is actually a 100-year-old branch of mathematics. A topology is the physical configuration of a network. The term is used to describe a network layout.

A topology is the architectural "drawing" of a network that shows the overall structure of a given communications system. Topologies are important to a network as, not only do they describe a network, a topology can easily describe a particular type of network. This drawing should show a company's layout of their network. Generally, this will not include such items such as PCs or printers, but it will show the access method (Ethernet, Token Ring, and so on) and specific names and network addresses that are used to identify parts of the network.

There are four main types of network topologies: star, ring, bus, and tree.

Topologies

- Topologies are the architectural "drawings" that show the overall physical configuration for a given communications system.

- A topology will indicate the access methods and will govern the rules that are used to design and implement the communications system.

- Topologies represent the drawing of your network cable plant.

- There are four main types of network topology: star, ring, bus, and tree.

STAR TOPOLOGY

The star topology is probably the oldest topology used for communications. It was first used with the telephone system.

In the star topology, all stations are attached by cable to a common point, usually a wiring hub. Since the network stations are on a point-to-point link with the central wiring hub, the cost may be higher than for other topologies. There are many different types of cable used in this topology.

The advantage of the star topology is that there is no cabling single point of failure that could effect the whole network, which allows for better network management of the network. If one of the cables should develop a problem, only the station that is attached to it is affected; all other stations remain operational.

The one disadvantage to this topology is its central hub, which can be a single point of failure—if the hub becomes disabled, any attachment to the hub becomes disabled. Hubs (or their more common name, *concentrators*) have become fault resilient with the advent of such things as multiple power supplies and multiple backplanes that will allow only certain components to become inoperable in the event of a failure.

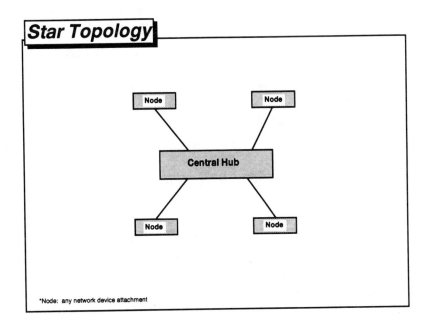

*Node: any network device attachment

- It is probably the oldest topology used in communications.

- It was first used with the PBX and DPBX telephone switches.

- It consists of a centralized hub with all stations connecting to it.

- No single point of failure that would affect the whole network.
    The one exception is the hub. The hubs are usually fault-resilient with dual power supplies, multiple backplanes, redundant controller cards, and so forth.

- The star topology allows for better network management.

- The star topology is the most popular type of topology for all networks.

RING TOPOLOGY

In the ring topology all stations are considered repeaters and are enclosed in a loop. There are no endpoints to this cable topology. The repeater, for our purposes, is the controller board in the station that is attached to the LAN.

Each station will receive a transmission on one end of the repeater and repeat the transmission, bit by bit with no buffering, on the other end of the repeater. Data is transmitted in one direction only and is received by the next repeater in the loop. The transmissions from the stations can be received by any station attached to the same cable; this is called a broadcast medium.

Since each controller in a network station is a repeater, each station repeats any signal that is on the network whether or not the signal is destined for that particular station. This could have a disastrous effect on the ring. If for any reason a repeater should break and quit repeating, this could bring the whole network down. Although the chances of this occurring are slim, the possibility does exist. The controller is capable of handling this problem and the defective repeater may pull itself off the ring allowing the ring to stabilize and continue to run.

The LAN that best represents the ring topology is the Token Ring. Although a Token Ring network is physically cabled as a star topology, a Token Ring LAN is logically a ring topology. Its commonly referred as a star-wired ring. A further example of this topology will be presented in chapter 3.

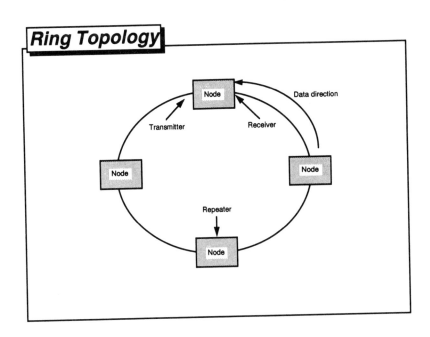

- All stations are considered repeaters and are enclosed in a loop.

- Each active attachment receives the signal at one end of the repeater and repeats it on the other side to its "downstream" neighbor.

- Data is transmitted in one direction only.

- There may be a single point of failure in that one station could quit repeating.
  There are usually management processes invoked in the attachment that are able to dynamically remove a station that has quit repeating allowing the ring to return to an operational state.

- A ring topology usually has a centralized control mechanism for cable access.

BUS TOPOLOGY

The bus topology is sometimes known as the linear-bus topology. It is a simple design that uses a single length of cable (also known as the *medium*) with network stations attached to it. All stations share this single cable. The transmissions from the stations can be received by any station attached to the same cable; this is called a broadcast medium. There are definite endpoints to the cable segment which are commonly known as terminating points.

Given the simplicity of this topology, the cost of implementing it is usually low. The single cable configuration can lead to a major problem, however: the single point of failure. If the single cable breaks, no station will have the ability to transmit. Although the cable is a passive device, anything as simple as a cut in the cable will cause the network to become inoperative.

If this type of cable is used, the LAN that best represents this topology is an Ethernet network. Ethernet has the ability to incorporate many different types of cable schemes, as will be shown later.

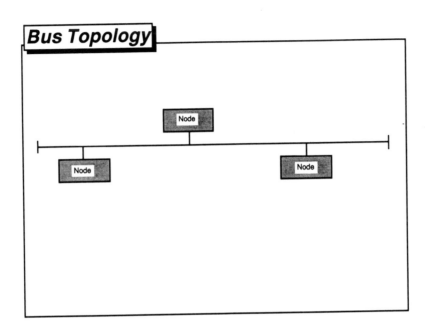

- The bus topology is also known as the linear bus topology.

- It uses a single length of cable with all stations attached to it.

- All stations share this single cable.

- The network is terminated at its endpoints (not a closed loop).

- A break on the single cable will bring down all attachments on the network.

- The bus topology is most commonly used for Ethernet networks.

TREE TOPOLOGY

The tree topology is a generalization of the bus topology. The cable plant is known as a *branching tree*, and all stations attach to it. The tree topology has a pinnacle point known as the *root*. This where the tree begins. From here, the tree branches in many different directions from the root. Its branches extend to the endpoints of a network. This allows a network to dynamically expand but there will only be one active data path between any two points in the network.

The network that best represents the tree topology is one that does not employ loops in its topology. An example of this is the Spanning Tree Algorithm for Ethernet networks. This algorithm disables loops in an otherwise looped topology and it expands throughout a network to ensure that only one active data path exists between any two communicating stations. The Spanning Tree Algorithm will be shown further in Part 3 of this book.

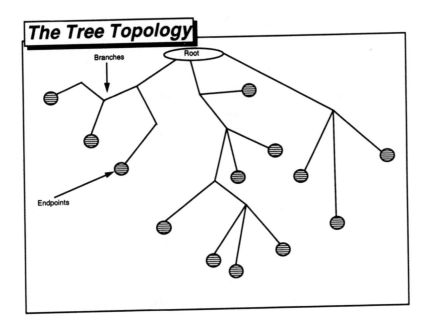

The Tree Topology

Branches

Root

Endpoints

- The tree topology is a generalization of the bus topology.

- It contains a point known as the root, from which all branches stem.

- It provides a single data path to any endpoint on the network.

- It is used in bridging and routing algorithms (explained in Part 3).

ETHERNET WIRING—WIRING SUMMARY

Thick Coaxial

When the Ethernet network was first introduced in 1980 as a standardized commercial network product, the cabling scheme required bus cable known as *thick coaxial cable*. This cable is similar to a commercially available cable known as RG-8 but is used with Ethernet networks only. It was specially manufactured and therefore very expensive, also it was hard to work with and required special tools for station attachment But it did allow for a tremendous cable length to be achieved without having to repeat the original signal (500 meters). It also provided two layers of shielding so that it could be used in any type environment (factory, office building, etc.).

Thin Coaxial

About five years later, Ethernet's cabling scheme was revised. Over the years, it was found that thick Ethernet cable was "over built," making it difficult to work with and to implement for most Ethernet applications. The new cable is called *thin coaxial cable*. Thin coaxial cable uses a common commercially available cable type (RG-58 A/U). It is easier to work with, costs less, and is shielded adequately for more installations. From 1985 to 1990, thin coaxial cable was the most common type of cable system found in the commercial marketplace. In small networks (two to ten stations) thin coaxial cable is still the most common cabling scheme used. Placing a station onto the cable was reduced from around five minutes to about one. Cable installation was also easier.

Unshielded Twisted Pair (UTP)

The bus topology has many restrictions and soon the technology advanced and the cost of certain components was reduced so that common household telephone wire could be easily adapted to use as Ethernet cable. This cable is very inexpensive as it has been manufactured for the telephone companies for decades. The Ethernet controllers were rebuilt so that they could handle the inefficiencies of this type of cable. Unlike the bus topology, UTP also allows for a star wired cabling system which allows network management down to a single workstation. Today, this is the most common cabling scheme used for Ethernet networks.

Fiber

Fiber cable is used in Ethernet systems, but since it has not yet been standardized by any committee, it will not be discussed here.

Ethernet Wiring - Wiring Summary

- There are four main types of wiring systems for Ethernet:

  - Thick coaxial cable

  - Thin coaxial cable

  - Unshielded Twisted Pair (UTP)

  - Fiber

- All may be used as one or intermixed on an Ethernet network.

- Thick Ethernet cable:
  is a specially manufactured cable to be used only in certain Ethernet environments.
  is a very expensive cable.
  provides many layers of shielding.

- Thin Ethernet cable:
  was designed in 1984 as an alternative to thick Ethernet cable.
  provides a simplification of the Ethernet cabling scheme.
  uses a commonly manufactured cable type.
  reduced installation time from about five minutes to around one minute.
  eliminated or moved certain thick coaxial components, which reduced the cost of the cabling.
  introduced new connectors.

- Unshielded Twisted Pair (UTP) cable:
  provided an alternative, easy to use, less expensive cable type for Ethernet networks.
  used common telephone wire.
  implements the star topology on Ethernet, which allows for better network management.
  introduced a new component called the *concentrator* which allows for network cabling to be collapsed into
      one entity.

- Fiber is used for Ethernet in proprietary systems. It is not standardized.

ETHERNET CABLE NAMES

Over the years, Ethernet has changed its cabling schemes to make it easier to use and manage and to make it more cost effective. Unfortunately, each type of cable took on more than one name. The chart on the following page summarizes the four Ethernet cable types. It has the following format:

- The first row contains the most commonly used name of a particular wire type.

- The second row, wire type, identifies the type of wire in the cable. If the cable was given an official name by the cable manufacturer, then it is stated. In the case of Unshielded Twisted Pair wire, this row identifies the diameter of the wire.

- IEEE name—<Speed of the network><Signal type used><Longest unrepeated cable segment x 100 meters>. It represents a kind of shorthand explanation for some of the characteristics of the cable type. The name 10BASE5, for instance is a cable with a 10 megabit per second transmission rate and baseband signaling (as opposed to broadband) that is 500 meters long (5 x 100 meters). 10BASET is the IEEE name for Unshielded Twisted Pair (UTP) and the T stands for twisted pair. The longest cable length is 100 meters.

- IEEE standard number—represents the standard or an addendum to the standard for a particular cable type. For example, the IEEE 802.3i represents an addendum to the original IEEE 802.3 standard to include UTP wire for Ethernet.

- "Other names" are names that are associated with a cable type but are not often used.

Ethernet Cable Names

Name	Thick coaxial	Thin coaxial	Unshielded Twisted Pair	Fiber
Wire Type	RG-8	RG-58	22 - 26 AWG	62.5/125 micron
IEEE Name	10BASE5	10BASE2	10BASET	10BASEF
Standard Number	IEEE 802.3	IEEE 802.3a	IEEE 802.3i	N/A
Other names	Thick net	Thin net	UTP	

- When Ethernet cable types changed so did the names.

- "Wire type" identifies the manufacturer's name for the cable.

- "IEEE name" represents a kind of shorthand:
  <Speed><Signal type><Longest cable segment without repeating>
  Example: 10BASE5.
  — This means that the cable has a 10 Megabit per second signal speed, a baseband signal, and can run for 500 meters.

- "Standard number" is the IEEE document specification or revision number.
  IEEE 802.3 is the official document specification number from the IEEE
  — The alpha number represents the revision or addition specification number to the original specification.

- "Other names" are those names that are not commonly heard but are still used.

THICK COAXIAL MAKEUP

Thick coaxial cable is made up of many layers. The *center conductor* is the innermost wire which carries the signals; it is a tin-plated solid copper wire (as opposed to a braided copper wire). Surrounding this conductor is a special foam covering, which in turn is surrounded by a foil shield.

Covering these pieces is the electromagnetic shielding. It consists of a thin braided shield, a foil, then a thick braided shield, and is used to shield the center conductor from outside electrical elements. Thick coaxial cable was built to withstand brutal punishment. It can be used indoors or out, and resists almost any type of electromagnetic interference (EMI).

A common example of EMI occurs when the television is turned on and you run the vacuum beside it; the picture fills with snow. The vacuum's electrical emanations are received by the television's antennae and amplified to the screen. Imagine what the data signal would look like if these same emanations were able to invade the Ethernet cable. This is part of the reason for all the shielding of thick Ethernet cable.

The outside layer of thick coaxial cable is polyvinyl chloride (PVC, a plastic) that is usually colored yellow (although not always). A special type of outside coating known as Teflon is used for fire code regulations. The reason behind this is: When PVC burns it emits a toxic smoke. Therefore, where PVC cannot be concealed within a conduit, Teflon cable must be used. This is true for all wire types. Teflon cable is very rigid and usually has brown covering.

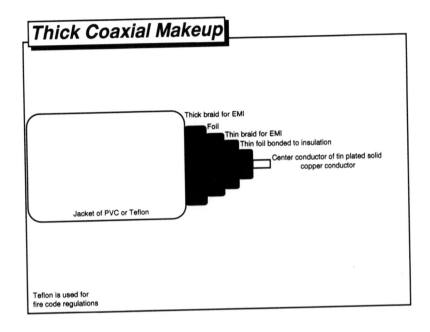

Thick Coaxial Makeup

Thick braid for EMI

Foil

Thin braid for EMI

Thin foil bonded to insulation

Center conductor of tin plated solid
copper conductor

Jacket of PVC or Teflon

Teflon is used for
fire code regulations

- Thick coaxial cable is made up of many different layers:
    Outside coating is polyvinyl chloride (PVC) and is usually yellow in color.
        — Different colors can be used in multiple Ethernet cable run installations.
        — Each color can be used to represent a different run that may have different attachments to it.
    After the PVC jacket are three layers of electrostatic shielding.
    Below the electro-static shielding is a foam that is covered by a foil.
    The center conductor carries the signals.

THICK COAXIAL CONNECTION

There are many components on a thick coaxial connection:

- The Ethernet controller card

- The external transceiver

- The transceiver cable

- The thick coaxial cable

The Ethernet controller card is an interface card also known as the network interface controller (NIC). The controller card is the component that takes information from a computer and transforms it to a format the Ethernet system can transmit or receive. It is usually found internally on a computer.

Transceivers couple the bus cable plant to the controller (explained later). Because of the cable design and the component density of the controller card, transceivers are external on thick coaxial cable plants. Every 2.5 meters there will be a black mark on the thick coaxial cable which indicates the proper placement for a transceiver. At each of the black marks the thick coaxial cable is cored with a special tool (a hand coring tool). Part of the transceiver (known as the clamp) is placed on the coaxial cable, and you place the drill in the opening of this clamp and core out the cable, drilling through all the shielding and foam to expose a pin hole to the center conductor. The transceiver is then placed onto the clamp with the thick coaxial cable between the clamp and transceiver. A pin located on the transceiver is inserted into the precut pin hole, providing a electrical contact for signals to travel off the cable plant and to the controller. This procedure is nonintrusive may be accomplished while the coaxial cable plant is being used.

To connect a controller card to the thick coaxial cable plant, a transceiver cable must be placed between the controller card and transceiver. This cable carries signals to and from the controller card and to and from the transceiver and may be no longer than 50 meters (165 feet). The connector is a female connector on the controller and a male connector on the transceiver cable itself. The connector that attaches to the controller is known by many names. It can be called a DB-15, a DIX, or an AUI connector. *DB-15* represents the physical attributes of the connector. It is a D-shaped connector shell with 15 pins. *DIX* comes from the initials of the three companies that collaborated on standardizing Ethernet: Digital Equipment Corporation, Xerox (which originated Ethernet), and Intel. *AUI* stands for Attachment Unit Interface, which comes from the IEEE which defines the AUI as the interface between the controller and the coaxial cable plant.

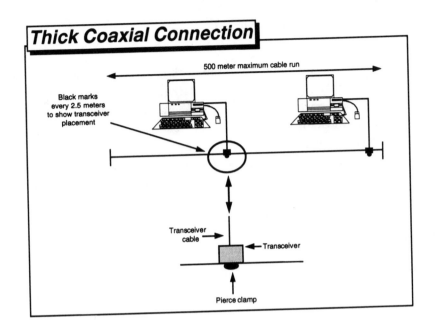

Thick Coaxial Connection

500 meter maximum cable run

Black marks
every 2.5 meters
to show transceiver
placement

Transceiver
cable

Transceiver

Pierce clamp

• Components are:

    The Ethernet controller card.

        — This allows information to flow between the network attachment and the network bus cable.

    The external transceiver.

        — This couples the bus cable plant to the controller.

    A transceiver cable.

        — This is placed between the controller and the transceiver.

    The thick coaxial cable.

        — This is used as the bus medium.

• Thick coaxial cable uses special coaxial cable (similar to RG–8) as the bus cable.

• It must use a special tool to core the coaxial cable for transceiver placement.

• The transceiver cable attaches to the controller and the coaxial cable plant.

• The connector on the Ethernet controller card and the external transceiver is known as the DB-15, DIX, or AUI connector.

THICK COAXIAL CONNECTION (CONT.)

Again, the Ethernet controller is connected to the thick coaxial cable plant through the use of a transceiver and transceiver cable. This cable may be attached to the controller card with a slide lock attachment or a positive lock attachment. The slide lock attachment is located on the controller card and the transceiver end of the transceiver cable. This slide surrounds the connector. The transceiver cable is placed onto the controller and the slide lock bar is moved to lock the cable to the controller card. The transceiver end of the transceiver cable attaches to the transceiver and the lock bar slides to lock the cable to the transceiver. This locks the cable to its attachments. Not very effective, but it works. It has a tendency to fall off. The positive attachment uses screws in place of the slide lock. The provides for a more secure attachment. Care must be used when ordering, for most thick coaxial connections use the slide lock.

There may be no more than 100 attachments to a single segment of thick coaxial cable and a single segment may be no more than 500 meters long. A network attachment is any device that has the capability to attach to the cable plant. As mentioned before, there are black marks on the coaxial cable every 2.5 meters. The Ethernet standard states that Ethernet controllers may be attached anywhere on the 500-meter cable but no closer together than 2.5 meters; 100 attachments times 2.5 meters adds up to only 250 meters. This still leaves 250 meters that may be used for Ethernet controller attachment. If there are more attachments than specified, they may cause unwanted distortions on the cable plant, which other transceivers may perceive incorrectly as an error. The method for allowing more attachments to this cable is explained under the repeater section.

The bus topology requires that at each end of the coaxial cable segment a component known as the terminator be placed. This is a 50 ohm terminator that allows for 50 ohm impedance to be maintained on the cable plant. Even if coaxial cables are concatenated together through the use of a repeater (explained later in the book), each cable segment must have two terminators, one on each end of each cable segment.

Thick coaxial cable is very expensive, hard to attach to, and hard to work with. With very few exceptions, this type of cable is used only for backbone and factory implementations. It is not used for simple office connections.

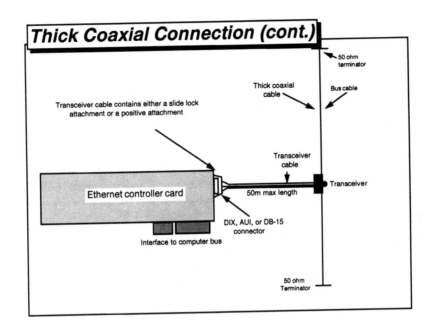

- The transceiver cable attaches directly to the DB-15 connector on the controller and the other end of the transceiver cable attaches to the DB-15 connector on the transceiver.

- To ensure a good connection there is a slide lock or a positive attachment connection:
  Positive attachment connector contains two screws that are screwed into the controller card.
  Slide lock attachment contains a bar that slides over set screw post to lock the cable to the controller.
  The transceiver attachment usually has the slide lock type of connector.

- Each end of the bus cable must be terminated by a 50 ohm terminator.

- The longest bus coaxial segment may run no longer than 500 meters.

- A bus cable segment may have up to 100 attachments.

- Attachments on the bus cable must be a least 2.5 meters apart.

- Thick coaxial cable is usually used as a backbone cable or in factory installations for its long length and shielding capacities.

TRANSCEIVERS

In order to transmit or receive on an Ethernet cable plant, a transceiver must be used. Transceivers (transmitter/receiver) couple the Ethernet controller to the cable plant and provide the controller with a means of transmitting and receiving signals on the cable plant. The transceiver also detects errors on the cable plant and notifies the Ethernet controller of an error so that the Ethernet controller may take the appropriate action. All Ethernet cabling schemes use transceivers.

Only on thick coaxial cable plants will the transceiver be external to the controller card. All other cable implementations place the transceiver on the Ethernet controller card. At the time of Ethernet's introduction there was not an inexpensive and efficient method to attach the thick coaxial cable directly to the controller card; thick coaxial cable ran through an office building and the transceiver cable ran from the host computer to the transceiver, which was directly attached to the thick coaxial cable plant.

Most external transceivers have light emitting diode (LED) status indicators on them to indicate certain conditions. These show:

- Power: Indicates if the transceiver is receiving power from the controller.

- Data Transmission: Data transmission has been detected on the cable plant

- Collision: Two stations have transmitted on the cable plant at the same time (an error condition)

- SQE: A signal condition that is used to tell the Ethernet controller the status of the transceiver.

With external transceivers being placed outside the Ethernet controller, the controller had no way of telling if the transceiver was operating. With the latest IEEE revision of the transceiver, the Signal Quality Error (SQE, also known as the heartbeat signal) was implemented (only for external transceivers). The SQE signal is transmitted from the transceiver to the controller upon the end of every transmission to indicate to the Ethernet controller that the transceiver is operational. Not all Ethernet controllers understand this signal; the ones that don't will log every one of their transmissions as an error. If excessive errors are being logged, turn off the SQE on the transceiver .

The transceiver is also responsible for terminating a transmission when the controller has transmitted beyond a specified length of time (150 ms or more). This is known as a *babble error,* and it eliminates one transceiver from constantly tying up the network.

Transceivers

- Transmitter/Receiver

- Used on all Ethernet networks and is the device that allows data to flow between the controller card and the network.

- Detects errors on the bus cable plant and reports them to the station's controller card.

- For thick coaxial cable, the transceiver is external to the controller card and attaches directly to the thick coaxial cable via a special cable known as the transceiver cable.

- External transceivers have a SQE function that enables the controller to determine the status of the transceiver.

- Transceivers ensure that the data is transmitted not longer than a specified time period.

- Usually has status indicators (LEDs) physically located on it to indicate the state of the transceiver (transmitting, receiving, collision, and power.)

THIN COAXIAL CABLE MAKEUP

After the introduction of Ethernet, it was quickly learned that the thick coaxial cable was "overdone," which made it hard to work with and very expensive. If the idea of Ethernet LANs was to succeed, the cable plant had to be revised. The cabling makeup changed with the introduction of thin coaxial cable. It was still a bus topology and all network stations were connected to one common cable bus. It was added as an addendum to the IEEE 802.3 standard and was known as IEEE 802.3a. The IEEE representation for thin coaxial cable was called 10BASE2 because it had a a 10-Megabit transmission, baseband signaling, and a 185-meter maximum cable segment run (without the use of a repeater).

The biggest difference between thick coaxial cable and thin is that most of the shielding has been removed. Thin coaxial cable has an outside plastic coating that is usually black in color (although not always). Below this plastic covering is a thin shielding of braided wire which is adequate for almost all Ethernet installations. It provides the shielding necessary to keep signals from escaping from the cable plant and ensures that EMI signals do not get into the cable plant. Below this shielding is the polyethylene foam and below this is the center conductor made up of tinned copper wire.

A few restrictions are placed on thin coaxial cable plants, including that it may have fewer attachments per cable segment and less total cable length. Despite these restrictions, thin coaxial cable became the most popular cable plant in use until 1990, when unshielded twisted pair (UTP) took over.

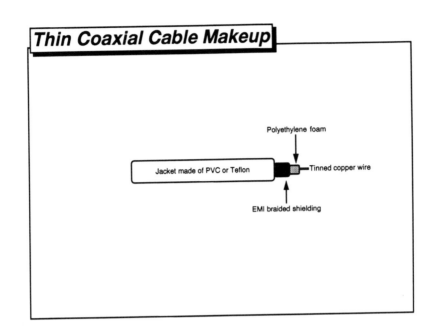

Thin Coaxial Cable Makeup

Polyethylene foam

Jacket made of PVC or Teflon — Tinned copper wire

EMI braided shielding

• Thin coaxial cable is used in the bus topology and is adequate for most Ethernet installations.

• It was introduced in 1984 because thick coaxial cable was expensive and hard to work with.

• It was added as an addendum to the IEEE 802.3 specification:
    IEEE 802.3a.
    Known as 10BASE2 cable.

• The PVC jacket is usually black in color.

• Uses common cabling found in wire manufacturers (RG-58 A/U).

• At the core of this cable is the copper tinned center conductor.
    Center conductor is surrounded by a foam.
    Foam is covered by a braided shield.

• It allows for lower overall maximum cable length and fewer attachments per cable segment than thick coaxial cable.

• Thin coaxial cable became the most popular type of bus cable for Ethernet installations until 1990.

THIN COAXIAL CONNECTION

With the introduction of a new wiring system came a new way to connect Ethernet controllers to a cable plant. Thin coaxial connections eliminated the need to core the bus cable, as well as eliminating the external transceiver and the transceiver cable. It introduced a two new connectors known as the BNC connector and T connector.

A piece of thin coaxial cable runs between each of the attached devices. Each cable segment is precut to a specified length no shorter than 0.5 meters and no longer than 185 meters. Controller cards are now concatenated with one another through a common bus cable. The cable plant is now directly attached to the controller card through the use of a T connector. There are three points of contact on the T connector: one point of the T connector attaches directly to the controller card and the other two points attach to the cable plant.

The ends of the cable run (not each piece of cable) still have the 50 ohm terminators. In other words, the two network attachments that are at the ends of the coaxial cable have terminators applied to them. Terminators are applied only to each end of the cable run. A cable run is defined as the total of all the individual cable segments between the network attachments. The cable run cannot be any longer than 185 meters. The last attachment on each end of the cable plant has a terminator placed on its T connector.

This type of wiring scheme has some restrictions. There can be no more than thirty attachments to the cable plant, stations can be placed no closer than 0.5 meters to each other, and the ends of the cable plant had to be terminated with a 50 ohm terminator. With the exception of PCMCIA (Personal Computer Memory Card International Association) network controller cards for laptop computers, the T connector must be attached directly to the Ethernet controller. You cannot run a piece of thin coaxial cable out to another cable plant. These restrictions proved inconsequential, and thin coaxial cable became the most popular cable scheme for Ethernet until the introduction of unshielded twisted pair cable in 1990.

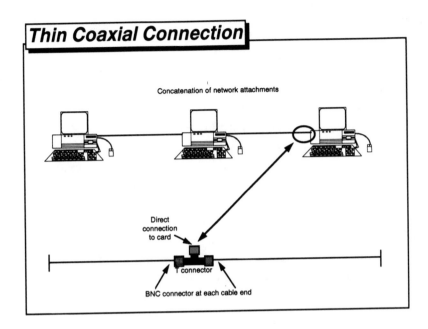

Thin Coaxial Connection

Concatenation of network attachments

Direct connection to card

T connector

BNC connector at each cable end

- Thin coaxial cable eliminated the coring of the bus cable, the external transceiver, and the transceiver cable.

- It introduced two new connectors: the BNC and the T connector.

- Stations are concatenated with thin coaxial cable precut to a specified length.

- Stations are placed from 0.5 meters to 185 meters apart.

- Cable plant attachment to an Ethernet controller uses a T connector that has three connection points:
    One point connects directly to the controller card.
    The other two points attach to the cable segments.

- The T connector must be directly attached to the controller. The only exception to this is the PCMCIA "credit card" controllers for laptop computers.

THIN COAXIAL CONNECTION (CONT.)

The external transceiver used on thick coaxial cable plants is placed directly on the controller card with thin coaxial cable plants, though the controller card costs about the same. The T connector attaches to the end of the coaxial cable and then to the controller card. The transceiver is still present and performs the same functions as the external transceiver.

Even though thin coaxial cable Ethernet was being introduced, there were still a tremendous number of companies that had standardized on the thick coaxial cable scheme. Instead of manufacturing two controller cards, the new controller cards implemented two connectors enabling the controller card to support both types of cable plants. This was not expensive for the Ethernet vendors to implement so connectors for both thick and thin cable appeared on the controller card. Ethernet stations choose which connector to use by either a jumper setting on the controller card, or a software configuration utility. Some controllers can self-sense—the controller "senses" which connector is active and then uses that connector. Only one connector can be used at a time.

The cable plant is simply "twisted together" to form a network.

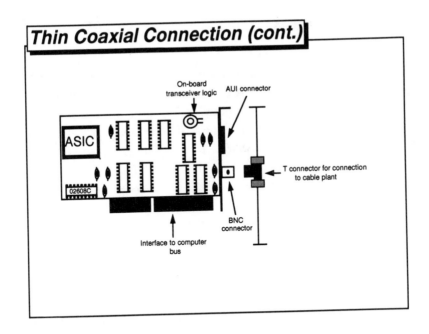

- With this type of coaxial cable, the transceiver moved "on-board" the controller card.

    It eliminated costly components.

    It allows for this Ethernet controller card to be less expensive than its predecessor

- Controller cards usually contain both the Ethernet DB-15 (AUI or DIX) connector and the BNC connector.

    The controller card chooses between thick and thin connectors by using software or hardware switches, or it can be self-sensing.

    Only one connector can be enabled on the controller card.

- The cable plant is simply twisted together to form a physical network.

UNSHIELDED TWISTED PAIR MAKEUP

In October of 1990, the IEEE standardized on a new wiring type known as unshielded twisted pair (UTP). Initially, this was the same type of wire that is found in common telephone wiring. It was 24 American Wire Gauge (AWG) wire that has between 75–150 ohms impedance. Today, there are multiple classifications for this type of wire now standardized by the Electronic Industries Association (EIA) under the standard of TIA568A. This standard includes UTP for many cable types but for our purposes it is used for Ethernet, Token Ring, and FDDI.

Unshielded twisted pair is now defined as data grade category 3, 4, and 5.

- Category 3 is used for up to LANs up to 10 Mbps.

- Category 4 is used for LANs up to 16 Mbps.

- Category 5 is used for LANs up to 100 Mbps.

The makeup of the cable is very simple. There are four pairs of wire (eight strands). The plastic coating covering the copper wire is color coded blue, orange, green, and brown. Each color pair must be twisted with at least two twists per foot. The higher the category, the more twists per foot, which allows for higher speeds to be achieved. Each pair color is mixed with white. Therefore, pair one is blue with white stripes and white with blue stripes; pair two is orange with white stripes and white with orange stripes; pair three is green with white stripes and white with green stripes; pair four is brown with white stripes and white with brown stripes. Since the impedance of this cable can range from 75–150 ohms, there are jumpers on a LAN controller card that enable the card to be matched to the impedance of the cable.

The pin out configuration for Ethernet UTP (10BASET) is the blue pair on pins 1 and 2 and the orange pair on pins 3 and 6. A cable made of category 5 wire can be used on any of the three LANs using the TIA568A standard shown below. Since the UTP connector is standardized as the RJ-45 for all three LAN types listed, a cable made up following the TIA568A standard can be used on any of the three listed LAN types. Otherwise, only two or the four pairs are needed for connection on an individual LAN. A simple matrix is shown below:

Pair	T568A	10BASET	Token Ring	FDDI
One	5 and 4	1 and 2	4 and 5	1 and 2
Two	3 and 6	3 and 6	3 and 6	7 and 8
Three	1 and 2			
Four	7 and 8			

UTP Makeup

- UTP was standardized by the IEEE 802.3 committee in October of 1990.

- Standardized by the EIA under TIA 568A.

- UTP for LANs is now classified as:
    - Category 3 - used for LANs up to 10 Mbps.
    - Category 4 - used for LANs up to 16 Mbps.
    - Category 5 - used for LANs up to 100 Mbps.

- Cable is made up of 8 strands of 24 AWG wire.

UNSHIELDED TWISTED PAIR

It was found that using the right components, the Ethernet system could be run on common tele-phone wire (what is now known as type 3 wire). Synoptics was the first company to mass produce this idea around 1985. This type of wiring scheme introduced the star topology, which is tremen-dous for individual network station management. At the same time, Ethernet was under attack by IBM's introduction of Token Ring for its network standard. Token Ring, which will be explained later, implemented a physical star topology. As it turned out, IBM was late with the Token Ring net-work, which was based on a physical star wire topology, and the new topology and cable scheme for Ethernet took hold.

With both thick and thin coaxial cable, network management of individual workstations was hard to implement. This is characteristic of a bus topology. Also, with coaxial cable all stations are attached to a common cable, allowing for a single point of failure. If the cable plant became disabled, all stations attached to that cable plant also became disabled. Also, if any one station on the cable plant needed to be individually managed, this was nearly impossible to accomplish.

UTP not only introduced a new topology, it introduced new components. With the star topol-ogy, there is a central component to which all stations attach. This is the central hub and is known as a *wiring hub* or a *wiring concentrator*. It is the termination point for all stations on the network and is necessary with UTP. Stations may be hooked back-to-back, but this is valid only for two stations. There is a one-to-one relationship between the Ethernet controller card and the repeater. The con-troller attaches to an individual port on the concentrator.

The connectors were changed to the RJ-45 connector. The RJ-45 connector is an 8-pin plastic connector with a small plastic tab on it that locks the connector shell into its plug. The pins that are used in this connector are pins 1, 2, 3, and 6. The transceiver is still located on the controller card. The transceiver was changed to accommodate the cable type but its functions are still the same as previous controller cards.

Incidentally, this is the same type of connector that is used on unshielded twisted pair for Token Ring connections.

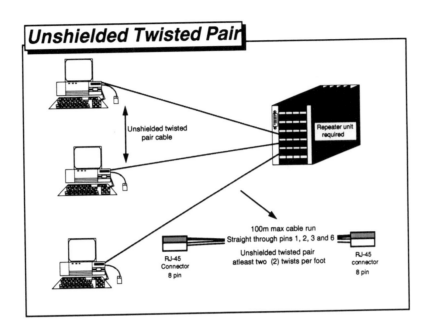

- The wire scheme changed to common telephone wire which is relatively inexpensive.
    The original wire used was called category 3.
        — This type of wire can sustain up to 10 Mbits of data transmission.
        — Most installations are using category 5.

- This new type of cable forced a change to the star topology, which provides better network management.

- This wire type introduced a new component known as the wiring concentrator.
    All network attachments were connected directly to this concentrator.
    There is a one-to-one relationship between the Ethernet controller and the concentrator.

- RJ-45 (8-pin) connectors are used with UTP.
    These are used with the business telephone system.
    These connectors are located on each end of the cable.

- Wires in the connector are placed on pins 1, 2, 3, and 6.

- The transceiver is still "on-board" the controller card.

Unshielded Twisted Pair (Cont.)

An interesting aspect of this wiring scheme is that the 50 ohm terminators are no longer used. Since impedance[1] on UTP wire can vary in the range of 75–150 ohms there are jumpers to match the controller card to the impedance value of the wire. Thick and thin coaxial cable is manufactured to strict specifications and when the 50 ohm terminators are applied the impedance is held to 50 ohm plus or minus 2 ohms. These jumpers have numbers beside them that could read 75, 100, and 150. This indicates the number that most closely matches the impedance found on the particular cable that is attached to a station. Before an Ethernet controller is placed on the cable, the cable must be "ohmed out." This means finding the impedance of the cable, using a relatively inexpensive ($1,000) cable tester. Once an impedance value is found, the jumper is moved to the number that is closest to the number found on the cable tester. Each network attachment cable should be checked.

The controller card may be no more than 100 meters from the repeater. When the IEEE was trying to standardize UTP, there was a question as to how long a cable run should be. In most corporations, if there is a phone, a computer is probably located nearby. Since the wiring hub is presumed to be located in the telephone closet near the telephone computer system, it was found that most telephones in business were within 100 meters of the telephone wiring closet. Therefore it was standardized at 100 meters. There are companies that claim further distances, and which may be okay for a few installations, but keep in mind that the standard is 100 meters. If you place an Ethernet controller card beyond this using a specific vendor, and find that the controller card has to be replaced, you will probably have to replace it from the same vendor. This can be cost prohibitive.

Repeater hubs, in the case of UTP wire, are the central point for wire concentration. All attachments on the Ethernet network are terminated into this repeater module. This is called a *point-to-point* cable run. Once a signal enters the repeater, it is regenerated to every port that is active on that repeater. In a sense, you may think of the repeater hub taking the place of the thick or thin coaxial cable. Repeaters will be explained in more detail later.

---

[1]Impedance is the natural ability for the cable to resist current flow.

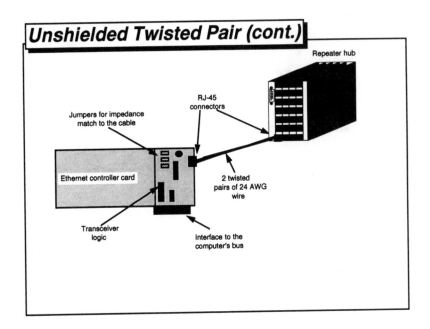

- UTP cable consists of 4 strands of 24 gauge wire, although 22–26 gauge is allowed.

- On each end of the cable, there are RJ-45 (8 pin) connectors.

- Four wires are twisted together with at least two twists per foot of cable.
    It may contain more than two twists per foot.
    The greater the number of twists per foot, the less the attenuation on the cable.

- Fifty ohm terminators are not used.
    The termination selection is via a jumper on the controller card and the concentrator.

- The cable that runs between the network attachment and the repeater can run a maximum of 100 meters.

- UTP requires the use of a concentrator.
    It is sometimes called a repeater hub.
    No other connections are allowed between the hub and the controller card.
    There is a single cable plant for each connection to the hub.

- If any individual cable fails, only the attachment on that cable segment is down. All other connections on the repeater are still active.

TRANSCEIVERS REVISITED

As the wiring schemes for the Ethernet network changed so did transceivers. Currently there are four types of transceivers available:

- 10BASE5 transceiver—explained previously

- 10BASE2 transceiver

- 10BASET transceiver

- Parallel Adapter Transceiver available in any of the above flavors

The 10BASE2 transceiver has a DB-15 connector on one side and a BNC connector on the other. This allows those Ethernet controllers that have only a DB-15 connection to a thin coaxial cable plant. For example, if you have installed a thin coaxial cable plant and some of the controllers that need a connection support only thick coaxial cable (that is, if they only have a DB-15 connector shell on the controller card), the controller card must use the 10BASE2 transceiver. The transceiver will connect directly to the controller card using the DB-15 connector and then will attach to the thin coaxial cable plant using the BNC connector.

The 10BASET transceiver allows for a DB-15 connection to a UTP cable plant. The 10BASET transceiver connects directly to the DB-15 connector on the controller card, and to the UTP cable plant using the RJ-45 connector on the other end.

The parallel adapter transceiver is used for laptop computers that possess a parallel port. This type of transceiver connects to the parallel port of a computer on one end. Then (depending on the type of cable plant to which you wish to connect) the adapter will connect to the Ethernet cable plant. There is a parallel adapter transceiver for each type of wiring used on Ethernet.

The transceivers explained above usually connect directly to the Ethernet controller card. When space is limited there are alternative means of connection. They come in all shapes and sizes. Some have a small DB-15 transceiver cable (two to three feet of cable) with the transceiver attached to the end of this cable, away from the controller card. Still, most will be a small rectangular box that connects directly to the Ethernet controller and the cable plant.

Transceivers Revisited

- Normally, transceivers are used to connect thick coaxial cable to a network station.

- Transceivers are available with many different connection options:

  - 10BASE5 transceiver
    - » used to connect a network station to thick coaxial cable.

  - 10BASE2 transceiver
    - » used to connect a network station that supports only the DB-15 connector to a thin coaxial cable plant.

  - 10BASET transceiver
    - » used to connect a network station that supports only the DB-15 connector to a segment of Unshielded Twisted Pair.

  - Parallel adapter transceiver
    - » used for laptop computers.

ETHERNET CABLE COMPONENTS

Now that all the wiring types have been explained, the following text will summarize all the components needed in each type.

When making an Ethernet decision, the type of cable plant used will determine the type of wire used. Any of the three types of cabling schemes may be intermixed by using a repeater, which will be explained later. Each type of cabling scheme has its own cable run limitations (without the use of a repeater): 500 meters for thick coaxial cable, 185 meters for thin coaxial cable, and 100 meters for UTP cable.

If the type of wire used is thick coaxial cable, there must be at least one external transceiver and one transceiver cable per attachment. Along with this, there must be one transceiver connection per attachment on a thick coaxial cable plant[2]. Likewise a coring tool (or two, one for a spare) must be purchased to core the thick coaxial cable for proper transceiver placement.

With each type of cabling scheme will come a new connector type. For thick Ethernet, the connector is the DB-15, female on the controller card and male on the transceiver.

Thin coaxial cable uses BNC connectors and T connectors. The BNC connector is located on the controller card and the end pieces of thin coaxial cable segments. The only separate item needed is the T connector, which is used to connect the cable to the controller card.

10BASET uses the RJ-45 connector on each end of the cable. Also remember with 10BASE2 and 10BASET controllers, the transceiver has been moved to the controller card.

Thick and thin coaxial cable plants use a common cable for all station attachments. This cable plant must be terminated at each end of the cable plant using 50 ohm terminators.

The final component is required only for UTP cable plants. Since the physical topology of UTP is the star, all stations must be terminated into a central hub. With UTP this is known as a repeater hub. The other two cabling schemes may use repeaters but this is only to extend the cable run beyond its longest cable run restriction, stated above, or to collapse all wiring connections into one common point.

---

[2]There are alternatives to this, and this is explained in the next section

Ethernet Cable Components

- Type of cable plant
- Transceivers and transceiver cables for 10BASE5
- Coring tools for 10BASE5
- Connector types
- Terminators
- Wire concentrators for 10BASET
- Repeaters for extension of the cabling plant beyond specifications

ETHERNET REPEATER HUBS

The repeater hub is a device invented to overcome the problems created by three types of wiring schemes and restrictions on the number of attachments per cable segment as well as on total cable length. The repeater is also used in certain topology designs that required a multiple-cable interconnection device even without cable length restrictions. With a repeater, cable runs can be extended and more network attachments can be connected without violating any rules. Some repeaters even connect network attachments without the use of a cable plant of any type.

When first introduced, repeaters simply extended a cable plant and allowed for more network stations to be attached. These simple devices did not have any network management capabilities. With the introduction of each new wiring scheme, a new repeater was created. When UTP came along, a more advanced repeater was invented called the wiring concentrator (also known as the wiring hub or just the hub). This type of repeater hub collapsed multiple wire types into one termination point.

Repeaters can be classified into three groups:

1. Multiport transceiver unit (MTU)—allows connections for 10BASE5 networks.

2. Multiport repeater unit (MPR)—allows connections for 10BASE2 networks.

3. Wiring concentrator—allows connections for all three types of wiring for Ethernet.

The MTU and the MPR are not widely used anymore. Their functionality has been condensed into the wiring concentrator. There are still plenty of them out there and they are used in special situations. Wiring concentrators offer not only the repeater functions but also special functions that enable better utilization of the cable plant. For example, they restrict errors to single cable plants, determine the quality of given cable, and so forth. But what they are most noted for is a greatly increased level of network management, which will be discussed later in the book.

All repeater functions, no matter which type, are standardized by the IEEE 802.3c standard. The specification for Ethernet states that the data path between two communicating stations may traverse more than four repeaters.

Ethernet Repeater Hubs

- They allow all three wiring schemes to be connected to a common point.

- They collapse all wiring types into a single component.

- They provide greater network management.

- They allow for a greater number of network stations to be attached in a single cable plant.

- Repeaters or concentrators repeat a signal to other cable plants.

- Early repeaters were not intelligent devices.
  - No network management.
  - Repeated every signal including errors to other cable plants.

- Repeaters have transformed into wiring concentrators (formerly called hubs).

- Repeaters are available in three varieties, all of which conform to the IEEE 802.3c repeater specification:
  - Multiport Transceiver Unit (MTU, 10BASE5 only).
  - Multiport Repeater Unit (MPR, 10BASE2 only).
  - Wiring Concentrator (10BASE5, 10BASE2, and 10BASET combination).

EXTENDING THE NETWORK

Repeaters allow a single network segment to be "stretched" beyond its maximum single cable segment run. They also allow for the concentration of cables into a single point. You will recall that a single cable segment run for thick coaxial cable is 500 meters, for thin coaxial cable it is 185 meters, and for UTP it is 100 meters.

To fully extend a cable plant, repeaters may be concatenated. With up to four repeaters, thick and thin coaxial cable segments may be connected together to allow a maximum cable run of 2,500 meters for thick coaxial and 1,000 meters for thin coaxial cable. This means that five cable segments can use four repeaters to extend the length to five times the maximum single cable run length.

With a repeated cable plant, if there are five segments that are repeated, two of the segments must remain with no attachments to the cable plant. These are called *link segments*. The link segments have only the repeater connection on them. No other attachments are allowed on these cable segments. Even with a network using concentrators, stations may not be separated by more than four concentrators.

Repeaters do act as a single attachment to the cable plant; therefore, there will be one less connection available to any cable plant that has a repeater connection. For example, instead of the thirty attachments allowed for thin coaxial cable, there are now twenty-nine other attachments and the thirtieth attachment is the repeater. The maximum number of attachments is specified in the IEEE 802.3 specification for each cable type.

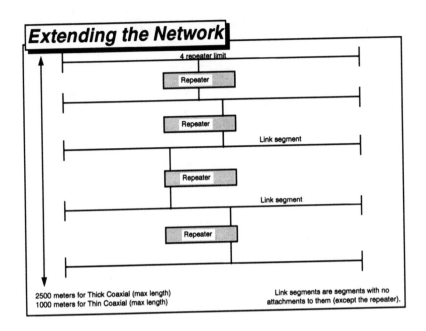

- Repeaters can be used to "stretch" the length of a single Ethernet cable segment.
    Four repeaters extend a thick coaxial cable plant to 2,500 meter.
    Four repeaters extend a thin coaxial cable plant to 1,000 meters.

- No more than four repeaters may be placed between to communicating stations
    More than four repeaters are allowed on a network, just not between the data path.

- If there are four repeaters to extend to the maximum cable segment length, two of those segments must remain nodeless.

- Repeaters do not separate the cable segments logically. They are only separated physically.
    All traffic on one cable segment is repeated to all other cable segments.

MULTIPORT TRANSCEIVER UNIT FOR 10BASE5 NETWORKS— THEORETICAL TOP VIEW

The workings of the MTU may be confusing, but if we look at the MTU from the top how it works may become more apparent. Remember, that this is only a functional view. If you open the MTU, you will see a printed circuit board with a lot of components on it. It will not look the way it is described in this book.

The MTU is a single unit that houses multiple transceivers. Remember that in the thick coaxial cable plants, an Ethernet controller is physically attached to the thick coaxial cable via a transceiver and transceiver cable.

These transceivers are then connected to an internal cable bus inside of the MTU. Therefore, there is no need for a external thick coaxial cable plant if all network stations are attached to the MTU. The drawback is that the largest MTU will only have eight connectors on it for attachment to eight network stations. For connectivity of more stations, you must use another MTU.

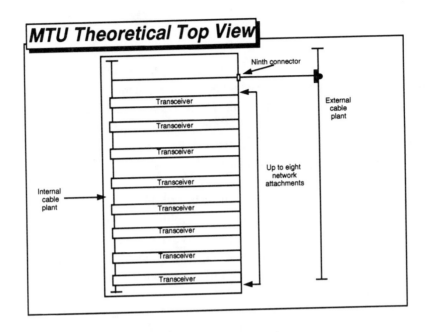

- The MTU internally houses eight transceivers that are connected to an internal bus (emulating a cable plant).

- MTUs are restricted to eight network attachments; further connectivity requires another MTU.

- The ninth connector is for a connection to an external cable plant.
    This connector requires the use of an external transceiver for connection to that cable plant.
    No connection other than an external cable plant hook-up may be made to the ninth connector.

10BASE5 MTU

Digital Equipment Corporation was first on the market with the MTU and other vendors followed suit. The MTU must conform to the IEEE 802.3c repeater specification but there is no standard on the physical or logical configuration of this unit. The MTU is available in many different sizes. It can be a rectangular box that has eight DB-15 male connectors and one DB-15 female connector on it. The male connectors are for attachments to network stations. The female connector is for attachment to a backbone thick coaxial cable plant. It is also available in smaller versions of two and four ports.

Network stations attach directly to one of the male DB-15 connectors using a transceiver cable. This device serves many purposes. The unique aspect of this unit is that no central cable plant (the thick coaxial cable) is needed unless the MTU is connected to a backbone cable (a backbone cable is shown later under the heading of a typical office environment.) All Ethernet controllers attach directly to the unit itself. The only cable that is needed is a transceiver cable that is run between the network station and the MTU.

Up to eight network stations may be connected to the MTU. If more stations are needed to communicate with one another then another MTU device is needed. MTUs can communicate with each other through a backbone cable or by being connected to each other shown later.

Another positive aspect of the MTU is that it can extend the restriction of one hundred attachments to a single thick coaxial cable segment. Remember that with thick coaxial you are allowed one hundred attachments total per cable plant, including not only network stations but repeaters and other devices. The MTU may be attached to a thick coaxial cable plant and it will be counted as one attachment even though there may be eight network stations connected to the MTU. Therefore, up to eight hundred network stations may be attached to a single thick coaxial cable segment using the MTU.

MTUs are not as popular as they once were but they are still used and they provide easy LAN connectivity. This is especially true in small environments, or maybe as support for old Ethernet controllers that have only a DB-15 connector. The MTU is also called the DEC DELNI (Digital Equipment Local Network Interconnect). It is commonly referred to as a DELNI and not as an MTU.

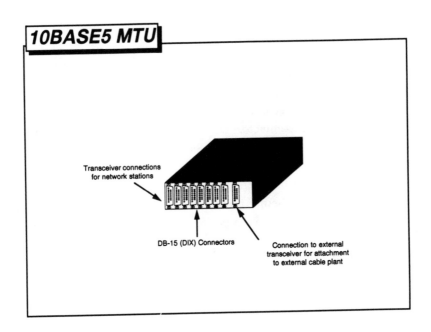

10BASE5 MTU

Transceiver connections
for network stations

DB-15 (DIX) Connectors

Connection to external
transceiver for attachment
to external cable plant

• Available with two, four, or eight ports.
    The eight-port models allow for connection to an external cable plant.

• The eight connectors are male DB-15 and the ninth connector is a female DB-15.

• Network attachments connect to one of the male DB-15s with transceiver cable running from the MTU to the network attachment.

• Since each MTU can have eight connectors, up to eight hundred network stations may now be attached to a single thick coaxial cable plant.

• The MTU is also known as the DEC DELNI.

MTU Connection

Although available in two and four DB-15 port connections, the MTU connection that will be shown in this book will contain eight DB-15 connectors and one DB-15 female connector that can be used only for connection to an external MTU or an external cable plant.

Each of the eight male DB-15 connectors can have an attachment to a single network station. The connectors are the slide lock type in that the cable is placed on the connector and then locked on by sliding the latch into the lock position. The female connection will not have the slide lock lever. The transceiver cable that attaches to this port will have the slide lock lever on the cable. Some units contain a switch to indicate whether there is a connection to an external cable plant. This switch can cause problems if left in the open position with no cable attached to that port. Most MTUs are self-sensing.

A DB-15 connector is attached to a network station using a transceiver cable that runs no longer than 50 meters.

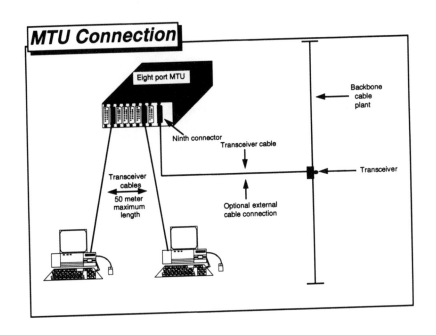

- Usually only the eight port MTU will have a connector for an external cable plant.

- Some units have a switch to enable or disable the ninth connector.

- Each of the eight male DB-15 connectors may attach to a network attachment.

- The connectors are the slide lock type on the MTU.

- The single female connector connects to a thick coaxial external cable.

- The transceiver cable may run for a maximum of 50 meters (165 feet).

CASCADED MTUs

A network can be designed so that more than eight network attachments may be connected without the use of an external cable plant. MTUs may be connected in a partial tree configuration called *cascaded MTUs*. With this, one MTU is considered the *root* MTU which may connect to an external cable plant. Usually there is a special device known as a *bridge* or a *router* that will allow this type of connection to a backbone cable plant. These devices are discussed later. All other MTUs are connected to the root MTU's transceiver ports (one MTU per port), and are free to connect network stations.

The cable connecting between the root MTU and the secondary MTUs may be a maximum of 45 meters. The specification is true for all MTUs and transceiver connections.

There is no exact specification for this type of cascaded MTU topology or for the MTU itself.

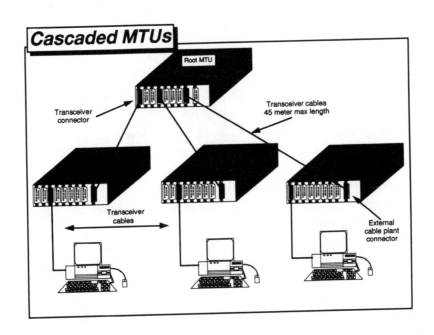

Cascaded MTUs

- Cascaded MTUs allow for more than eight network attachments without an external cable plant.

- One MTU acts as the root MTU with all others connected to it.
  The external cable plant connectors (the ninth connector) of all the secondary MTUs connect to the transceiver port connectors of the root MTU.

- This allows for 64 active stations without the use of coaxial cable.

- The root MTU is the only one in this configuration that can be externally attached to a coaxial cable plant.
  The transceiver cables connecting the active stations on the lower MTUs must not exceed 45 meters in length.

10BASE2 MPR

The Multiport Repeater, or MPR, is used with the 10BASE2 wiring scheme, whose coaxial wire scheme imposed new restrictions: no more than thirty attachments to one cable segment run, no more than 185 meters for a single cable run, and so forth.

As with all repeaters, the MPR conforms to the IEEE 802.3c repeater specification, and is similar in connectivity to the MTU except that the connectors conform to the 10BASE2 mechanism. In other words, it has eight BNC connectors on it for attachment to eight thin coaxial cable runs. It also possesses one DB-15 connector for attachment to a thick coaxial cable plant. The repeater is considered a network attachment so the maximum number of attachments per cable segment—excluding the repeater—is reduced to twenty-nine.

MPRs can be cascaded using one of their BNC ports. That is, one port of an MPR is directly connected to a port of another MPR. The MPR may be connected to a backbone cable, allowing many more stations to communicate.

Up to eight thin coaxial cable segments are allowed to be attached to one MPR, with each cable run holding twenty-nine network attachments. The cable attachment to the MPR does not require a T connector; it is connected directly. The other end of the cable run does require a T connector and terminator. This allows for 232 total network attachments to one MPR.

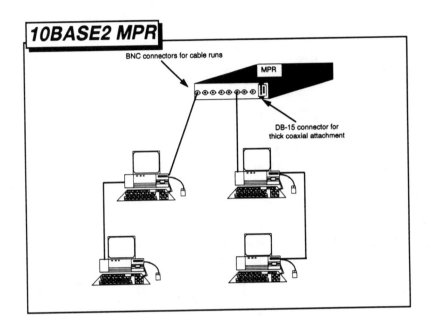

- Like the MTU, the Multiport Repeater (MPR) extends the distance limitations of the thin coaxial cable plant.

- This type of repeater usually has eight BNC connectors with one external transceiver connection used for connection to an external cable plant.

- It will connect up to eight thin coaxial cable segments.
    Each segment may have up to twenty-nine attachments.
    Up to 232 network stations may be attached to a single repeater.

- Using an MPR reduces the amount of network stations allowed on a single cable segment.
    Thirty stations on a non-repeated cable plant; twenty-nine with an MPR.
    The repeater is considered an attachment.

- The maximum cable run on each of the eight segments is still 185 meters.

- You may concatenate up to four MPRs (the four repeater limit) using one BNC port on each MPR that is cascaded.

- When the cable plant is connected to the MPR, the physical connection does not necessarily require a T connector and terminator.
    The cable may be placed directly on the BNC port of the MPR.
    The terminator is internal to the MPR.

WIRING CONCENTRATORS—HUBS

Unshielded Twisted Pair wire was being installed about five years prior to its actual adoption as a cable method by the IEEE 802.3i committee. The use of this wire type required a new type of repeater; instead of building one repeater strictly for UTP wire, vendors decided to develop a repeater that could be used with all cabling methods This is how the wiring concentrator (or hub) came about.

The wiring concentrator has connections for 10BASET, 10BASE2, and 10BASE5 networks all within one housing. This type of connection allows it to still act as one repeater. A network attachment on UTP is able to talk to a network attachment on thin coaxial wire. All connections on this repeater have the ability to talk to any other connection.

This is possible because the wiring concentrator houses what are known as *repeater modules*. Each module slides into a slot in the wiring concentrator, and is a separate repeater for a certain wire type. The modules communicate together through the *backplane* of the wiring concentrator. This is a common wired socket that all modules plug into that runs the length of the repeater.

In 1985, the concentrator added life to the Ethernet standard. Housing all wiring types into one unit and the subsequent implementation of the star configuration for Ethernet cable allowed for better network management. It became more popular with the announcement in 1985 that IBM would be late in shipping its Token Ring products. But the main selling attribute of this device is its ability to allow better network management.

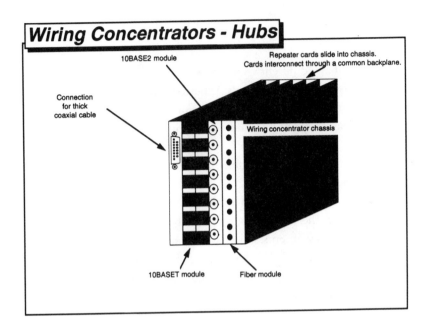

- This device was introduced around 1985 after UTP wire began being used.

- Usually called a concentrator although some still call it a hub.

- Houses repeater modules that slide into the concentrator chassis.

- Concentrators house all repeater types into one unit using repeater modules that are connected together with a common backplane.
    It allows the concentrator to act as one repeater.
    It reduces the number of repeaters on a network.

- Concentrators usually have connections for fiber, 10BASET, 10BASE2, and one connector for 10BASE5 (connection to external cable plant).

- Added life to the Ethernet standard by providing a physical star topology.
    The concentrator allows for better network management.

WIRING CONCENTRATOR

A concentrator can house many different wiring types. Some concentrators can house not only different media types but different access methods (Ethernet, Token Ring, and so on) as well. They are maintained on separate backplanes and cannot communicate with each other without the use of a bridge or a router but at least they can be housed into one unit, which again leads to better network management.

Each wiring type is contained in one module that slides into the concentrator which allows them to act as one wiring scheme for Ethernet.

10BASET connections have their point-to-point attachments to one of the modules in the repeater. Another module in the repeater allows for the 10BASE2 attachments. Finally, another module allows for 10BASE5 attachments. There is not a set configuration for any one type of wiring module. A concentrator can house all 10BASET modules or mostly 10BASET modules and a few 10BASE2, and so forth. There is no restriction on the type or number of cards that can be placed in the concentrator; this is vendor specific.

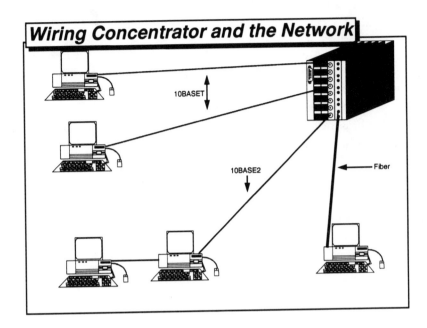

Wiring Concentrator and the Network

10BASET

10BASE2

Fiber

• Concentrators allow all media types to communicate in a single housing in any combination.

• Concentrators collapse all wiring into one single unit.

• The media modules may all be of one type.

• Each module supports one media type.
    All connectors on each repeater module will be of one wire type.

• Some concentrators allow for multiple LAN wire types to be housed in one concentrator.
    Ethernet, Token Ring and FDDI repeater modules are all housed in one concentrator.
        — Each type will be connected to a different backplane in the concentrator.
        — No interconnection of these boards without the use of a bridge or router module (discussed later).

MIXING REPEATER TYPES

With the advent of the wiring concentrator, it may seem that all other repeaters were replaced; in fact, many of the older repeaters are still in use today. Today, heterogeneous networks encompass many different types of equipment and this includes repeaters.

All repeaters, as long as they conform to the IEEE 802.3c repeater specification, may coexist on any Ethernet network. Usually they coexist via connection to one cable scheme through a backbone cable plant. This backbone cable plant is usually thick or thin coaxial cable but it may be fiber.

Without the use of a bridge or router (discussed later), there still may be no more than 1,024 network attachments on any Ethernet network (an Ethernet specification). Each repeater, no matter what type, acts as one repeater and the data path of any two communicating stations may traverse no more than four repeaters.

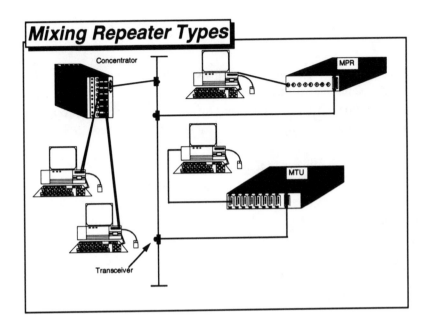

- All three repeater types are still in use.

- All conform to the IEEE 802.3c repeater specification.

- All three repeater types may exist on the same physical cable plant.

- The connecting medium (backbone) may be thick coaxial, thin coaxial or fiber.

- The connecting medium may be the concentrator.
    The MPR and MTU may connect directly to the concentrator.

- No matter what type of repeaters are used, you must still maintain the four repeater limit.

OFFICE ENVIRONMENT

You will often hear the term *wiring closet*. This is the termination point for any wiring that is installed, including electrical, telephone, and data communications wiring. This closet contains the wiring concentrator if there is one. If not, concentrators are connected together through the use of a back-bone cable. What exactly is meant by a backbone cable and how do repeaters or repeater hubs connect to this backbone?

The backbone cable of an office is a cable that runs up the "backbone" of the building. All buildings with multiple floors contain a riser that runs up through the building. It may house the elevator shaft, telephone cables, and so forth. It is also where the backbone LAN cable usually runs. The backbone cable can be of any LAN or cable type but the rule to remember is that the backbone should be of a higher speed than the speed of any of the floor networks attached to it. For instance, if the floor networks are 10-Mbps Ethernet, the backbone should be faster than 10 Mbps—either Fiber Data Distributed Interface (FDDI, which runs at 100 Mbps, explained later) or a 16-Mbps Token Ring (not common).

Attached to the backbone will be the repeater concentrators which allow multiple repeaters to communicate with one another. Even with all these repeaters, the LAN is not segmented and still acts as one LAN.

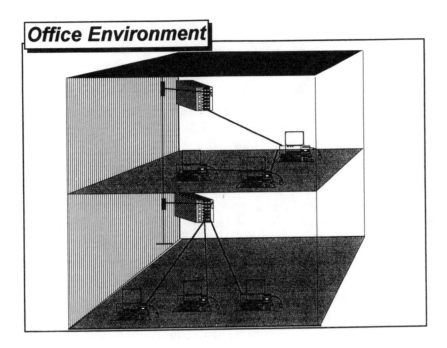

- The backbone cable plant runs up the "spine" of a building.

- Concentrators are connected to the backbone and also provide the "ribs" to the local connections on each floor.

- Backbone cable capacity is usually faster than the floor interconnections.
  If the floor LANs are 10 Mbps, the backbone should be 16 Mbps or 100 Mbps.

- This system still acts as one cable segment or LAN.

NETWORK MANAGEMENT OF THE CONCENTRATORS

Wiring concentrators have come a long way since the early repeaters. They are really required only for 10BASET connections, but do allow for a single point of termination for all network wiring. But by far the biggest advantage of placing all wiring in the concentrator is that network management is improved. Although it is beyond the scope of this book to detail the aspects of network management, it will be mentioned here in relation to concentrators.

Since all wiring is terminated in the concentrator and therefore all data passes through this device, keeping statistical data on the network occurs here. Network management also encompasses the ability to control the network and management of concentrator allows for this control. Each port on the concentrator can be controlled. For example, an individual 10BASET port can be turned on or off, thereby controlling a single network attachment. This is convenient when the station that is attached to it is having problems or a new network station is being added; this port can be disabled and the station can then be physically attached and remotely enabled. A BNC connector on the concentrator will control a single cable plant, and this port can be controlled in the same manner with the exception that all stations attached to that cable plant will be controlled from the concentrator.

During the normal operation of the concentrator, statistics can be gathered and stored, such as how much data has passed through an individual port, how many times an error has occurred, and whether the concentrator has disabled the port due to excessive errors. All information is "stamped," meaning that any statistic will have the date and time appended as to when an event occurred. This information can be retrieved at any time by a network management station polling for the information.

How is such management enabled? Usually, one workstation on the network is tasked with this operation. Software that resides on this workstation will send commands to the controller requesting information of it or passing a control command to effect an action to be taken. The concentrator will respond to the commands with replies back to the workstation. The workstation software can display any management information on the workstation screen in any format desired, including charts, graphs, and text. This type of management is known as *in-band*. In-band means the management is taking place over the network. *Out-of-band* management means the concentrator is being managed outside of the network, through a console port on the concentrator or a dial-in port through the use of a modem.

Network Management of the Concentrators

- With the concentration of the wiring into a common point, network managers can manage the hub with specialized software.

- Network management software resides not only in the concentrator but on an external workstation's device (a PC, for example).

   - The workstation can query the concentrator for information.

- Concentrators also allow the control of individual ports.

- This software allows managers to extract information from each card that is inserted in the repeater. You could query the hub for statistics such as:

   - number of packets (bytes),

   - number of collisions (single and multiple),

   - number of framing errors,

   - number of time the particular card de-inserted itself from the network,

   - ability to turn on/off any repeater card in the hub, and

   - all information is time and date stamped.

- With 10BASET, all information is provided on an individual-connection basis, giving a manager information right from the desktop.

TOKEN RING PHYSICAL LAYER—OVERVIEW

Token Ring is a combination of topologies; physically it is a star and logically it is a ring. It is known as the *star-wired ring*. This will be shown in the next few examples.

There are only two versions of Token Ring cable: shielded or unshielded twisted pair. Token Ring does not use coaxial cable for its cabling scheme though coaxial cable can be used through the use of devices known as *baluns*. It is not a recommended practice.

The connectors used for Token Ring cable can be DB-9, RJ-11, RJ-45, or hermaphroditic (Universal Data Connector, UDC).

Since the physical topology is the star, all cable will be terminated into a central location. This is called the *multistation access unit*, or MAU. When IBM introduced Token Ring in 1984, there was only one type of MAU available. Currently MAUs have transformed into wiring concentrators that are similar in function to the Ethernet wiring concentrator.

Also as with Ethernet, Token Ring has cable extending devices known as repeaters. Fiber can be used between the MAU and the network attachment, but this is not a part of the IBM cabling scheme. Fiber is specified to run between MAUs.

The network controller card is also specific to Token Ring. In order to place a network attachment onto a Token Ring cable plant, the controller must be a Token Ring Controller card. Network controller cards do not have the ability to run different access method types.

Token Ring Physical Layer - Overview

- The Token Ring topology combines the physical star and the logical ring and is known as the star-wired ring.

- The wire that is used is either shielded or unshielded twisted pair.
  - Fiber may be used as a repeater connection but it can also be used for connections to the network stations.

- There are four types of connectors:
  - RJ-11 for UTP.
  - The hermaphroditic connector (also called Universal Data Connector or UDC) for shielded twisted pair.
  - The DB-9 and RJ-45 connectors can be used for both wire types.

- All wiring is concentrated at a common point known as the Multistation Access Unit (MAU).

- There is no concatenation of network stations, nor is there a single cable to which all stations attach.

- There are physical layer extending devices known as copper repeaters which can extend the length of MAU-to-MAU interconnection.

TOKEN RING CABLE TYPES

Even though the cable used on Token Ring is shielded or unshielded twisted pair there are different versions of this cable.

Type 1   This is a shielded data grade cable (as specified by the Electronic Industries Association, EIA) that contains two solid twisted pairs with a wire mesh shield around them that keeps unwanted signals from entering the cable and also retains any signals on the cable. There are two pairs of wires (totaling four individual wires) that separated each other. Each wire in a pair is twisted with the other wire in the same pair and then the pair is covered in a foil shield. The two pairs together are then covered in braided shield and wrapped in a covering of PVC that is usually black in color.

Type 2   This cable is the same as Type 1 cable with the exception of four voice grade wires that are wrapped in it. This is used in new or changed installations that require a voice and data cable to be run. It allows for simpler installation in that both data and voice are wrapped into one cable type.

Type 3   This is the UTP cable for Token Ring and it is the same UTP cable used by Ethernet (the pinouts in the connectors are different). Originally, it was specified to be voice grade cable but has since changed to be specified for UTP data grade cable. Because UTP is prone to noise, this type of cable requires a hardware filter known as a *media filter*. This allows for only certain signals to pass to the controller from the cable plant. The filter may be built directly onto the controller card or it may be a separate device external to the controller card.

Type 5   This type of cable is 100/140 micron fiber, which is the fiber specification for Token Ring. It is primarily used for inter-MAU connections and it has not been specified for network attachment to MAU cable.

Type 6   This is a shielded data grade cable that is used as a patch cable. The size of the wire is 26 AWG.

Token Ring Cable Types

- Type 1
    - A shielded data grade cable with two solid wire twisted pairs.
    - Available in indoor and outdoor versions.

- Type 2
    - A Type 1 indoor cable with four solid twisted pairs of 24 AWG wire.
    - Contains four voice grade wires along with four data grade wires.

- Type 3
    - Unused existing telephone wire or EIA category 3 wire (4 Mbps operation).
    - Category 4 is needed for 16 Mbps (speed of the Token Ring) operation.
    - Must use a special media filter.

- Type 5
    - 100/140 micron fiber cable used for fiber optic repeater links.

- Type 6
    - Often used for patch cables.
        » Patch cables can be used for MAU-to-MAU connection or from a wall outlet to a network attachment.

Token Ring Cable Types (Cont.)

Type 8   26 AWG wire cable with a plastic covering so that it may be run under carpeting.

Type 9   26 AWG flat cable covered in Teflon used in plenum areas. This is used in areas where the cable is not run through a sealed container known as a conduit. The PVC coating on the outside of the cable is toxic if it catches on fire. Therefore, Teflon cable must be used where the cable will be run in open areas (known as plenum) without a conduit.

Token Ring Cable Types (cont.)

- Type 8
  - 26 AWG flat cable for use under carpets.

- Type 9
  - 26 AWG in a plenum jacket (for fire code regulations).

Cable Connectors

A Token Ring controller card is attached to the cable plant with a cable known as the *lobe* cable. Lobe cables consist of Type 1, 2, or 3 and patch cables consist of Type 6. MAUs are connected together with patch cables. Whatever the cable, there are four types of connectors that may be used on the Token Ring cable system.

There are two connection points in a Token Ring network: on the controller card and on the MAU. The DB-9 connector is always located on the controller card and it allows for a cable connection from the controller card to the MAU. The DB-9 connector has an outside shell shaped like a D and nine pins are inside the shell. The DB-9 connector will support both UTP and shielded twisted pair wire.

The RJ-11 is a connector that was used when the Token Ring network scheme was first introduced. It was used with UTP wire and is mainly found on older Token Ring controller cards. Currently, the RJ-11 is rarely used at all.

The other end (the MAU end) of the controller cable can be of two types: hermaphroditic or RJ-45. If the cable is plugging into an IBM 8228 MAU the connector will be hermaphroditic. Most other concentrators use the RJ-45 connector.

A hermaphroditic connector is a black rectangular connector that snaps into a port on the MAU. Due to its expense and size, this connector has been replaced by many MAU vendors. The connector that is commonly used on new MAUs is the RJ-45 connector. This is the same connector that is used on Ethernet 10BASET concentrators but the pinouts are different. IBM has switched its MAUs to use the RJ-45 connector on the 8230 and 8250 MAUs. The IBM 8228 is the only IBM MAU that uses the hermaphroditic connector.

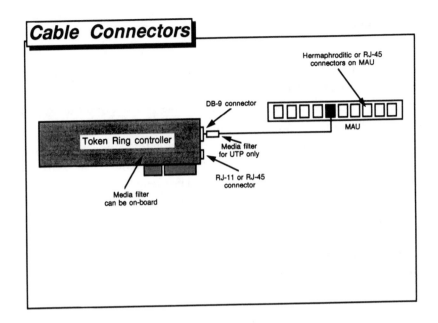

- There are four types of connectors:

   The DB-9 is always located on the controller card.

   The RJ-11 is always located on the controller card.

   The RJ-45 can be located on the controller card or on the MAU.

      — The RJ-45 connector costs less than the hermaphroditic.

      — It is used with most modern types of MAUs.

   The hermaphroditic (or universal data connector, UDC).

   If it is used, it is always located on the MAU or on a cable that attaches to the MAU.

      — It is used with the IBM 8228 MAU.

      — The MAU connection is actually vendor specific.

      — Most concentrator vendors have switched to the RJ-45 connector.

      — IBM has switched to the RJ-45 connection with its 8250 hub.

- With the exception of RJ-11, any of the connectors can be used for shielded or unshielded twisted pair cable.

TYPE 3 MEDIA FILTER

As mentioned earlier, there is another device that must be used on cable plants that use Type 3 cable. It is known as a *media filter*. The media filter is only used with UTP wire for Token Ring. This filter is a small rectangular box that is usually part of the UTP cable itself and must be located within close proximity of the controller card or directly attached to the controller card.

Its purpose is to filter out unwanted signals that may have entered the cable en route from the previous station. UTP cable does not use any shielding, and electrical noise may easily enter this type of cable. Any signals that are not within a certain range will be filtered out through this filter.

The media filter may be a separate item (placed directly on the DB-9 connector) or it may be an integral part of the UTP cable or it may be built on-board the Token Ring controller card that is in the network attachment. This filter may be part of the controller card, though it is not usually found there. If the media filter is built into the card, a UTP cable may be directly attached to the controller card through the connector on the controller card.

Type 3 Media Filter

- Type 3 cable requires a device known as a media filter.

- Its purpose is to filter out any unwanted signals.

- It is a small rectangular device that is usually part of the UTP cable itself.

- It can be a separate device that attaches to the UTP cable at the end of the cable that attaches to the controller card.

- It can be used on 16- or 4-mb Token Rings.

- It is only used with Type 3 (UTP) cable.

Token Ring Wiring Concentrators

The terminating point for all wiring in a Token Ring network is the wiring concentrator commonly called the MAU, or Multistation Access Unit; it is similar to the Ethernet concentrator. There are many styles of this concentrator and each is vendor specific. The one that will be discussed first will be the IBM 8228. This is the original MAU used with the introduction of Token Ring from IBM in 1985. No matter which type of MAU is used, they all operate in the same manner.

There are ten ports on the 8228 of which eight are used for network attachments. The other two are used for connecting to another MAU and are called the Ring In (RI) and Ring Out (RO) ports. This type of MAU does not require any external power.

IBM recommends for shielded twisted pair that up to 260 devices may be connected to one ring. Therefore up to thirty-three MAUs may be connected together (through the Ring In and Ring Out ports). Four ports will be left empty. For UTP wire only seventy-two devices may be connected up to one ring. Therefore only nine MAUs may be connected together. Modern MAUs that are really concentrators go beyond this specification for UTP, usually allowing for up to 120–150 UTP attachments to one ring. This type of MAU is covered later in the Modern MAU section.

The IBM 8228 is a nonintelligent device that does not contain any logic to allow for network management. IBM introduced the 8230 a few years back. The 8230 looks like four 8228 MAUs put together, and can connect to other MAUs through a copper or fiber repeater. The 8230 is available with RJ-45 connectors. This is an intelligent device that does allow for network management. This information may include how many data ports are active, whether any of the ports have problems, whether the RI or RO ports are active (indicating a connection to another MAU), the addresses of the network stations on the ring down to identity of addresses to a specific port, bytes and packets, lost tokens, and more.

Currently IBM is reselling a concentrator known as the 8250. This concentrator functions physically similar to the Ethernet concentrator. Modules slide into the concentrator as more connections are needed. Type 1, 2, or 3 cable can be used. There are only RJ-45 connections to this concentrator. The hermaphroditic connector is not used. Even with all the changes, any Token Ring concentrator is still called a MAU.

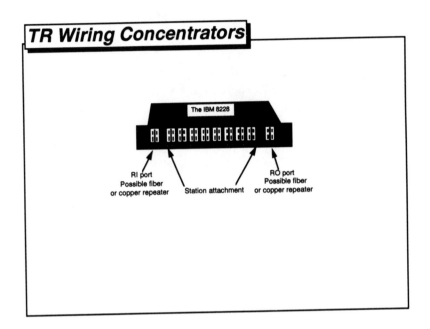

- When Token Ring was first introduced, all MAUs emulated IBM's concentrator for connection of all ring stations.

    It is called the IBM 8228.

    It has no network management capabilities.

    It requires the use of a special tool to set the relay into a known state.

- The 8228 contains ten connector ports.

    Eight for network station attachment and two for connection to another MAU.

- The outer two connectors will be labeled Ring In (RI) and Ring Out (RO).

    RI is for the incoming path of another MAU.

    RO is the outgoing path to another MAU.

- The above MAU is shown for Shielded Twisted Pair (STP) connections.

    UTP MAUs will have RJ-45 connectors in place of the hermaphroditic connectors.

- IBM recommends 260 stations as the maximum for a ring using Type 1 or Type 2 cable. Using Type 3 the maximum recommended number of stations is 72.

    This allows for up to thirty-three MAUs to be connected together for Type 1 or Type 2 cable.

    Up to nine MAUs may be connected together for UTP cable.

- Different vendors support different physical configurations of the MAU.

MULTIPLE MAU CONNECTION

For more than eight attachments (using the IBM 8228), a MAU must be concatenated with another MAU. This is the purpose of the RI and RO ports. These ports are not used for network attachments but only to connect to other MAUs. The RI port of one MAU connects to the RO of another MAU. For example, in a three-MAU network (allowing up to twenty-four network attachments), the RI from the first MAU will be connected to the RO of the second MAU. The RI of the second MAU will be connected to the RO of the third MAU and the RI of the third MAU will be connected to the RO of the first MAU. It should now be apparent why this is called the star wired ring topology: logically, the network is a true ring; physically network attachments are connected to the ring in a star pattern.

If there are fewer than eight connections, only one MAU needs to be used and the RI and RO ports need not have any attachments to them (for the IBM 8228). In other words, for a single MAU, the RI and RO ports are empty.

Finally, as stated before, STP cable can handle up to 260 stations on one ring, which requires 33 MAUs to be connected to one another. Even with this many MAUs, the last MAU should be connected back to the first MAU on the ring.

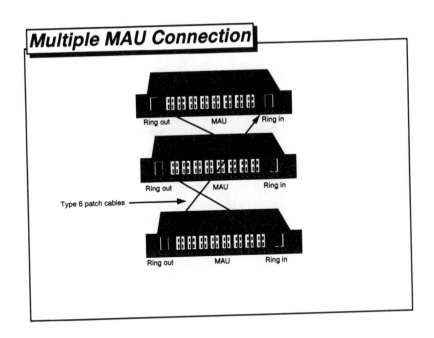

- The RI from one MAU is connected to the RO of the next MAU.

- The RO from one MAU is connected to the RI of the next MAU.

- The last MAU should have a connection back to the first MAU.

- If there is only one MAU, no connection from its RI to RO is necessary. This is vendor-specific, though.

- Interconnection of the MAUs is used when there are two or more MAUs that will be placed on the same ring.

- Up to thirty-three MAUs may be interconnected in an STP configuration to allow for one ring.

- Up to nine MAUs can be used for UTP to allow for one ring.

CONTROLLER ATTACHMENT TO A MAU

A MAU's data ports connect to network attachments. The cables that run from the MAU to the network attachment are called *lobe* cables. The cables are of Type 1, 2, or 3 cable. The IBM 8228 uses the hermaphroditic connector on the MAU data ports.

The cable run from the MAU to the network attachment can be from one to three-hundred meters long. The current accepted maximum is one-hundred meters for both UTP and STP cable. Typically all Token Ring cable terminates in one room. These cables are run through patch panels and may be separated into different rings. The rings may be tied together through devices known as bridges or routers, which are discussed later in this book.

There is one stipulation when running cable. UTP and STP cable cannot both be used on the same ring. Although there are sites that do this and the ring appears to operate, in the long run, problems will inevitably occur (for example, when adding stations beyond the network attachment specification allowed for the media type).

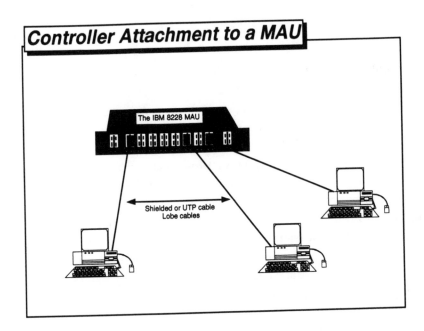

Controller Attachment to a MAU

The IBM 8228 MAU

Shielded or UTP cable
Lobe cables

- The connection of a network controller to the MAU is accomplished using Type 1, 2, or 3 cable. Using any type, the maximum recommended length is 100 meters.

- The cable that interconnects the network controller to the MAU is called the lobe cable.

- STP and UTP cable cannot be used on the same ring.

MAU Operation

When a station is attached to a data port on a MAU, the MAU does not automatically include it into the ring. There is an initialization procedure that must occur before the station is considered an active station on the ring. One part of this procedure is activating a relay in the MAU. Attaching to the ring is actually a five-stage process that is explained in detail later, in part 2 of this book.

There is a component in the MAU known as an *electronic relay* or simply a *relay*. This device is very similar to the relay that controls the turning signal in an automobile, in that when the voltage is applied to the relay, the relay will flip to a closed state allowing current to flow to the light bulb that illuminates on the outside and inside of the car. When the voltage is removed, the relay will flip to the opposite or normal state and the voltage is removed from the turning bulb and it is turned off.

In the MAU, when the controller in the network attachments initiates, it applies a small voltage to the lobe cable. This is called a *phantom* voltage because it will not be mistaken for a data signal, but will be applied while there is data running over the wire simultaneously. While this voltage is applied, the relay in the MAU flips to the closed state, which opens up the MAU's internal bus to the lobe cable and allows data to flow to the network attachment.

For example, with all stations active in a three-station network, the MAU will have three relays in the closed state; the other five relays will be in the open state. Therefore, data will flow only between the three stations that have their relays closed. Even if there were stations attached to the other ports, as long as the phantom voltage is not applied, the relay will not flip to the closed state. This will keep the network attachment from being connected to the MAU bus.

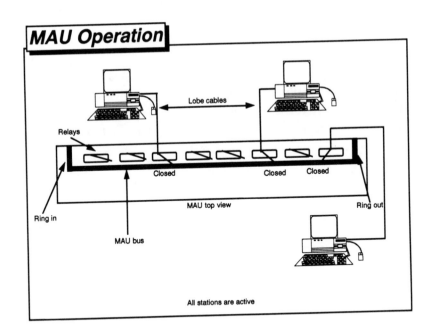

- A physical attachment to a MAU alone does not include it into the active ring; the relay in the MAU must be opened.

- Part of the controller initialization will activate the relay in the MAU by applying a phantom voltage on its transmit pair to the MAU.

- Applying the phantom voltage will energize the relay and allows the network attachment a logical connection into the active ring.

MAU Operation (Cont.)

An example of the same three stations in a network with one of the stations not having an active connection. That relay will be in the open state. Therefore there will only be two stations on the network and the data will flow between them. The data will be bypassed on the MAU port connected to the third inactive station. The data will not travel down the lobe cable of the third inactive station.

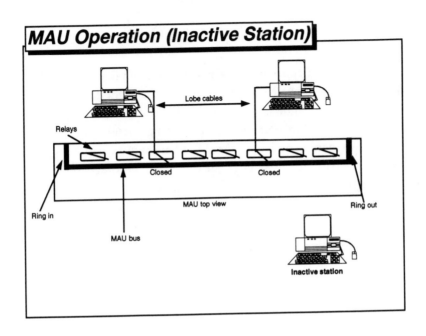

- Three stations are physically attached to the MAU.

- The inactive station is physically attached to the ring but not logically.

- The two active stations have energized the relay which allows a logical connection to the ring.

- The one station that is inactive does not apply the phantom voltage to the MAU and therefore the relay is not flipped.
  The station is physically connected to the MAU but not logically connected to the MAU.

RING LENGTH

There is a simple but important concept that relates to active and inactive stations on the ring. It is called the *ring length*. Say there is one MAU that has three of its eight data ports connected, the ring length is simply the sum of the lengths of the individual lobe cables.

For example, if each cable is 100 meters long, the ring length is 600 meters (100 meters out to the controller and 100 meters to travel back to the MAU). If one of those stations is not connected to the ring, its relay will be flipped to the closed state. The ring length becomes 200 meters shorter.

It becomes shorter since the relays are not flipped and the data on the ring will not flow out of those ports. Having one of those ports shut off subtracts 200 meters from the total ring length. This becomes important in terms of congestion, delays, and so forth. The more active stations that are placed on a ring, the longer the ring length and therefore the longer the delays. This concept is simply being introduced here for design considerations; it is not a fatal error or an error of any type, but you should know how the ring length can affect your operation.

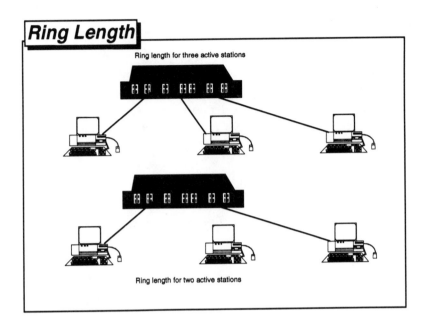

Ring Length

Ring length for three active stations

Ring length for two active stations

- Three active stations connected into one MAU makes the ring 600 meters in length assuming that each station is attached to a 100-meter lobe cable.

- If one station is not active on the ring it reduces the ring length by the length of its lobe cable, which in this case is 200 meters.

- Shorter ring lengths can produce a faster ring since there is less total cable for data to travel on.

Modern MAUs

Though IBM still makes the 8228, it has since developed the 8230 MAU. It really is just four 8228s connected to one repeater module that contains the one RI and one RO ports. The 8230 is an active repeater in that the data ports are actually repeater ports. It uses the expensive hermaphroditic connectors but is available with RJ-45 connectors as well. The 8230 is an intelligent device in that it contains network management capabilities. The 8230 has not been copied by any other Token Ring vendor.

Other concentrator manufacturers have detoured from IBM's MAU design and incorporated the MAU as a module card that can be slid into a concentrator. The Token Ring concentrator is physically very similar to the Ethernet concentrator. The following text is generic and not specific to any one vendor's hub.

Each module board can hold up to eight RJ-45 connections. Multiple boards can be arranged into one ring using a network management module (that occupies one slot). This means that if the chassis can hold eight cards, seven cards can be configured into one ring. Any of the boards in one concentrator can be split off into multiple rings. The rings in the hub are separated but may be connected through the RI and RO ports. It is up to the individual hub vendor as to how it is configured. Separated rings can communicate with each other by using a bridge or a router (bridges and routers are detailed in Part 3 of this book)

These concentrators do not use the large and expensive hermaphroditic connectors. They support both shielded and unshielded twisted pair using the RJ-45 connector but the two wire types cannot be intermixed on the same ring. Their technology in essence allows each data port on the concentrator to become a repeated port, allowing 130–150 UTP stations to attach to one ring.

Token Ring specifications allow for 260 stations to attach to one ring using the more expensive STP cable, but this is poor design. One hundred to 150 stations per ring is the ideal maximum per ring, no matter which cable type is used. The point to be made here is that shielded twisted pair cable is expensive and if Type 3 cable can be used and the concentrator can support 130–150 stations per ring, Type 3 will suffice for most installations. This reduces the cost of a Token Ring installation.

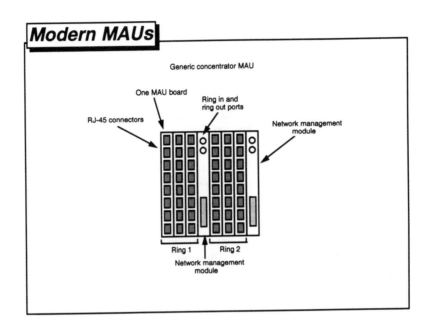

- The 8228 was the first MAU presented with Token Ring's introduction in 1985. It is still used today.

- After the 8228, came the 8230.
    It looks like four 8228s that are physically connected together.

- Other Token Ring MAU vendors took a different approach from IBM.
    The concentrator "boards" slide into a slot in the concentrator.
    Each board that slides into the concentrator can operate as a single MAU or the boards may be grouped together to form a single MAU.
        — Each board operates like a single 8228 MAU.
    The connector shell on the boards is an RJ-45, which is less expensive and enables high port density.
    These MAU boards will not have the RI and RO ports on them.
    A separate network management board that does not contain data ports contains the RI and RO ports.
        — This separate board also contains the network management software for the hub.
        — It can logically group any combination of MAU boards into one ring in the hub.

- This type of concentrator can house multiple independent rings.
        — Grouped MAU boards are separated by different backplanes in the concentrator.

- This type of concentrator uses a technology known as an "active hub," which allows for up to 130 stations to attach to one concentrator using UTP wire.

FDDI Physical Layer—Brief Overview

Fiber Data Distributed Interface (FDDI) offers an advancement in technology for LAN topologies. The FDDI standard is actually of a set of standards as established by the American National Standards Institute (ANSI). FDDI is a ring access method that uses a special bit pattern, called a token, that continuously circulates the ring for stations to gain access to a cable plant, which operates at 100 Mbps. It can connect up to five hundred dual attach stations in a two-hundred-km network. It differs from other ring access methods in that FDDI is a timed-token protocol; that is, each network station is guaranteed network access for a certain time period that is negotiated between all active stations upon startup and when a new station joins the ring.

FDDI stations may be of two types: Dual Attachment Stations (DAS) and Single Attachment Stations (SAS). To allow for simpler connection and better fault tolerance of the ring, stations may be attached to a concentrator which is connected to the ring.

An FDDI dual ring can consist of two rings (known as the primary and the secondary ring) that normally operate independently. Data can travel on each ring; the rings are counter-rotating to each other. Although data is allowed to travel on both rings, it is commonly found that data is transmitted only on the primary ring until a certain fault occurs in which the two rings may become one ring. When a fault does occur, such as a DAS station powering down or a cable break, the two rings combine to form one ring. This is known as *wrapping*.

The cable most often used with FDDI is fiber optic cable, though copper cable may also be used. This will be discussed in greater detail later in the book. Each ring is allowed to be 100 km. In the event of wrapping, the total ring length is allowed to be a maximum of 200 km. Twisted pair cable (UTP) is allowed to run up to 100 meters. An FDDI ring operates at 100 Mbps.

The use of concentrators is not required but is heavily recommended. These concentrators are functionally similar to the cable concentrators, as explained before under the Ethernet and Token Ring concentrator topics. Stations (both DAS and SAS) may attach to the concentrator and offer many efficiencies for the design of an FDDI network.

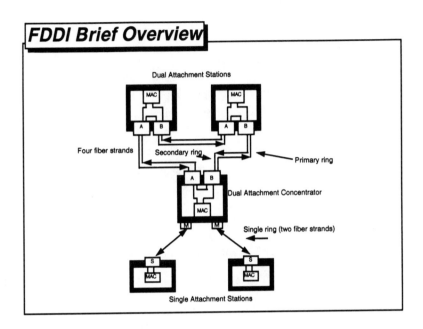

- FDDI is a set of standards published by the American National Standards Institute.
  FDDI is known as standard number X3T9.5

- Network attachments may be of two types: Dual Attachment Station (DAS) or Single Attachment Station (SAS).
  These attachments may be any device, such as a user's workstation, a bridge or router, or even a wiring concentrator.

- An FDDI network can connect up to 500 DASs or 1,000 SASs and operates at 100 Mbps.

- Stations access the ring by capturing a special bit pattern that continuously circulates the ring. This bit pattern is called a token.

- An FDDI ring actually comprises primary and secondary rings.
  In normal operation data only travels on the primary ring.
  In the event of a fault, wrapping causes the primary and secondary ring to combine.

- The primary cable that is used is fiber optic.
  Copper cable has been approved for FDDI.
  Fiber stations are allowed to be 2 km apart for multimode fiber.
  Stations can be 20 kilometers apart using single mode fiber.

- Although not required, FDDI networks generally rely on a concentrator.
  They are similar to the Ethernet and Token Ring concentrators previously mentioned.

OSI COMPARISON

FDDI operates at the physical and data link layers of the OSI model. The physical layer is split into two sublayers: The physical layer protocol (PHY) and the physical layer medium dependent (PMD).

The PHY is specified as the upper sublayer of the physical layer. It is responsible for symbols, line states, encoding/decoding techniques, clocking requirements, and data framing requirements.

The PMD sublayer is responsible the transmit/receive power levels, transmitter and receiver interface requirements, error rates, and cable and connector specifications. It comprises four standards:

1) Physical Layer Medium Dependent (PMD)

2) Single Mode Fiber Physical Layer Medium Dependent (SMF-PMD)

3) Low Cost Fiber Physical Layer Medium Dependent (LCF-PMD)—under development

4) Twisted Pair Physical Layer Medium Dependent (TP-PMD, also known as CDDI, for Copper Distributed Data Interface.

At the data link layer, FDDI is defined at the Media Access Control (MAC) layer. The MAC is located at the lower sublayer of the data link layer. It is responsible for data link addressing (the MAC address), media access, error detecting, and token handling.

Station Management (SMT) is defined at the physical layer and at the MAC sublayer of the data link layer. It is responsible for management services including connection management, node configuration, recovery from error conditions, and the encoding of SMT frames.

FDDI assumes the use of another protocol called IEEE 802.2 protocol, which is discussed later in this book. The IEEE 802.2 protocol is adopted to run on all four LAN standardized protocols. The IEEE 802.1 standard is also adopted to run over all four LAN protocols. The most noted of the IEEE 802.1 protocols is the 802.1 standards for bridging.

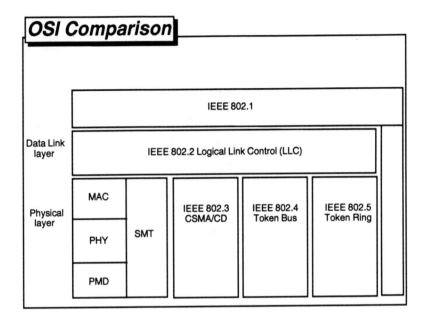

- The physical layer is split into two entities:
    The physical layer protocol (PHY), which is responsible for:
        — symbols (signals),
        — line states,
        — encoding/decoding techniques, and
        — clocking and data framing.
    The physical layer medium (PMD), which is responsible for:
        — transmit/receive power levels,
        — transmitter receiver interface requirements,
        — error rates, and
        — cable and connector specifications.

- At the MAC sublayer of the data link layer FDDI is defined as handling:
    data link addressing (the MAC address),
    media access,
    error detection, and
    token handling.

- Station management (SMT) covers all the above functions and is responsible for:
    connection management,
    node configuration,
    recovery from error conditions, and
    encoding of SMT frames.

FDDI CABLE

By far the most common cable choice for FDDI is fiber optic cable. There are two types used: PMD (multimode) and SMF-PMD (single mode). First, a look into fiber optic cable.

There are actually three pieces that make up fiber optic cable: the core, the cladding, and the protective coating. The core is a glass cylinder through which the light rays travel. The cladding is a glass tube that surrounds the core; its main purpose is to reflect any light rays back into the core. The protective coating is exactly that—a plastic coating that surrounds the core and cladding and protects it. The color of this cable is generic to the manufacturer of the cable.

The core and cladding are most commonly referred to by their diameters. The most common found are 50/100 micron, 62.5/125 micron, and 100/140 micron. In each, the first number refers to the diameter of the core and the second refers to the diameter of the cladding.

Light that travels through the fiber is called a *light ray*. Light is transmitted at one end of the cable and is received at the other end. In essence the connection of any two attachments is a point-to-point connection. A cable that is capable of handling many different light rays is called *multimode* fiber. Therefore a mode is a single light ray. Multimode fiber generally uses light emitting diodes (LEDs) as its light source. There is a large attenuation with multimode fiber. Attenuation is the loss of signal strength as the signal travels through the cable. High attenuation means a signal cannot travel as far down a cable when compared to a cable that has a low attenuation rate.

Single mode fiber (SMF) allows only a single light ray to travel through the fiber cable. It uses lasers as its light source and does not have a large attenuation rate like that of multimode fiber. The core of the fiber is usually 8–10 microns in diameter with a cladding diameter of 125 microns. Single mode comes at a higher cost partly because of the use of lasers as the light source. Stations may be up to 2 km apart using multimode fiber, while single mode fiber allows for the separation of up to 20 km.

Copper has been approved for FDDI cable and this standard has publicly adopted the name Copper Data Distributed Interface (CDDI). The cable run is allowed to be 100 meters and must be of Category 5 rating as rated by the Electronics Industry Association (EIA).

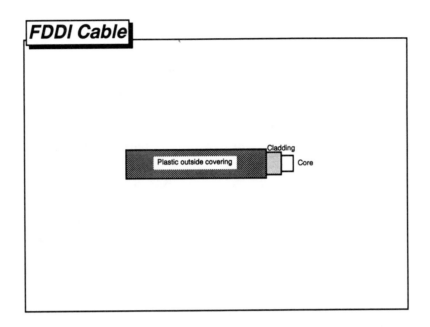

• The largest installation of cable for FDDI networks is fiber.

• The fiber cable is made up of three pieces:
    the core, which is the glass through which the light actually travels,
    the cladding, which is a covering of the core that reflects light back to the core, and
    the protective coating, which protects the fiber cable from hostile elements.

• FDDI cable is available in four common sizes (the first number refers to the core and the second number refers to the cladding):
    9/125 micron for single mode fiber.
    50/100 micron for multimode fiber.
    62.5/125 micron for multimode fiber.
    100/140 micron for multimode fiber.

• The recommendation from ANSI is 62.5/125 for multimode fiber and 9/125 single mode fiber.

• Copper has been approved for FDDI.
    It can be used only on Category 5 UTP type cable.
    The maximum cable run is 100 meters.

CONNECTORS

Although the FDDI standard allows for many types of connectors, two types of connectors are commonly used. These are the media interface connector (MIC) and the ST connector. The MIC is a flat rectangular connector used to connect multimode fiber to any type of FDDI network attachment. It is constructed with "keys" that are defined by the PMD standard. These are small plastic pieces that are inserted into the top of the connector to ensure the connector is placed on the correct port type (port types are explained in a moment). Although there are many ways to use these connectors, there are two types of common cables: MIC to MIC and MIC to ST.

The MIC houses one fiber pair. One fiber pair is the minimum needed to attach to an FDDI network. There are two MICs for dual ring attachment and one MIC used for single ring attachment. One fiber pair connects into each MIC; in this pair, one fiber is used to transmit and the other to receive.

ST connectors are commonly used to connect the fiber to an FDDI patch panel ST connectors are not keyed and care must be taken to ensure proper connection. One end of this type of cable will have the MIC connector, which can be used to plug in to an end station. The other end of the cable will have two ST connectors; one for transmit and one for receive, which is commonly used for attaching to a patch panel. Other cables in the patch panel will connect to the FDDI ring. ST connectors are less expensive than MIC connectors. The ST connector can be found on single attached stations.

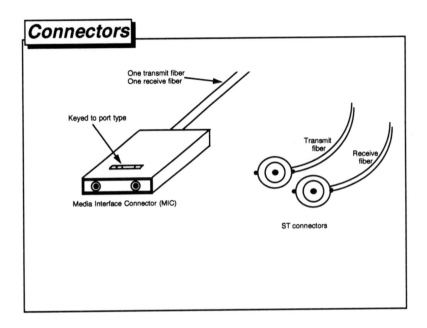

- FDDI allows for multiple types of connectors; two are commonly found:
    the Media Interface Connector (MIC), and
    the ST connector.

- The MIC is a flat rectangular connector and used to connect multimode attachments.
    It contains a small plastic "key" that enables correctly attaching ports types (explained later).
    There are two fibers in one MIC. One to transmit and one to receive.

- ST connectors are commonly used to connect fiber to an FDDI patch panel.
    The connector shell looks like a BNC connector (only smaller).
    STs are not keyed and care must be taken when attaching a station with ST connectors.
    They can be used with single attachment stations (SAS) and are less expensive than MIC.

PORT TYPES

To guard against illegal topologies, the FDDI standard identifies use of four port types: A, B, M, and S. Ports are the connectors on all FDDI attachments—concentrators, bridges, routers, and network end stations. The attachment can be a concentrator or a network end station. It may also be a bridge or a router. Any network attachment may use any of the port types; dual attachment stations have A and B port types, concentrators have A, B, M, or S port types, single attachment stations have only the S port type. The FDDI standard also mandates which port types are allowed to be connected to one another. A FDDI network uses a structured cable system and it will be cabled together to form a network by making sure the port types are legal connections.

In normal operation, an FDDI network is actually two rings. A DAS will have two ports: A and B. A DAS that enters the ring uses port A to connect to the incoming primary ring and the outgoing secondary ring. A DAS can be an end station or it can be a Dual Attachment Concentrator (DAC).

Port B is the opposite of port A. It connects to the outgoing primary ring and the incoming secondary ring.

Port M connects a concentrator port to a SAS port, DAS port, or another concentrator (DAC or SAC) port. This type of port is found only in a DAC or a SAC.

Port S connects a SAS or SAC to a concentrator (DAC or SAC).

The next topic will show the legal connections. Simple enough—almost all connections are allowed (whether desired or not) but one hard and fast rule must be adhered to: no S ports are allowed to connect directly to an A or a B port.

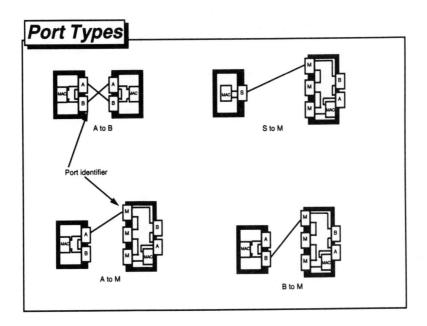

Valid FDDI Port Configurations

The following chart is a summary of the valid FDDI port configurations.

Valid FDDI Port Configurations

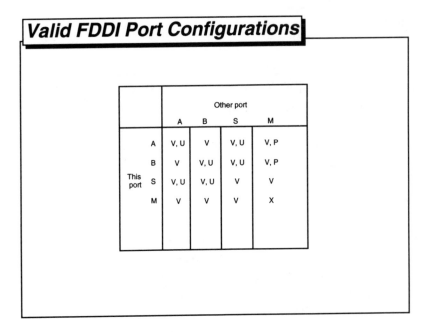

		Other port			
		A	B	S	M
This port	A	V, U	V	V, U	V, P
	B	V	V, U	V, U	V, P
	S	V, U	V, U	V	V
	M	V	V	V	X

• Legend:

    V indicates a valid connection.

    X indicates an illegal connection with SMT notification required.

    U indicates an undesirable connection with SMT notification required.

    P indicates a topology known as dual homing is in effect; B port takes precedence (FDDI topologies are covered in Part 2).

FDDI Station Classes

A station is any device that may connect to the ring—a concentrator, bridge, router, or an end user workstation. FDDI has two station classes: Dual Attachment Station (DAS) and a Single Attachment Station (SAS). A SAS provides the least expensive and simplest means of connection to an FDDI network. It has one S port and connects to the FDDI ring through the M port of a concentrator. It is a reliable, cost effective method of connecting to an FDDI network. It provides a single attachment to the ring and does not have a connection to the dual ring. Therefore, if the SAS connection is disabled, all ring connectivity is lost for that station.

SAS connections are used in network stations that may be powered off and on periodically. Since the S port of a SAS is connected to a M port of a concentrator, the M port of the concentrator provides port isolation from the rest of the ring network. This will cause little or no disruption of the main ring, since when the SAS port is inactive, the topology does not change.

The DAS connects to both the primary and secondary ring of an FDDI network. It has two instances of the PHY and PMD and one or two instances of the MAC; it may have a connection to an optical bypass relay. The optical bypass relay is an electromechanical device that allows for no disruption of the dual ring should the DAS become inactive. It allows the light to reflect to the next station as if the station were still active. However, the light will not be regenerated as it is reflected to the next station which can cause attenuation of the light. As we will see later, disruption of the dual ring can create problems.

The DAS has two ports: A and B. The A port connects to another station's B port, and the B port connects to another station's A port. It is important to note that a DAS does not require a concentrator for attachment to the ring; it is a full-function dual ring attachment. In case of a failure, the DAS can wrap the ring to isolate the failure. FDDI networks should not be designed using only DAS connections. This can lead to complications; for instance, if there is a failure, the dual ring may segment itself into separate autonomous rings. The purpose of wrapping is to isolate the failed components and bring the ring back up even if there are two or more rings. DAS is more expensive but more resilient than SAS.

A different type of connection known as dual-homing allows for different port types to be connected which will allow for fault resiliency. The B port of a DAS can connect to the M port of a concentrator. This isolates the DAS from the dual ring and allows the concentrator to bypass the DAS in the event of a failure. A DAS station may be dual homed to a concentrator if both its A and B ports are used. Each port is connected to an M port but on different concentrators. This is illustrated in the FDDI topology section.

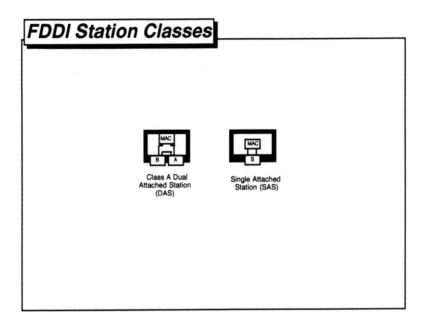

FDDI Station Classes

Class A Dual
Attached Station
(DAS)

Single Attached
Station (SAS)

• A Dual Attachment Station (DAS):
> is an FDDI station that can attach directly to the dual ring.
> can optionally attach to a single ring (M port of a concentrator).
> does not require a concentrator for attachment.

• A Single Attachment Station (SAS):
> is an FDDI station that attaches to the FDDI single ring through a port on a concentrator.
> is an inherent single point of failure.
> cannot attach directly to the dual ring.
> can attach to another SAS (creates a maximum limit of a two-station ring).
> has no fault tolerance.
> is lower in cost.

FDDI CONCENTRATORS

FDDI concentrators provide many benefits. The FDDI concentrator functions like the Token Ring concentrator or the Ethernet concentrator, but is technologically advanced. The FDDI concentrator is a repeater that operates at the physical layer. Concentrators allow for an FDDI network to be collapsed into a single node. It is simply a device that provides multiple ports for connection of network stations into the ring. It allows for multiple single attachment stations, dual attachment stations, and even other concentrators. Concentrators are not necessary to form an FDDI ring, but they allow for better network management, better topology designs, and greater efficiency.

One of the primary goals of an FDDI concentrator is to provide an FDDI service to those devices that may be powered on and off periodically. This normally would cause a disruption of the ring and may even segment the ring into two or more autonomous rings; the concentrator isolates its network attachments from the dual ring. Concentrators may be cascaded to form one of the most popular FDDI topologies: dual ring of trees. They provide the root of the tree topology. Topologies are discussed at the end of Part 1.

A concentrator may possess any of the four port types. To provide for this, there are two types of concentrators: dual attachment concentrators (DACs) and single attachment concentrators (SACs). DACs attach to the ring as a full dual ring device via its A and B ports. They provide multiple single attachment connections to SASs through their M ports. The DAC does not posses any S ports and does not require connection to a dual ring for it to become active. An FDDI network can be as simple as SAS connections to a standalone DAC.

The SAC attaches to the ring as a single ring device. It appears as a single attachment device and cannot connect directly to a dual ring, except through a DAC. A SAC will have one S port for connection to another concentrator's M port, and provides for multiple SAS connections through its M ports. The SAC does not need any connection on its S port to operate. It can provide FDDI connectivity to SAS stations as a standalone concentrator.

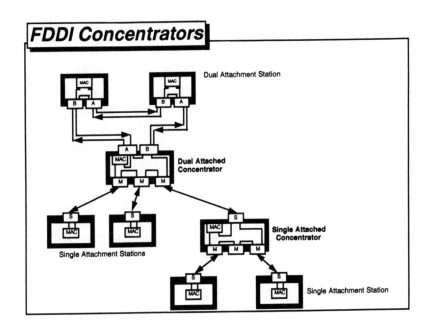

- A concentrator:
    is an FDDI network in a box.
    is a device that provides multiple ports on the FDDI cable plant for stations to insert.
    is primarily used for those stations that will be inserted on and off the ring often.
    provides for better management of the ring.
    provides the root of the tree topology.

- Two types:
    Dual Attachment Concentrator (DAC) which attaches to the ring as a full dual ring device.
    Single Attachment Concentrator (SAC) which attaches to the ring as a single ring device (attaches to a
        DAC).

CONCENTRATOR FUNCTIONS

Concentrators perform two functions: port bypass for inactive stations and port insertion for active stations. Port bypass is a concentrator port that is closed. This means that the attachment to that port does not have access to the FDDI network. No data from the FDDI network will flow out this port. The port being closed may have been caused by: an inactive station (powered off) connected to its port, network management shut the port down due to excessive errors, or a another management entity requested the shut down of the port. This usually does not affect the normal operation of the ring. Only those ports that have their port shut off will be affected and denied FDDI services.

Port insertion is the process by which the network attachment and its concentrator port have a good physical connection and the concentrator port inserts the attachment into the FDDI ring. This provides access to the services of the ring for the network attachment. The network attachment is an active participant of the FDDI ring.

The insertion process causes a momentary disruption of the active ring, but the ring corrects itself quickly and will return to normal operation. This process is accomplished in a very short amount of time.

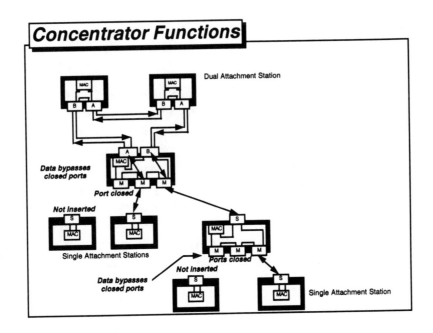

- Port bypass:
    is simply a concentrator port that is closed.
    does not allow data to flow to the attachment.
    may be due to the attachment being powered off.

- Station management (SMT) may have closed the port.

- Port insertion:
    is the process by which the network station and the concentrator port have a good physical connection.
    allows the port on the concentrator to be opened.
    allows the network attachment to become active on the ring.

FDDI PHYSICAL LAYER OPERATION

FDDI stations are connected into a network in a point-to-point, bi-directional physical connection formed between the physical layers of two stations, connected by their FDDI cable. Each attachment to the network has the ability to transmit and receive. A single physical connection has two fibers. A dual attachment will possess four fibers. This allows connection to each of the dual rings. The transmit fiber from one station is connected to the receive fiber of another station, and the receive fiber of one station will be connected to the transmit fiber of another station.

In the dual ring environment, data is allowed to flow in opposite directions on each ring. This is not common for it requires more expensive equipment to accommodate this. In most cases, data flows only on the primary ring. The secondary ring is used for backup. Each ring can be 100 km long, giving a total length of 200 km. Data on the primary ring flows counter-clockwise. Depending on the location of the break in a dual ring, the ring is said to wrap and the primary and secondary rings will collapse into one ring.

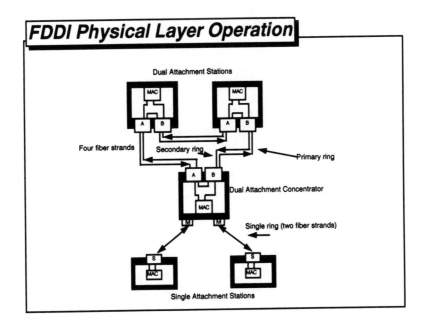

- FDDI defines the standards for the functions that control ring operation and the maintenance necessary for proper operation of the ring.

- Data may flow in opposite direction on the two rings.
    Data on the primary ring flows in a counterclockwise direction until a fault occurs.
    During normal operation data does not flow on the secondary ring.
    Most implementations use only the primary ring until a fault occurs.
      — It is lower in cost to implement this (only one MAC is implemented).

- Data is transmitted and received using two fibers (one for transmission and one for reception).

- Dual ring operation requires the use of four fibers (two for transmission and two for reception).

- Due to default timers, the total length of one ring is limited to 200 kilometers.

- Each ring is limited to 100 kilometers, allowing for 200 kilometers in the event of a fault.

FDDI Station or Ring Breaks

An FDDI ring can operate on two rings: the primary and the secondary ring. In normal operation, data will flow only on the primary ring. The secondary ring will remain inactive until there is a failure. In this case, the ring will wrap and the primary and secondary rings will act as one ring.

There are many conditions that will cause a ring to wrap. What breaks determines how the ring will wrap. An FDDI dual ring will continue to wrap until the failure is isolated. For example, in a network that has five dual attachment stations, data will normally flow in a counter-rotating fashion. If there is a break in the fiber between stations B and C, they will wrap the ring between station B to A and C to D. This will create a single ring topology. This will allow the network to continue operating. Network management will indicate the at the ring is wrapped and will identify which stations wrapped it. This allows network administrators to find the cable break and fix it. Once the FDDI stations have determined the cable has been restored, they will automatically rewrap the ring to again provide a dual ring topology.

Not only will the ring wrap if a cable becomes disabled, but if a dual attached station becomes disabled. If station B became disabled, stations A and C would wrap the ring again. Station A would wrap the ring with station E and station C would wrap the ring with station D. If station B has the optical bypass switch installed, the ring may not wrap. The signal would be reflected to station A just as if station B was still active. If the distance between station C and A is more than 2 km, the ring may wrap. This would occur because a multimode fiber run more than 2 km could deplete the strength of the signal; station A would not be able to receive and process it as a valid signal. Station A loses connectivity with station B and the ring wraps.

In another scenario, station B and D become disabled, station A will wrap with station E and station C will become isolated. If the fiber broke between Stations A and B (not shown) and the fiber broke between station E and D, station A would wrap with station E and B, C, and D would wrap to each other. This will provide two dual attach rings. Something as simple as powering off a DAS attachment will cause a disruption. This is the why stations that attach to the dual ring should be stable devices. All other devices should attach to the FDDI topology through the use of a concentrator.

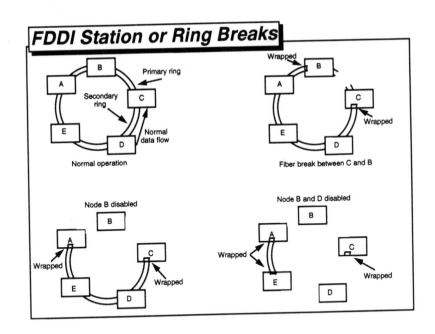

- During normal operation of the ring, data flows on the primary ring in a counter-clockwise fashion.

- If a fault occurs, the ring will wrap.

- For example:
    If there is a break in the fiber between attachments B and C,
        — B and C will wrap, creating a single ring for all stations.
    If station B becomes disabled,
        — A and C will wrap creating a single ring with stations A, C, D, and E.
    If station B and D become disabled,
        — A and E will wrap, creating a single ring with stations A and E.
        — Station C is still active but both its ports are wrapped to itself.

THE DATA LINK LAYER FOR ETHERNET, TOKEN RING, AND FDDI

DATA LINK DEFINITION

The second layer of the OSI model is the data link layer. This is the layer that is responsible for physical addressing, framing, and ensuring that error correction is added to the data that is handed to it by the upper layer protocols of the OSI model. It will then pass the data (now known as a *packet*) to the physical layer for transmission to the network. This layer is also responsible for the algorithms that control the reception and transmission of data on the network.

Defined at this layer is a concept known as access methods known as Ethernet, Token Ring, and FDDI. Their true names for the algorithm they perform will be explained later.

An access method is a set of procedures or rules (an algorithm) that defines a method of how to access the LAN. As the name implies, it is simply a method that determines access. Somehow, data must be transmitted and received in good form. All stations that attach to a single LAN attach to one cable plant (without the use of bridges or routers, which are explained later), and this singular access must be controlled so that all are allowed fair access.

Data travels to and from network stations, but the access method does not care about this. An access method is concerned about whether it can transmit and receive reliably. It is also concerned about whether it can receive the data in good form. Notifying a source station that a destination station received the packet is not a matter for the access method. Access methods are simply the vehicles used to acquire a given communications channel and permit the data to be transmitted and received.

Although they are not difficult to learn, access methods required years of research and even more years of laboratory experiments before they were actually implemented. Ethernet took seven years before it became available to commercial business and much more research had been done before that acted as a catalyst for Ethernet.

Data Link Definition

- Access methods
  - The second layer of the OSI model is the data link.
  - Access methods are defined here.
  - An access method is a set of procedures or rules (an algorithm) that defines the methods to access the LAN.
  - Access methods are the vehicles used to acquire a given communications channel and permit the data to be transmitted and received.
    » LAN access methods care only about whether they can transmit and receive data on the network.

  - Albeit not complex to understand, the access methods of Ethernet, Token Ring, and FDDI, took years of research and development just to develop the prototypes.

PACKETS

Ethernet, as used in this book, is a generic term than can mean an Ethernet network or an IEEE 802.3 network. Unless otherwise stated, Ethernet will imply either IEEE 802.3 or Ethernet. Both will be explained later in the chapter.

Network stations can communicate only through the use of packets. There are many different types of packets, depending on the access method (Ethernet, Token Ring, FDDI) and software protocols (TCP/IP, IPX, etc.) that you may be using. But there is a general format that can be used to show what a packet looks like.

Each packet has a definite beginning, middle, and end. It contains network headers, a data field (for data or control information), and network trailers. Network headers and trailers are information that is used by the network hardware and software in the network station. This can be control information, network addressing, error detection schemes, etc. Network headers and trailers are for use only by the network components, which provide information to the network hardware and software as to how to process the packet.

Say, for example, that a workstation is connected to a file server and requests that a block of data from a file be read and transmitted to the workstation. The workstation addresses the packet to the file server; the network headers contain some type of control field that the file server would recognize as a file read, as well as how much to read. Once the requested information is found, it is readied for transmission back to the requester.

The file server addresses a new packet, puts the response data in the data field, calculates a checksum[1] and submits the packet back to the originator of the request. Each OSI layer of the protocol stack adds its network header or trailer information to the packet, then transmits it to the network. If the packet requires multiple responses, all responses will be sent back in the same manner.

---

[1] A *checksum* can be thought of as a fancy parity checker. It is an algorithm that applies a calculated number based on the number of bits in the original packet. When the packet is received, the same checksum algorithm is used and the result is compared to the received checksum number. If the two match, the packet is accepted. If the two are different, the packet is discarded.

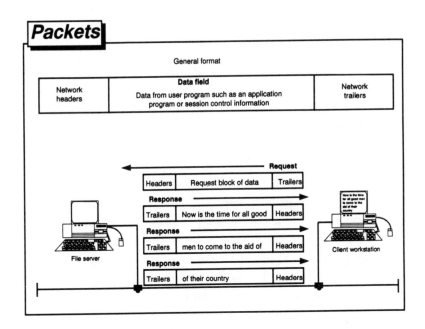

• Network stations communicate through the use of packets.
   There are different packet types depending on the access method and network software used.

• Packets have a maximum and minimum size and a definite beginning and ending.

• Generally, the format of the packet is: network headers, a data field, and network trailers.
   Network headers and trailers are placed in there by the network hardware and software.

• For example:
   A network station requests a block of data from its file server.
      — The network station builds a request packet and transmits it to the network.
      — The file server receives this request and builds response packets.
• The file server sends the response packets back to the requesting network station.

DATA PACKETS

Before the data link layer is explained, the concept of how communication takes place between two stations needs to be discussed. How do stations pass information back and forth over a network?

Communication on a network occurs when stations send and receive data. This data could be user data or some type of command/response message indicating an action needs to be performed, such as open, create, write, or close a file. Simply reading information off a remote station's hard disk and transmitting to the network is not enough; the data must be formatted for transmission onto the network. The transfer of information between stations is accomplished when the source station packages the data for transmission over the network. The packet contains the user data or control information for the remote station; each network type, Ethernet, Token Ring, or FDDI, formats its information differently. A packet is sent to another station that unformats it and acts upon its information. The formatting of the data is called *data encapsulation*.

But what exactly are packets? Basically, a packet is a unit of information that one station addresses to one or more other stations on the network to relay certain data or control information. A packet may contain user data or it may contain control information upon which a receiver station may act. User data could be data that was received from a Lotus 1-2-3 or WordPerfect file, for instance. Control data may, for example, ask another station to read a file and send the contents of that file to the requesting station.

In a sense, you may think of packets as sentences. A packet has a definite beginning, or network header, and ending, or network trailers, that is pertinent to the network controller card or the network software that is operating in the network station. Like an English sentence, which is usually directed to one or more persons, packets at the data link layer have source and destination addresses that specify what station initiated the packet and what station the packet is intended for. A sentence could contain command or control information. For example, asking someone to sit down or to move can be a command or control sentence. This is the same type of information that network stations send to each other. Network stations can communicate only through the use of packets.

Data Packets

- Communication on a network occurs by network stations building and sending packets.

- You may think of packets as sentences.

- A packet is a unit of information that one station on the network addresses to one or more stations to relay certain data or control information.

- The packet may contain:
  - user data (such as information from Lotus or WordPerfect).
  - control information that is specific to the network operating software (such as acknowledgements, errors, and so forth) or both.

OSI Layers as Packet Headers

With the exception of the physical layer, each layer of the OSI model may add the network header or trailer information into a packet. The position of each layer's information is formatted as it resides in the OSI model. Each layer of the OSI model will create its own header or trailer information. Since the data link layer is closest to the physical layer (which transmits the data), the beginning of each data packet contains data link header information. Following this in the packet is network, transport, session, and application header information. Presentation layer information is not usually present in the packet since this layer deals with data encryption and data formatting (EBCDIC to ASCII translation, etc). Again, the physical layer is not part of the packet. Its function is to transmit the raw data onto the media.

Each layer of information is placed into a packet at a certain location. An Ethernet packet's maximum size is 1,518 bytes. Adding the header and trailer information will not increase the size of this packet to over 1,518 bytes. The headers consume part of the data field, which leaves less room for the actual data.

As information travels down the OSI stack (starting from the application layer), each layer that is active in the model[2] adds its appropriate header. For example, when data is received by the session layer from the application layer, the session layer will add its header before the application layer information. The session layer then passes the whole unit of information down to the transport layer. This layer adds a transport layer header before the session header. This unit information is then passed to the network layer. The network layer then adds addressing information and passes the unit information down to the data link layer for addressing and error detection fields. The packet would then be passed down to the physical layer for transmission onto the network.

The receiver of this packet strips off the data link headers and passes the information to the network layer. The network layer reads, processes, and strips off the network layer header and passes the rest of the information to the transport layer. Each layer reads, processes, and strips off its respective headers until the information reaches the application layer.

---

[2]Not all layers are active in every network protocol. For example, a protocol known as NetBIOS implements only the session layer. Therefore this protocol places only session layer and data link layer information into the packet. Other protocols implement the full OSI stack, which places each layer's header into the packet.

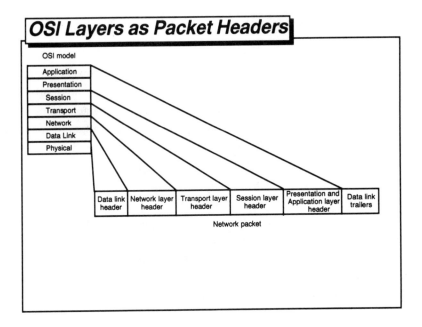

- Each OSI layer that is present in the network software or hardware adds its respective header to the packet.

- When the packet is received at the remote end of a connection, this header information is stripped off by the same OSI layer software.

- For example, the transport layer software processes only the transport layer header in the packet.
    The other layers will process their headers and leave the other headers alone.

- The maximum and minimum packet size for any network does not increase.
    The layers use the existing data field of the packet to place their information.

LAN Controller Types

Ethernet, Token Ring, and FDDI possess similar controller types which vary from manufacturer to manufacturer. They come in all shapes and sizes, and can be configured differently. They all adhere to their respective access method but the configuration and physical characteristics vary.

There are network controllers for almost every type of computer system made today. IBM supports the Token Ring, Ethernet, and FDDI standard through a front-end processor known as the 3172. Digital Equipment Corporation (DEC) supports Ethernet, Token Ring, and FDDI for its complete range of mini computer and personal computer systems. The controller card will be different for each type of computer bus design involved.

There are two types of network controller cards: intelligent and non-intelligent controllers. Intelligent controllers contain "computer on a board" technology; that is, they can run network software on the card, instead of through the computer system. Non-intelligent controllers do not have this capability and take all their instructions (except for the handling of the LAN protocol) from the particular computer systems in which they reside. A certain type of controller may affect the data throughput speed but not the transmission speed of a particular access method.

LAN Controller Types

- A LAN controller is the interface to the network for attached devices
  - Device could be a mainframe, mini, personal computer, laser printer, bridge, router, etc.
  - Basically, any device that has the ability to communicate over a network.

- There are different controllers for any type of computer system.

- Controllers vary in their capabilities (intelligent and non-intelligent controllers).
  - Intelligent controllers perform protocol processing on the controller
  - Nonintelligent controllers depend on their computing device for protocol processing.

- Controllers are available to attach to all types of cabling schemes.

Non-intelligent Controllers

When controller cards were first developed for host computers (mainframes, minis, and personal computers), the controller developed was a non-intelligent controller card. This means that the cards contained very little intelligence or memory. Their primary function was to accept data from the cable (usually up to 8 kb buffering) and from the computer to transmit onto the LAN.

For personal computers, this was the original type of controller developed. It does not contain any intelligence that allows network software to be downloaded to the card; all network software runs as an application on the PC. Most network software is a small program that runs in the background of the operating system, allowing user applications to run concurrently. Network software is becoming an integral part of a computer's operating system.

A non-intelligent controller card consumes a half-slot in a PCs expansion bus. Personal computers today are powerful and fast, and this allows the non-intelligent card to run in them. Non-intelligent cards are inexpensive when compared to the intelligent cards and are available in 8-, 16-, or 32-bit data paths. The data path is the "highway" over which information is exchanged between the LAN controller and the computer's memory. The larger the data path, the faster the information can be transferred.

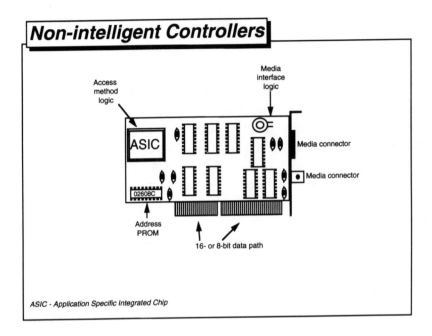

Non-intelligent Controllers

ASIC - Application Specific Integrated Chip

- Non-intelligent controller cards are the most popular type of controller cards.

- They do not contain any intelligence except for access method protocol.

- All network software resides on the associated computing device and is becoming part of the computer's operation system.

- The non-intelligent controller allows for concurrent operation of multiple network software protocols.

- The controllers are available in 8-, 16-, or 32-bit data paths.

INTELLIGENT CONTROLLERS

Around 1985, intelligent cards started to emerge into the marketplace. The reason behind this emergence was that the networking software that ran on a workstation was generally very large. Though mainframe and mini computers were not necessarily strapped to a memory constraint, personal computers (IBM PCs running under the DOS operating system) were bound to a memory space that barely allowed enough room to run applications. Intelligent controllers could hold a large part of the downloaded network software, while a small amount—primarily used to allow a data path between the intelligent controller and the personal computer—still ran on the PC. Mainframe and mini computer controllers adopted the philosophy that networking software should be able to run on the controller card. These cards were also the first to hold 16-bit paths. This means that data can be transferred on a 16-bit data path as compared to an 8-bit data path previously available.

The intelligent controller card has several disadvantages, however. First, it is expensive. Though, it allows for the downloading of protocols, offloading of network processing, and large packet buffering, and was the first controller card that contained the 16-bit interface, the expense of this card prevented widespread popularity. Also, the intelligent card slows down faster computer systems, which must wait for it to finish processing before they can continue with another task.

The non-intelligent card again became very popular when the network software that ran on the personal computer became smaller, tighter, and faster. Also, when the availability to use more memory on a DOS PC became available, network protocols were loaded into this memory space and not into a memory space for applications.

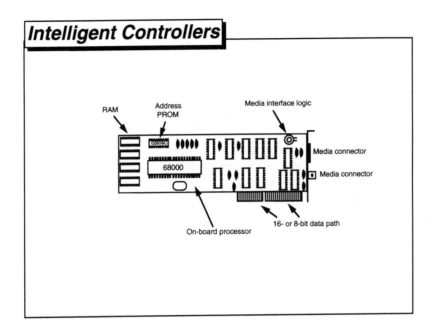

Intelligent Controllers

- Intelligent controllers:
    download network protocols.
    offload the protocol processing from the computer's CPU.
    allow for large send and receive packet buffering.
    use either an 8- or 16-bit data path.
    are very expensive.
    are not the primary controller card in use today.

- They are still used in file servers and protocol analyzers.

MAC Layer Addressing

LANs were developed to be protocol-independent (independent of the upper-layer protocol) and therefore each attachment to a LAN has a unique address called the media access control or MAC address. It is called the MAC address because it is at the MAC sublayer of the data link layer that this address is defined.

On Ethernet, Token Ring, and FDDI networks, each network attachment has a unique address that is 48 bits (6 bytes) long. Two-byte addresses are permitted with the IEEE 802.3 and the IEEE 802.5 network, though they are rarely implemented. Six-byte addresses are the norm for Ethernet/IEEE 802.3, Token Ring, and FDDI networks. The beginning of each packet header will contain physical addresses known as the destination and source address. The source address is the address of the network attachment that transmitted the packet and the destination address is the address of the intended recipient of the packet.

There are three types of addresses on a LAN: unique, multicast, and broadcast. A *unique address* is an address that is not replicated by any other station in the network. A *multicast address* is an address intended for a group of network attachments. In other words, if a packet is addressed (meaning the destination address) to a multicast address, the intended recipient is a group of network stations that have been programmed to accept that address. One address can be used to reach multiple destination stations. A *broadcast address* is a form of multicast address that is intended for all network stations on the network. This is usually indicated by all 1s (binary) in the destination address. When a packet has a broadcast address, all stations on the network will receive and process this packet, except those separated by a router.

LANs are broadcast-oriented, which means that when a packet is transmitted it will be received by every active network attachment—though it may not be destined for every active network attachment. When a network attachment receives a packet, it will compare the destination address with its own address. If there is a match, the packet is processed; otherwise the packet is discarded. There is a reserved bit in the destination address only that is designated as the multicast bit, and when the controller reads this bit it will know whether the address is unique (the bit will be a zero) or a multicast (the bit will be a binary 1).

MAC Layer Addressing

- LANs were developed to be independent of the network software protocol.

- The only way that one station can talk directly to another on a LAN is through the MAC address.

- There are three types of of 48-bit (6-byte) addresses.
    - Unique
        » also known as unicast.
    - Multicast
        » one packet intended for a specific group of workstations on a LAN.
    - Broadcast
        » A special type of multicast in which the packet is intended for all stations.
        » Broadcast and multicast packets are determined by one bit in the destination field.
        » A source address cannot be broadcast or multicast.

- LANs are broadcast-oriented (not to be confused with broadcast packets).
    - Every station can see every packet transmitted.
    - Each address in a network station is unique.
    - Each packet received is checked for an address match.

- Addresses are assigned by the IEEE.

GENERALLY DEFINING THE ADDRESS FIELDS

The MAC addresses are 6-byte addresses that physically identify the network attachment on the LAN. Each address must be unique, since two stations with the same MAC address on the same cable segment can be disruptive, i.e., may cause a packet to be received by the wrong station.

The address can be any combination of hexadecimal numbers as long as it is not duplicated by any other node in the network. Unique addresses are guaranteed in that the IEEE oversees the addressing. The 6-byte address is split into two 3-byte fields. The first three bytes are assigned by the IEEE to a single LAN vendor. Once those three bytes are assigned to a vendor, the IEEE will reserve that address for that vendor and will not distribute that address to any other requesting vendor. Another vendor will receive three different bytes. The vendor is allowed to use the last three bytes for controller addressing. The vendor should not assign the same three bytes twice. Usually, a vendor will increment by 1 the address of every controller it manufactures. This allows the vendor to create 2^{24} addresses. This address is burned into a PROM on each controller card. It is known as the *PROM address*. Token Ring allows for this address to be overwritten in that the network administrator may assign the address but it is rare that an Ethernet PROM address is overwritten. This is discussed later.

For example, the IEEE committee assigned the three bytes 02-60-8C to 3Com Corporation; 3Com may then assign to their network controllers (Ethernet, Token Ring, or FDDI cards) the following range of addresses 00-00-00 through FF-FF-FF. Thus, 3Com's full range of addresses is 02-60-8C-00-00-00 through 02-60-8C-FF-FF-FF. This allows for 16,777,216 addresses to be applied to 3Com's LAN controller boards; if a vendor runs out of addresses, it applies for another 3-byte block.

Thus, the first 3 bytes identify the vendor and the last 3 bytes identify the unique node on the network. But, just because the first 3 bytes are an identification of the vendor makes no difference to the controller card; it still reads all 6 bytes of any address upon receiving the packet.

Controllers from two different manufacturers may establish communications with one another; they make no differentiation based on the manufacturer of the card. Therefore, if a 3Com Ethernet controller card running on a PC establishes communications with a SUN Microsystems workstation on an Ethernet LAN at the data link layer, there is nothing prohibiting them from doing so. The first 3 bytes of the address would be different, but the controller cards do not care. The purpose of assigning each vendor a unique 3-byte address was to ensure uniqueness on a heterogeneous computing environment.

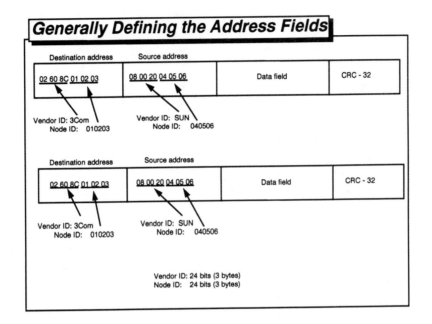

- The source and destination fields are placed at the beginning of each packet and contain 48 bits (6 bytes).
    The address is the sum of two parts.
    Physically identifies the address of the network attachment.

- The first three bytes indicate the vendor ID as assigned by the IEEE.
    IEEE reserves that address for the vendor.
    This ensures uniqueness in a heterogeneous environment.

- The last three bytes indicate the physical node address that is assigned by the vendor.
    This creates 2^{24} unique addresses for that vendor's controller cards.

- This address is known as the hardware or the PROM address.
    There is one PROM address per controller card.
    The address is "burned" into a PROM on the card.
    Upon controller initialization, software drivers will read the unique address from the PROM.

- Taken together, the numbers constitute a MAC address.

Overview of IEEE 802.3 and Ethernet

Electrical

Although Ethernet transceivers are virtually nonexistent (the original Ethernet transceivers have been superseded by the IEEE 802.3 transceivers), some IEEE 802.3 transceiver features should be mentioned. On the physical layer there are differences between the two. They are the signal quality error (SQE) test and the jabber control. SQE was added to the IEEE 802.3 specification to allow the transceiver to tell the controller that it is operating in good condition. This signal is for external transceivers only. External transceivers are separate from the controller card itself, and the controller card has no way of telling whether the transceiver is operating. This means that after every transmission, the transceiver will transmit a short signal to the controller board indicating an "I am alive" message. This message is transmitted up the collision detect wire in the transceiver cable. This signal is also sent when the transceiver detects a problem with the electrical signals on the cable plant. A problem arises with SQE when the controller card connected to a transceiver does not support it. The IEEE 802.3 transceiver transmits a SQE signal after every transmission; if the controller does not support this, it detects every transmission as a collision, and erroneously thinks it had a collision when it transmitted a good packet. This is an option and it should be turned off on a transceiver.

Jabber control is used by the transceiver to indicate when it has been transmitting for a certain length of time. If this timer expires, the transceiver stops transmitting. Ethernet is allowed to transmit one packet at a maximum of 1,518 bytes. This was implemented in case a faulty transceiver decided that it continuously had information to transmit. If a transceiver continually transmits, no other station can transmit. Before the jabber control circuitry was added, transceivers had to be removed from the cable plant one at a time until the faulty transceiver was found.

Packet Format

Ethernet and the IEEE 802.3 packet format are different. This discussion begins on the next page.

Link Control Services

Ethernet allows for a *connectionless service* only, meaning that there is no session setup before data is transmitted between two stations. A transmitting station assumes that the destination station is able and ready and immediately begins transmitting when requested. The transmitter also does not expect any acknowledgments. Generic IEEE 802.3 provides only for connectionless service as well. IEEE 802.3 with the IEEE 802.2 protocol allows for both connectionless and connection–oriented service. It is expected that IEEE 802.3 will use one type of service or the other. *Connection-oriented service* means that a session is set up (including sequencing and acknowledgments) between two stations before data is transmitted. IEEE 802.2 is discussed in greater detail later in the book.

Overview of IEEE 802.3 and Ethernet

- Electrical functions
  - The SQE test is used on IEEE 802.3 transceivers.
    - » Enables the controller to learn the status of an external transceiver.
  - Jabber control used on IEEE 802.3 transceivers.
    - » Disables a transceiver that talks for longer than it should.
  - Ethernet transceivers were only made with Ethernet V1.0.
    - » Virtually nonexistent today and not compatible with IEEE 802.3 transceivers.

- Packet format
  - Ethernet and IEEE 802.3 use different packet formats, as shown on the next few pages.

- Link control services
  - Ethernet has only unacknowledged connectionless service.
  - IEEE 802.3 can implement either connectionless or connection-oriented protocols when used with IEEE 802.2.

The Preamble, Ethernet

Now that MAC addresses have been explained, the rest of the packet header (at least the data link headers) will be easier to understand. The packet format for each LAN type will be shown in this section.

The start of an Ethernet frame contains the preamble. In order for data to be transmitted and received on an Ethernet network, the signal must be synchronized. A clocking mechanism is provided to accomplish this. Clocking provides for the synchronization of the bits in the frame. It allows for the differentiation between the 0 and the 1 bits. The clock signal is embedded with the data signal.

Every station on the network that transmits a packet will provide its own clock for the packet. The clock rate for Ethernet is 20 Megahertz, which combined with the data signal, yields a 10 Mbits per second transmission rate for Ethernet. Since there is not a master clock (that is, one station that provides the clock for the rest of the active stations) on an Ethernet LAN, an Ethernet controller's clock is provided by a chip on the transceiver. There may be a slight deviation of the clock signal from controller card to the next controller card and there must be a mechanism in place so that all Ethernet controllers may synchronize their receiver logic to that clock from the transmitting station. Therefore, the preamble is a 64-bit transmission to ensure that all Ethernet controllers synchronize their receiver logic with the clock of the incoming packet.

The Preamble, Ethernet

	MAC layer header			OSI layer 3 - 7 headers and data	MAC trailer
Preamble	Destination address	Source address	Type field	Data field	CRC-32

- There is no master clock on an Ethernet network.

- Each transceiver possesses its own clock.
    Not all clock chips will transmit with the same clock signal.
    The preamble is sent before the data packet to ensure that all receivers synchronize their clocks to the transmitter's clock.

- The preamble is 64 bits long.

BIT ORDER AND TRANSMISSION FOR ETHERNET AND IEEE 802.3

A packet is transmitted on a bit-by-bit sequence known as a *serial stream*—rather than a byte at a time—until all bits in the packet have been transmitted. This is true whether the network is Ethernet, Token Ring, or FDDI, although the order of transmission is different for Ethernet compared to Token Ring and FDDI. This may not seem important to understand but when the section on the Ethernet to Token Ring bridging is discussed, it will be readily noticeable why this section is important. The first bit transmitted is the multicast (M) bit, which indicates whether the packet has a multicast or unique address. If this bit is set to a 1 (binary) it is a multicast packet and the packet is destined for a group of stations on the network If the bit is set to a 0 (binary), the packet is destined for one station on the network. Therefore, in Ethernet packets, if the address starts with an odd number, it is a multicast packet.

For example the Ethernet address 02–60–8C–01–02–03 translated to binary will be:

02	60	8C	01	02	03
00000010	01100000	10001100	00000001	00000010	00000011

but the order in which it is transmitted onto the network will be:

01000000	00000110	00110001	10000000	01000000	11000000

Note that the bits in each byte are reversed during transmission. This is only for Ethernet transmission onto the cable plant. When the serial stream of bits is received by the Ethernet controller, the stream is reversed again. Only at the MAC layer (the source and destination address), is this important. The bit order for transmission is different for Token Ring and FDDI and this will again be explained in their respective sections. All of the different transmission methods will be brought together under the IBM 8209 section of the book.

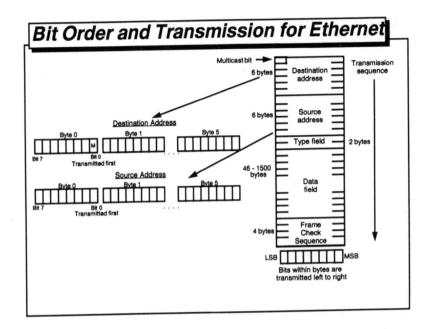

- Information transmitted on a LAN is transmitted bit by bit rather than a byte at a time.
    This is called a serial stream.

- Each LAN type transmits the bits differently to the LAN.

- Ethernet places bit 0 as the rightmost bit of a byte.
    For example, the address 02-60-8C translated into binary is 00000010 01100000
        10001100 . . . .
    The first three bytes transmitted on the cable are 01000000 00000110 00110001.
        — Each of the bits in each of the bytes is transmitted in reverse order of the way they are in the computer's memory.
        — The receiving controller reverses the bits when the packet is received.

- This reversal process is important to note.
    This is only important at the MAC layer header.
        — The rest of the packet is not effected.
    Ethernet transmits the bits differently from Token Ring or FDDI
        — This causes translation problems when trying to bridge the two (Ethernet to either method).

THE ETHERNET PACKET

The Ethernet packet is where the upper layer software puts its data to be transmitted onto the network. The MAC format of the Ethernet frame contains five fields:

1. the destination address,

2. the source address,

3. the type field,

4. the data field, and

5. the Cyclic Redundancy Check (CRC).

The source and destination address were explained earlier. The 2-byte type field identifies the network protocol that sent the packet. There are many network protocols that may run on a network. If the client server system of Novell NetWare is being used on a network, the Type field will contain a unique number that identifies the owner of the packet as Novell NetWare. If the packet is originated by the Transmission Control Protocol/Internet Protocol (TCP/IP), then another unique number would be in this field. The recipient of the packet would also have to be running the TCP/IP protocol to receive a TCP/IP packet. It will be received only by a similar protocol at the receiver end of the communication. In other words, a NetWare packet cannot be received by a station that is only running the TCP/IP protocol. The type field was originally governed by Xerox, but control over this has been assigned to the IEEE. Each protocol is assigned a unique number.

The data field is used for anything else. It can be used for upper layer (the network layer through application layer) protocols, headers, trailers, and user data.

The CRC is a 4-byte field that is used to guarantee 99.999% accuracy of the packet. The CRC is not an error *correction* mechanism, merely an error *detection* mechanism. That is, it will not correct any errors in the packet, but merely records that there was a data integrity error (a CRC error) and has the controller discard the packet. In Ethernet, it is the responsibility of the upper layer protocols to identify a discard packet. The Ethernet controller may discard a packet without notifying the sender.

When a packet is transmitted, a CRC is generated for the whole packet (including the address headers). When the packet is received, the receiving controller will also generate a CRC for the incoming packet. It will then compare its CRC with the received packet's CRC and, if the two do not match, the packet is discarded.

The Ethernet Packet

Preamble	MAC layer header			OSI layers 3 - 7 headers and data	MAC trailer
	Destination address	Source address	Type field	Data field	CRC-32

• The fields in order of transmission are:
   the destination address,
   the source address,
   the Type Field—indicates the protocol type,
      — Assigned by the IEEE. For example
         + 0800 indicates a TCP/IP packet.
         + 0600 indicates a XNS packet.
         + 8137 indicates a Novell NetWare IPX packet.
   the Data Field—contains packet data,
   the Frame Check Sequence (CRC-32).
      — This guarantees 99.999% accuracy of the whole packet.

IEEE 802.3 Packet Format

Ethernet and IEEE 802.3 follow the same access method algorithm. This access method will be explained momentarily. The differences between the two really lie in the packet format; both standards peacefully coexist on the same cable.

At the beginning of the packet is the preamble and the start–of–frame delimiter (SFD). The IEEE split the Ethernet 8-byte preamble to a 7-byte preamble and a 1-byte SFD. It is the same bit pattern as the 8-byte preamble for Ethernet V2.0. There are two other differences in this frame in that the multicast bit was changed to the Individual/Group (I/G) bit. This bit is in the same location as the M bit for Ethernet but it is now called the individual or group address. The function is still the same in that if the bit is a 1, it is a a group address. If it is a 0, it is an individual address. The second bit is now reserved and is called the universally or locally administered address, the U/L bit. If this bit is set to a zero, the address was assigned by a central authority (the IEEE); if it set to a 1 (binary), the address is locally generated by the local site to this LAN.

It was stated earlier that all addresses on a LAN had at least the first three bytes assigned by the IEEE to indicate the vendor. The IEEE decided that locally administered addresses would be allowed. This means that the address on the PROM of the card (the address assigned by the manufacturer of the card) would be allowed to be overwritten by another address assigned by a network administrator of the network.

Does this lead to chaos? Not if it is properly handled. This address scheme does place the burden of address assignment to a local administration (usually a company's network administrator) and addresses easily can be duplicated. But it does allow for greater flexibility for addresses. For example, the address is now freed up for address assignments based on building and floor numbers. The LAA can be based on user's phone number. Whatever the case it must be carefully administered for no matter what the address administration type (IEEE or locally administered) every physical address on a LAN must be unique. It is best to leave the address as the PROM address

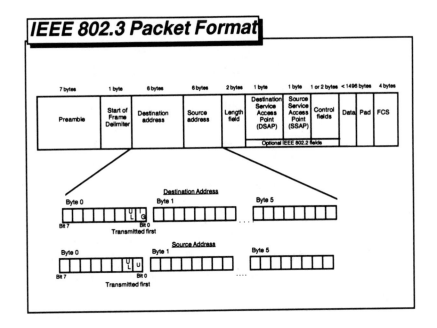

IEEE 802.3 Packet Format

- The IEEE 802.3 working group adopted the Ethernet V2.0 standard.
  It placed a few minor changes, mainly in the packet format.
  Both standards follow the CSMA/CD algorithm.

- The preamble was separated into a 7-byte preamble and a 1-byte Start-of-Frame Delimiter.
  Whether it is the IEEE 802.3 preamble and 1-byte SFD or the Ethernet preamble, there are the same
  number of bits in the same order in each and they are indistinguishable from each other.

- The first two bits of the address field for source and destination addresses are reserved.
  These bits are defined as the I/G and the U/L bits.
    — I/G—indicates whether this is a unique (individual) or group (multicast) address.
    — U/L—indicates whether this address is assigned by the IEEE (Universally administered) or vendor
      assigned (Locally administered). This bit is not generally used on IEEE 802.3. It should be set to
      zero.
    — The locally assigned address overwrites the PROM address.

DETAIL COMPARISON OF THE TWO PACKET FORMATS

Both the Ethernet and IEEE 802.3 packet formats have been shown. This topic is very important for both packet formats are used throughout a LAN.

IEEE 802.3 packets use 6-byte addresses (although a 2-byte address is allowed), a length, pad, a data field (that may be used with a pad field), and a 32-bit CRC. The maximum frame size for IEEE 802.3 or Ethernet packets is 1,518 bytes and the minimum frame size is 64 bytes. Data that has to be transmitted onto the network that allows a packet to become smaller than 64 bytes will be padded until it reaches 64 bytes. This is what the pad field is for. It is to ensure that a small frame is padded to the minimum 64 bytes.

The main difference between the Ethernet and IEEE 802.3 packets is the length field. This two-byte field is located directly after the source address field. The length field is used to indicate the exact length of the data field (not including the pad field). A number of bytes in the data field past this number are called *padding*. An Ethernet controller uses this number to indicate exactly how many bytes are in the data field.

If both packet types can be used on the same network, how do the controller cards know how to interpret a received packet? There is a trick to how Ethernet/IEEE 802.3 controllers determine whether the packet is an IEEE 802.3 packet or an Ethernet packet. For any protocol of a sublayer of a protocol, a Type field must be assigned. The Type field will be in the range of 0600–FFFF. The minimum value for a Type field in an Ethernet packet is 0600 (hex). Network protocols do not arbitrarily assign their Type fields. They are static numbers assigned by the IEEE.

The largest frame size for data on an IEEE 802.3/Ethernet network is 1,500 bytes which translates to 05DC (hex, just below 0600). Therefore, if the value at Type field location is 0600 or greater, then it is an Ethernet packet. If it is below 0600 then it is an IEEE 802.3 (indicating a length field and not a Type field) formatted packet.

It is very important that the controller be able to distinguish between the two packet formats, because it could incorrectly process the received frame.

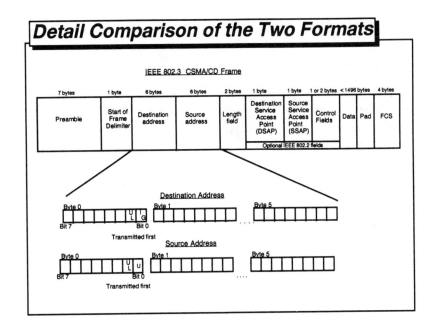

- The pad field is used to fill out a packet to the minimum 64-byte standard.

- The main difference between the two packet formats is the length field.
    The length field indicates the number of true data bytes in the data field.
        — The number does not include the pad field.

- Trick for Ethernet drivers to determine the packet format.
    The Type and Length field are located at the same position.
    The minimum Type field will start with 0600 (hex).
    Maximum packet size for Ethernet is 05DC (hex).
    Any number below 0600 is an IEEE 802.3 packet (length field)
    Any number above is an Ethernet packet.

- It is important for a controller to recognize the packet type.
    The controller could incorrectly read the packet which will cause error.
    Errors incurred could be anything from data corruption to network attachment disconnects.

ETHERNET AND IEEE 802.3 PACKETS

The following slide shows the IEEE 802.3 and the Ethernet V2.0 frame side by side to indicate the differences between them. The IEEE 802.2 (explained in a later section) information is added to the first three or four bytes of the data field. Therefore, the data field of an IEEE 802.3 packet is reduced to 1496 bytes for total possible length of the data field.

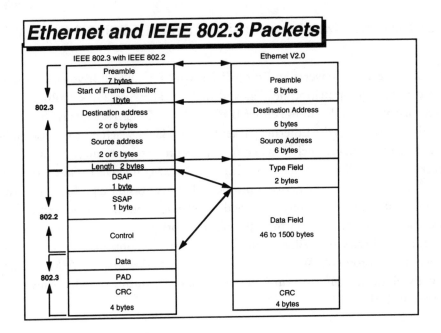

PROTOCOL IMPLEMENTATION OF ETHERNET OR IEEE 802.3 PACKET TYPES

Many types of packets may traverse an Ethernet network but all will have either the Ethernet or IEEE 802.3 data link encapsulation headers and trailers. The AppleTalk protocol uses the IEEE 802.3 packet format; TCP/IP can use either IEEE 802.3 or Ethernet (usually the Ethernet packet format is used). DECnet uses the Ethernet packet format. Having each protocol use different packet formats does lead to problems, such as when one station tries to communicate with another using different packet formats. A station that uses IEEE 802.3 packet formats cannot process an Ethernet V2.0 packet format using the same network protocol. This is a common problem but easy to fix. The network administrator must be acutely aware of the packet formats that are being used on a network.

The two packets can be used on the Ethernet network using the same physical components. Whether to run an Ethernet or IEEE network is not a matter of controller types, cables, etc. It really is a matter of network protocols. With the exception of the packet formats, IEEE 802.3 is Ethernet. In this book, I will use the generic term Ethernet. Unless specifically noted, the term Ethernet will mean Ethernet or IEEE 802.3.

Protocol Implementation of Ethernet

- Many different types of packets may traverse an Ethernet network.
  - All will use either the IEEE 802.3 or Ethernet packet format.
  - Packets differ based on network software protocols.
    - » AppleTalk and Novell NetWare generally use the IEEE 802.3 frame format.
    - » DECnet and TCP/IP generally use the Ethernet frame format.

- All protocols are slowly switching to the IEEE 802.3 frame format.

ETHERNET

Ethernet is an access method that is based on the carrier sense with multiple access and collision detection algorithm, commonly called CSMA/CD.

The Ethernet algorithm was started in 1973 by its inventor, Bob Metcalfe, at Xerox's Palo Alto Research Center (PARC). Bob Metcalfe has stated that he studied another type of early network known as the Aloha Network (so called because it originated at the University of Hawaii) and "fixed the mathematics." The first Ethernet network—known as the Experimental Ethernet—was designed and implemented in 1975.

A cooperative effort between DEC, Intel, and Xerox produced the standardized Ethernet Version 1.0 in 1980. This standard is known as the DIX standard for the three companies that designed the original specification. Their cooperation was significant, since at that time any advanced technology was closely guarded. These three companies worked together to establish an open standard that was known as the Blue Book. This is a public document, now known as Ethernet V2.0, that anyone can order from Xerox to design Ethernet components and build an Ethernet network. The standard was changed in 1982 to incorporate some changes (mainly transceiver changes), and it is version 2.0 that is used in today's Ethernet LANs.

In 1985, the DIX standard was adopted with modifications by the IEEE 802.3 committee. As shown before, the IEEE 802.3 committee made some changes to the standard mainly in the packet format. The IEEE 802.3 standard was then adopted by the American National Standards Institute (ANSI) and is known as the ANSI 8802/3 standard. The ANSI standard is the same as the IEEE 802.3 version.

Ethernet conforms to the bottom two layers of the OSI model (the physical and data link layers) but has nothing to do with the upper layers. Network software protocols reside at these layers and these protocols reside on top of Ethernet. Ethernet provides the upper-layer protocols with the ability to transmit and receive information on the network. These upper-layer protocols hand the information to the data link layer and then it is up to Ethernet to properly transmit and receive the data to and from the network.

Ethernet only allows for a communication mode known as *connectionless*. This means that two stations do not set up a connection before transmitting data to each other.

Ethernet

- An access method based on the Carrier Sense Multiple Access with Collision Detection (CSMA/CD) algorithm.
- Work started back in 1973 by Bob Metcalfe and David Boggs from Xerox Palo Alto Research Center (PARC).
  - He studied the Aloha network and "fixed" the mathematics.
- Experimental Ethernet implemented in 1975.
- Cooperative effort between Digital, Intel, and Xerox produced Ethernet Version 1.0 in 1980.
  - This also became known as the Blue Book specification or DIX standard. Ethernet V2.0 adopted in 1982.
- Ethernet was adopted with modifications by the standards committees IEEE 802.3 and ANSI 8802/3.
- Ethernet conforms only to the bottom two layers of the OSI model.
- Transmits information to other stations on the network through the use of packets.
- Ethernet allows for only connectionless communication.

Normal Ethernet Operation

The access method known as Ethernet controls the operation of multiple network attachments to transmit and receive data using one cable plant.

When a station needs to transmit a packet on the cable plant, the station listens to the cable plant to ensure that no other station is currently transmitting on the cable. If the cable plant is quiet (meaning there are no other stations transmitting), the controller immediately starts to transmit the packet to the cable. During the whole transmission, the controller listens to the cable plant to ensure that no other station is transmitting at the same time.

If 64 bytes of data are transmitted without incident (that is, no other station attempted to transmit at the same time), the controller has successfully passed the *collision window* which is the number of bytes that need to be transmitted at 10 megabits per second to travel 2,500 meters, the maximum cable run length for Ethernet. In other words, if a station at one end of the cable plant that extends 2,500 meters started to transmit, it would take 64 bytes of data traveling at 10 megabits per second to reach the end of 2,500 meters. This would ensure that any station would be able to detect that the cable is being used by another station on the cable plant. Any station that wishes to transmit and detects another station currently transmitting will defer transmission until the cable plant is quiet again. Once the cable plant is quiet again, another station is allowed to transmit. If there were no collisions during the transmission, the transmission is considered successful.

There is not a priority scheme used with Ethernet. All stations contend for the cable plant with all having equal chances of acquiring the cable plant. Under certain conditions, two or more stations will attempt to acquire the cable plant at the same time, and Ethernet has a method for handling this that will be explained next.

The largest packet an Ethernet station is allowed to transmit is 1,518 bytes. The minimum packet size is 64 bytes. Any packet smaller than 64 bytes or larger than 1,518 bytes is illegal.

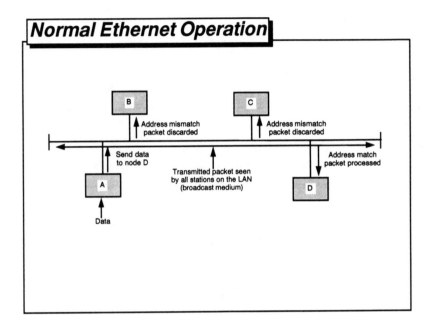

- Node A needs to transmit data to Node D.
  Node A builds a packet.
  Node A checks to see if the cable plant is clear (no one else is currently transmitting).
  Node A transmits packet while listening to the cable.

- If there were no collisions, node A returns to listen mode.

- Another station wishing to transmit should detect the cable plant is busy when node A is transmitting and enter into defer mode.
  It will try again later.

- No priority scheme used with Ethernet.
  All stations have equal access to the cable plant.

- An Ethernet station is allowed to transmit a packet as small as 64 bytes, as large as 1,518 bytes, or any size in between.

ETHERNET COLLISIONS

What happens if two or more stations happen to transmit at the same time? When an Ethernet controller starts to transmit, there is a small period of time during which other stations may not detect this earlier transmission and start to transmit as well. Since only one station is allowed to transmit on the cable at a time, two or more transmissions will interfere with one another. If two or more stations transmit at the same time, the result is known as a *collision*.

Collisions are inherent in the design of Ethernet. They are not fatal errors and most times will not cause the Ethernet network to crash. The Ethernet algorithm recovers from this error with a collision detection algorithm allowing the Ethernet controllers to recover from this condition. However if more than 0.5 percent of all transmissions on the Ethernet are collisions, the cable plant should be closely monitored. Excessive collisions are an indication that something is starting to go wrong on the network.

If a transmitting station detects a collision, that station will continue to transmit a signal for 4 to 6 bytes. This is called a *jam signal*. The reason behind this is to ensure that all stations on the cable plant detect the collision. Even if a station is not transmitting on the cable plant, it is still listening to the cable plant. All stations on a cable plant will detect the collision and *all stations that can sense the collision*—even those controllers that are not involved in the collision—will invoke the backoff algorithm.

The backoff algorithm is a random number and is measured in units. One unit is equal to 512 bit times or 51.2 microseconds. The random number is generated by the controller and is used as a timer to deter any future transmission on the cable plant. The delay (the number of units) is a uniformly distributed random number from [0 to $2^n - 1$] for $0 < n <= 10$ (n is the number of attempts to transmit with 0 as the original attempt). The number will be in the range of 0 to 1024 units. The more times that a network station has incurred a collision, the larger the random number. The larger this number, the longer the controller will wait before it attempts to retransmit the same packet.

It is the intent of the backoff algorithm that no two controllers will generate the same number and therefore attempt another transmission at the same time again. Controllers should generate different numbers and therefore will backoff for different times. Ethernet has no priority scheme, so after a collision, the cable is fair game for any controller wishing to transmit data. In other words, the stations involved in the collision have the same chance of acquiring the cable plant as a station that was not involved in the collision.

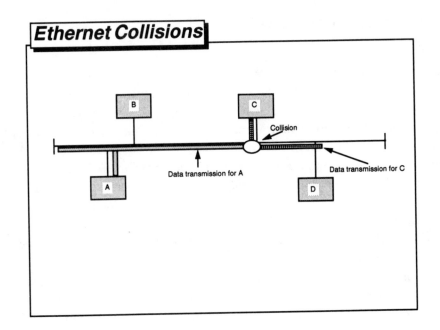

- Node A needs to transmit data to Node D.
    Node A builds a packet.
    Checks to see if the cable plant is clear (no one else is currently transmitting).
    Transmits packet while listening to the cable.

- Node C accomplishes the above steps and also starts to transmit.

- There is a collision on the cable plant caused by nodes A and C.

- All stations invoke the backoff algorithm.
    This deference should allow the cable plant to stabilize.
    When the cable is clear, it will be available for any station to transmit.
    No special priority treatment is given to the stations that were involved to the collision.

- The backoff algorithm assumes that no two controllers will generate the same two backoff times and attempt to simultaneously transmit.
    Even if they do, it is not a fatal error.
    Each controller's backoff algorithm will generate a longer backoff with each successive collision.

CSMA/CD—A Simple Definition

When a station wishes to transmit on the cable plant, it will listen to the cable plant to determine if there is anyone else currently transmitting on the cable plant. If there is any other transmission on the cable plant at this time, the controller will enter into a defer mode for a specified amount of time (at least 9.6 microseconds) before attempting a transmission again. This is known as *carrier sense*.

In an Ethernet system there may be up to 1024 stations (including repeaters) attached to a single cable plant. An access method must be used in order to allow fair access for all stations to the single cable plant. This is known as *multiple access*. If the controller has determined that the cable plant is clear, it immediately begins transmitting on the cable while continuing to listen. If at the end of its transmission, there have been no errors, the transmission is considered done.

If at any time during the transmission (even after the collision window has passed) a controller card detects another station is transmitting, the two stations will continue to transmit for four to six bytes. This is called the jam signal. A collision may occur at any time during a transmission. If the controller detects a collision, it will invoke the backoff algorithm, which produces a number that will indicate to the controller how long to wait before attempting the transmission again. This is known as *collision detection*. Remember, all stations participate in this backoff algorithm whether they were involved in the collision or not. This allows the cable plant a chance to stabilize after a collision.

CSMA/CD - A Simple Definition

- Ethernet uses the Carrier Sense Multiple Access with Collision Detection algorithm.

  – A network station wishing to transmit will first check the cable plant to ensure that no other station is currently transmitting (*CARRIER SENSE*).

  – The communications medium is one cable, therefore, it does allow multiple stations access to it with all being able to transmit and receive on the same cable (*MULTIPLE ACCESS*).

  – Error detection is implemented throughout the use of a station "listening" while it is transmitting its data.

    » Many ways to detect when another station has erroneously started to transmit.

      ◇ Two or more stations transmitting causes a collision (*COLLISION DETECTION*)

      ◇ A jam signal is transmitted to network by the transmitting stations that detected the collision, to ensure that all stations know of the collision. All stations will "backoff" for a random time.

      ◇ Detection and retransmission is accomplished in microseconds.

ETHERNET TRANSMISSION FLOWCHART

Some readers will find following a flowchart is easier to understand than trying to read text. Therefore, the following flowchart is provided to show the flow of an Ethernet transmission.

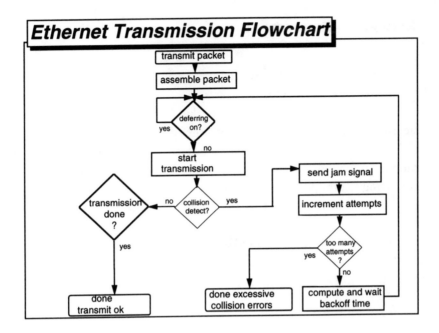

ETHERNET RECEPTION FLOWCHART

All packets being transmitted have unique source and destination addresses. Even with this, all stations on the Ethernet network will receive all packets.

Each network controller will receive the whole packet before carrying out any validity checks on the packet. If the packet is smaller than 64 bytes or larger than 1,518 bytes, it is discarded. The next check is to see if the packet is destined for that station. If the destination address and the station address of the station that receiving address do not match, the packet is discarded.

Finally, the receiving station performs a checksum on the packet. If the received checksum and the computed checksum (accomplished by the receiving controller) do not match, the packet is discarded.

If a packet passes all these checks, it is passed to its upper-layer software (layers three to seven) for further processing.

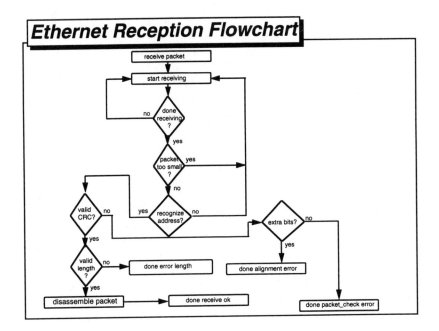

Ethernet Reception Flowchart

FINAL ETHERNET ISSUES

There are some issues that may be questionable in the reader's mind about the Ethernet protocol. For example, Ethernet is not a protocol in itself. It is a name that is applied to the access technique known as carrier sense multiple access with collision detection. CSMA/CD is the actual protocol and the IEEE 802.3 is the committee that standardized it from the Ethernet V2.0 specification. Ethernet is the name that was applied to it from the three-company consortium of DEC, Intel, and Xerox.

Ethernet applies to all of the first and second layer (actually only the MAC sublayer, explained later) of the OSI model. Therefore, Ethernet allows multiple protocols—such as TCP/IP, XNS, and AppleTalk—to run on top of it without changing the Ethernet specification. Ethernet is primarily implemented in hardware. There are software drivers for Ethernet but transmission and reception of raw data over the Ethernet is implemented in hardware.

Ethernet is known as a broadcast-oriented type of LAN. A broadcast oriented network is one in which all stations see all packets but discard those whose destination address does not match theirs. Token Ring and FDDI are also examples of broadcast-oriented networks. Theoretically, there is only one cable and all stations attached to that cable will transmit on it. Therefore, the packets that are transmitted onto the cable can be seen by all active stations on the network. If there are fifty stations attached to a single cable plant and one station transmits a packet to a uniquely addressed destination, forty-eight other stations receive the packet besides the intended recipient. Those forty-eight other station will discard the packet. Broadcast-oriented should not be confused with the broadcast physical address. Not every packet transmitted is a physically addressed to broadcast.

Ethernet does not guarantee the delivery of a packet. Ethernet's job is to transmit and receive packets to and from a cable plant. When a station successfully transmits a packet, the algorithm on that controller card considers its job done. It does not know whether the destination station accepted the packet, or even if the destination station is active on the network. Ethernet merely receives and transmits packets to a cable plant. The upper-layer network protocols accomplish what Ethernet does not.

Final Ethernet Issues

- Ethernet is an access method that strictly adheres to the CSMA/CD algorithm.

- Ethernet is a multiprotocol solution.

- Ethernet is hardware, not software.

- Ethernet is a broadcast oriented network.
  - All data packets are seen by all stations on the network.
  - This should not be confused with a broadcast packet.

- Ethernet does not guarantee delivery of a data packet.
  - It will detect an error in the packet via the CRC but Ethernet provides only connectionless service.
  - The upper layer protocols (layers 3 - 7) usually have some type of reliable protocol built to take care of this issue.

- An Ethernet controller is allowed to "miss" packets when the controller is busy.

ETHERNET MISCONCEPTIONS

Even though Ethernet runs at 10 Mbps, this does not mean that it is less efficient than 16 Mbps Token Ring. Token Ring is better suited to certain environments (heavily loaded networks such as imaging, graphics, and so on), and Ethernet is better suited for others (bursty traffic).

The size of the cable in no way affects the speed at which Ethernet transmits. There are four types of cable on which Ethernet may transmit and all transmit at 10 Mbps. Ethernet may transmit and receive at 10 Mbps but other factors directly affect the data throughput—the speed of the machine transmitting, the speed of the disk drive, the protocol used, and so forth. Ten Mbps transmission is only at the physical layer.

Collisions are inherent in the design of Ethernet and are not fatal errors. Collisions happen when two or more stations determine that the cable is quiet (not in use by any other station) and begin transmitting simultaneously. Ethernet easily recovers from this type of error and operation is quickly restored. Collision rates higher than 0.5 percent of the total transmissions on the Ethernet are an indicator that something is wrong and needs to be fixed.

The size of the packet on Ethernet does affect performance—64 byte packets do not allow better utilization of the bandwidth. They do, however, allow more stations to access the Ethernet (stations can transmit a packet quickly and then get off the Ethernet, allowing other stations to transmit packets). But smaller packets mean that more packets have to be transmitted to get the all the data transmitted between two stations. Fewer, larger packets each transmit more data between two stations but control the cable plant longer. The average or best packet size on Ethernet is hard to determine.

The topology of an Ethernet system directly affects performance. A poorly designed Ethernet causes many delays in the transmission and reception of packets. The design of an Ethernet network is the most critical aspect of building an Ethernet network.

Ethernet Misconceptions

- Ethernet is not necessarily less efficient than any other access method.
  - Depends on the application that is using Ethernet.

- Collisions are important in Ethernet but it is inherent in the design.

- Not all upper layer networking software was designed to run over Ethernet.

- Smaller packets are not more efficient on Ethernet.

- The size of the cable does not affect the speed of Ethernet.

- Ethernet may transmit and receive at 10 Megabits per second but the actual data throughput is much less.

- The design of the cabling system will affect performance.

- There are minimum or maximum packet size requirements.

IEEE 802.2

Logical Link Control (LLC) is the standard published by the IEEE 802.2 working group of the IEEE 802 committee, which produces LAN specifications. This protocol was allowed so that established LAN/WAN protocols, like TCP/IP, XNS, NetWare, etc., can migrate to the IEEE 802.2/802.3 protocol.

The IEEE 802.2 working group divided the data link layer into two entities: the MAC (media access control) layer and the LLC layer. LLC is placed between the MAC layer specification of the data link layer and a network layer implementation. This provides many benefits. First, it provides for a peer-to-peer connectivity between two network stations, which reduces the LAN's susceptibility to errors. The protocol of IEEE 802.2 is actually a subset of another protocol, high-level data-link control (HDLC), which is a specification presented by the international standards body, ISO. LLC uses a subclass of the HDLC specification called asynchronous balanced mode (ABM). The protocol of ABM allows network stations to operate as peers, in that all stations have equal status on the LAN. There is not a master-slave relationship.

As a subset of the HDLC architecture, LLC provides a more compatible interface for wide area networks. It is independent of the access method (Ethernet, Token Ring, etc.), meaning LLC may run on top of any access method. The MAC portion of the data link layer is protocol-specific, which allows an IEEE 802.2 network more flexibility.

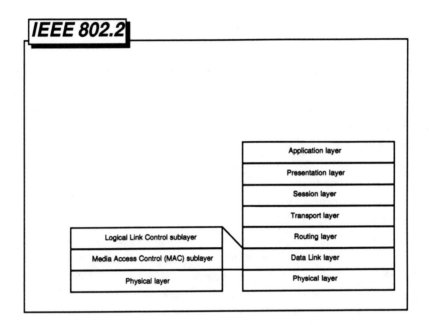

- Logical Link Control (LLC) is a standard published by the IEEE 802.2 working group of the IEEE.

- The standard splits the data link layer into two entities:
    Media Access Control (MAC), and
    Logical Link Control (LLC).

CONNECTION-ORIENTED VERSUS CONNECTIONLESS SERVICE

Connection-oriented link methods originated before LANs, and were originally used with data transfer through serial lines. Computers could communicate with one another either locally (in the same computer room) or remotely (together through the phone system). Just a few years ago, serial lines tended to be noisy. Part of the High Level Data Link Control (HDLC) protocol provides for the reliability of data. Although today, data lines from the phone company are conditioned to handle data, there still are some lines that will remain noisy and the connection-oriented services are used to handle this type of link. These functions are carried over the LAN with LLC2.

Connection-oriented service means that two stations that wish to communicate with each other must establish a connection at the data link layer before any data can pass between them. Two stations will pass certain frames between each other in order to establish a connection. After this conversation, data may flow on the connection. For example, when station A wants to connect to station B, it sends special frames to station B to indicate that a connection is wanted. Station B responds with a special frame indicating that a session may or may not be established. If a connection can be established, station A and station B will exchange a few more special packets that will set up sequence numbers and other control parameters. After this is accomplished, data may flow over the connection. The connection will be strictly maintained using sequence numbers, acknowledgments, retries, and so forth which can reduce the speed of data transfer between two stations.

Connectionless service is just the opposite. No connection is established at the data link level before data is allowed to flow between two stations. A connection will probably still be established but this is the responsibility of a particular network protocol (TCP/IP, NetWare, etc.). Connectionless service means that a frame will be transmitted on the network without regard to a connection at the data link layer. It is the responsibility of the upper layer software of a network operating system to perform these tasks. This is similar to the Ethernet connectionless operation. The data link layer simply provides the means for transmitting and receiving data to and from the network

Since there is not a connection established before the transmission of data, connectionless data transfer does not provide for error recovery, or flow or congestion control. There are also no acknowledgments upon receipt of data. This type of functionality requires less overhead and is implicitly faster.

Connection Oriented and Connectionless

- Connection oriented data communications arrived before connectionless

  - Used primarily over noisy serial lines.

  - Two stations must establish a connection before data is transmitted.

  - Connection is strictly maintained using sequence numbers, acknowledgments, retries and so on.

- Connectionless is the opposite of connection oriented.

  - Allows data to be transmitted without a pre-established connection between two stations.

  - This type of service flourished with the proliferation of LANs.

    » LANs tend to have a very low error rate and a connection need not be established to ensure the integrity of the data.

  - This type of service does not provide error recovery, flow or congestion control.

    » It is assumed that the upper layer network protocols can accomplish this.

  - It requires less overhead and is implicitly faster.

IEEE 802.2 Function Types

There are three types of frames that are transmitted or received in an connection oriented network. These are:

1. *The I frame or Information frame*
   Once a connection is setup, information transfers using the I frame. Included in the information frame will also be sequence numbers, or an acknowledgment receipt of previous data from the originating station.

2. *The S frame or Supervisory frame*
   This frame performs control functions between the two communicating stations. It may acknowledge a frame, request a retransmission of a frame, or request flow control of frames (rejecting any new data from the network). S frames do not contain user data; they simply supervise the connection using the frames shown on the next page. The supervisory frame provides for three commands or responses: Receiver Ready (RR), Reject (REJ), and Receive Not Ready (RNR).

3. *The U frame or Unnumbered frame*
   This frame is used for control functions. In LLC2, the frame is used for session initialization or session disconnect, though it can be used for other control functions. This frame has commands and responses and is used to extend the number of the data link control functions.

IEEE 802.2 Function Types

- The Information frame (I frame) - provides for information transfer over a connection.

- The Supervisory frame (S frame) - provides for the control of a connection.
  - These frames include the ability to reject and acknowledge a frame as well as the capability to poll a remote station or to tell the remote station that it is busy.

- The Unnumbered frame (U frame) - provides for an extension of the control functions.
  - These frames provide for setting up or disconnecting a session.

THE THREE TYPES OF SUPERVISORY FRAMES

Receive Ready (RR) is used by the source or destination station to indicate that it is ready to receive data and also to acknowledge any previously received frames. For example, when the station previously indicated that it could not receive any more data, it will send the RR frame to indicate it can again accept new data. A network station may also use this frame to poll a destination station (an "are you active" type of poll). When running a protocol over IEEE 802.2 (SNA over Token Ring for example), RR frames will traverse the ring even when there is no data to send. They are polling frames to ensure that the link is still good and are usually sent every few seconds. This polling uses non-data frames and will consume bandwidth.

Receive Not Ready (RNR) is used by a receiving network station to indicate that it saw the data packet but was too busy to accept it for some reason. Therefore, a network station will send this frame to indicate to the source not to send any more information until further notice. The receiving network station will again indicate that it is ready to receive data by using the RR frame.

Reject (REJ) is used to indicate a request for a retransmission of frames (more than one). Inside this frame will be a number which indicates to the recipient the starting frame number to repeat. All frames up to that number are considered acknowledged and need not be resent. Any frames after, including the frame indicated in the REJ packet, need to be resent.

The Three Types of Supervisory Frames

- Supervisory frames control a session after it is set up. The frames used are:
  - Receiver Ready (RR)
    - » Used by the source or destination station to indicate that it is ready to receive data.
    - » Used as a "keep alive" packet to ensure that each end of a connection is alive when there is no data to send.
  - Receiver not Ready (RNR)
    - » Transmitted by a station to indicate that it cannot receive any more data (busy indicator)
    - » Will signify that it is again ready by transmitting a Receiver Ready
  - Reject
    - » Used to request a retransmission of frames.

THE UNNUMBERED FRAME TYPES

Set Asynchronous Balance Mode Extended (SABME). This frame is used to establish a data link connection to a destination network station. It establishes the link in asynchronous balanced mode (ABM) which means that each end of the connection is equal. Either side of the connection is allowed to transmit unsolicited request or response frames. With ABM there is not a master–slave relationship, which means that one station does not control the session.

No user data is transferred with this frame. The destination, in response to this packet, will send a Unnumbered Acknowledge (UA, explained below) frame back to the originator. Since LLC2 requires sequencing between two stations, all sequence counters are set to zero upon receipt of a SABME and receipt of the UA. This frame can also be used to reset a connection. If a connection has been established between two stations and one end receives the SAMBE frame from its peer, the connection is not lost, it is simply returned to a known state. All sequence and acknowledge numbers are reset to a known state (usually set back to zero) and all previous unacknowledged data is discarded and must be resent.

A similar frame is the set asynchronous balance mode (SABM). This frame performs the same functions as the SABME but its sequencing numbering is smaller. It allows only eight sequence numbers.

Disconnect (DISC). This frame is used to disconnect a session between two communicating stations. No user data is sent with this frame. Upon receipt of the frame, the destination station should acknowledge it with a UA frame.

Unnumbered Acknowledge (UA). This frame is sent as an acknowledgment to the SABME and DISC commands.

Frame Reject (FRMR). This frame is different than the simple reject frame in that the sender of it is rejected. It is noncorrectable. The session is usually terminated.

Disconnect Mode (BM). This frame is used to indicate a disconnection is wanted or to indicate that a session is not allowed to be established. It can also be used in response to a DISC command.

Unnumbered Frame Type

- Unnumbered frames are used for control functions.

- Used for session set up and disconnection such as:

  » SABME - used to set up a connection

  » DISC - used to disconnect a session

  » UA - used to acknowledge a received unnumbered frame.

  » FRMR - used to indicate a frame was rejected and non-recoverable

IEEE 802.2 Implementation Types

The IEEE 802.2 working group allowed for three types of implementation for LLC:

Type 1, known as LLC1—uses the unsequenced information (UI) frame, which sets up communication between two network stations as unacknowledged connectionless service. When the IEEE started work on the LLC subset, the working group knew providing a connection-oriented service only, Type II or LLC2, would limit the capability of this protocol in the LAN arena. Time-sensitive applications cannot tolerate the tremendous overhead involved in establishing and maintaining a connection-oriented session. Since most LAN protocols already provided for this type of functionality in their software, the IEEE 802.2 working group provided the connectionless mode of the LLC protocol (LLC1) as well as a connection-oriented specification (LLC2).

Type 2, commonly known as LLC2, uses the conventional Information Frame (I) and sets up acknowledged connection-oriented service between two network stations. Most applications currently operating on a LAN do not need the data integrity functions provided for with the LLC2 protocol, since the LAN is a highly reliable medium. Adding LLC2 usually only slows down the speed of a network. LLC2 is used to link a LAN to a Wide Area Network (WAN, networks tied together that are geographically separated by serial [telephone] lines) and also between network stations on a local network. SNA over Token Ring uses LLC2 to establish connections between network stations and SNA hosts. Another example is the IBM Lan Server program. This is a network workgroup operating system based on a session layer protocol, NetBIOS, that operates functionally like Novell NetWare.

Type 3, using something called AC frames and sets up an Acknowledged Connectionless Service between two network stations. Type 3 is not widely implemented and is beyond the scope of this book.

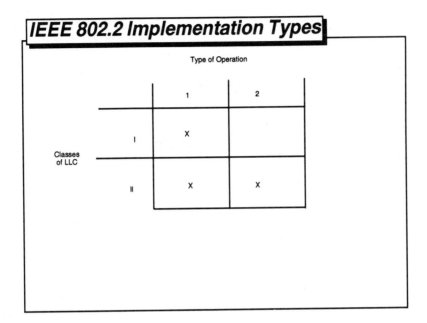

- Three classes of operation:
  - Type 1—provides for a connectionless operation.
    - — Type 1 is known as LLC1.
    - — It can only implement LLC1 services.
  - Type 2—provides for a connection-oriented operation.
    - — Type 2 is known as LLC2.
    - — It can implement LLC1 services as well as LLC2.
  - Type 3—provides for a connectionless service with acknowledgments.
    - — Type 3—is known as LLC3.

- Connection-oriented operation means that a session is established at the data link layer before data is transmitted.
  LLC2 uses sequence numbers, acknowledgments, and timers to maintain the session.
  The beginning sequence numbers and time out values are set at session establishment.

- Connectionless operation means that a session is not set up before data is transmitted.
  It does not provide for error recovery, or flow or congestion control
  It expects the upper-layer protocols to perform this.

LLC COMMANDS AND RESPONSES

The following table shows the commands and expected responses for each of the frame types used by LLC. The frame types cannot be interchanged between the two types of LLC service (LLC1 or LLC2).

Each LLC type uses its own frames that may be used to control or send and receive data between two stations. Each frame format has its own specific set of functions to perform. This will be shown over the next few pages. Realize for now that the above frames simply send and receive data and allow a connection to be set up, maintained, and disconnected. They also allow for sequencing and acknowledgments.

LLC Commands and Responses

Type of Frame	Format	Command	Response
Type 1		UI	
		XID	XID
		TEST	TEST
Type 2	I frame	I	I
	S frame	RR	RR
		RNR	RNR
		REJ	REJ
	U frame	SABME	UA
		DISC	UA
			DM
			FRMR

• The above table shows the command frame for each format and the expected response.

IEEE 802.2 FIELDS

An LLC header uses 3 or 4 bytes to place its information in a packet. It can start immediately after the source address field for any type of LAN packet, and contains the following fields:

The destination service access point (DSAP) field identifies one or more service access points to which the LLC information field should be delivered.

The source service access point (SSAP) field identifies which service access point originated the message.

The control field (CTRL) is one or two bytes long and it is used to control a session. It could be setting up, maintaining, or disconnecting a session. It is in this field that sequencing is performed.

There are four types of addresses:

1. An individual address is used by DSAP and SSAP to uniquely identify a SAP.

2. A null address, all zeros in the DSAP and/or SSAP.

3. A group address is used by the DSAP to indicate the type of multicast SAP.

4. A global address, indicated by all 1s (binary) in the DSAP field, is used to designate all active DSAPs on the network.

Each SAP address consumes exactly one octet (one byte). The DSAP address contains 7 bits of address space (indicated by the D bits) and one bit (I/G) that identifies the address as an individual SAP or a multicast SAP (intended for a group of SAPs). The I/G bit is the leftmost bit of the DSAP field. If this bit is set to a zero, it is an individual address. If it is set to a 1, it is a group address.

The SSAP contains 7 bits of address (indicated by the S bits) and one bit to indicate whether the packet is a command or response type of packet. If this C/R bit is a zero, it is a command packet; if it is set to a 1, it is a response packet. This bit is set to indicate to the recipient that an immediate response is requested by the SSAP.

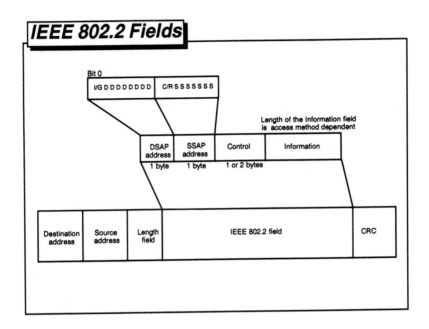

- LLC header uses a 3 or 4 byte header, depending on the operation which usually starts after the source address field of any frame type.

- The LLC header includes three fields:
    Destination Service Access Point (DSAP)—identifies a destination service.
    Source Service Access Point (SSAP)—identifies a source service.
    Control (CTRL)—used to control a session. This includes:
      — setting up,
      — maintaining, and
      — terminating a session.

- SAPs identify a service running on a station. Examples are:
    Network management,
    Novell NetWare, and
    NetBIOS.

- Four types of SAPs:
    Individual SAP
    Null SAP
    Group SAP—used only by the DSAP
    Global—used only by the DSAP

- There is one bit in SSAP to indicate whether the frame is a command or response frame.

SAP Types

For LANs implementing LLC1 or LLC2, service access points (SAPs) identify a particular service that resides on a network station. Each service is uniquely identified by a SAP, and all SAPs are registered with the IEEE committee. Once they are registered they are reserved and cannot be used for any other purpose.

SAPs are analogous to the Type field in the Ethernet frame. They allow multiple services to run on a single network attachment. For example, a SAP of FE indicates that the OSI protocol owns the packet. A SAP of F0 indicates NetBIOS, and so forth.

SAP Types

- E0 - Novell NetWare
- F0 - NetBIOS
- 06 - TCP/IP
- 42 - Spanning Tree BPDU
- FF - Global SAP
- F4 - IBM Network Management
- 7F - ISO 802.2
- 00 - NULL LSAP
- F8, FC - Remote Program Load
- 04, 05, 08, 0C - SNA
- AA - SNAP
- 80 - XNS
- FE - OSI

- There may be many different services that run on a network attachment.

- These services may be network management or specific protocol identifiers.

- To uniquely identify a service at the data link layer, numbers are assigned to the service.

- This is demultiplexed at the data link layer and the frame will be delivered to the service identified by the SAP.

CONTROL FIELD

The control field is used to supervise and control a session. It indicates to a station what type of frame has arrived. It occupies the third and fourth bytes of the IEEE 802.2 fields. The control field represents the function of the frame. For data (I frames), this field contains sequence numbers when needed.

The first two bits of the control field indicate what type of frame has arrived. This can be and information (I), supervisory (S), or unnumbered (U) frame. This information enables a network station to properly read the IEEE 802.2 field. First an explanation of the poll and final bits.

Poll and Final Bits

These bits are located at bit seven of the frame and are used between two communicating stations to solicit a status response or to indicate a response to that request. The P bit is used by the primary station (the requester) and an F bit is used by the secondary station (the responder). With LLC, any station can transmit a frame with the P bit set or the F bit set, since there is no master-slave relationship. Transmitting stations set these bits when an immediate response is needed.

A frame with the F bit set does not indicate the end of a transmission. It is used as a housecleaning method between two stations to clear up any ambiguity between them and it is used to indicate that the frame is an immediate response to a previously received frame that had the P bit set.

For example, when a station wants to set up a connection with another station, it will submit a frame known as the Set Asynchronous Balance Mode Extended (SABME[1]). In this frame the P bit will be set to a one. The destination station, upon accepting a connection request, will respond with a Unnumbered Acknowledgment (UA) frame and the F bit will be set to a one. A P bit frame is acknowledged immediately with a frame that has the F bit set.

The N(R) and N(S) fields are used to indicate sequence numbers. Sequencing is explained next.

---

[1]SABM and SABME are the same frame. SABME tells the destination station that the requesting station would like to use extended sequencing (modulo 128).

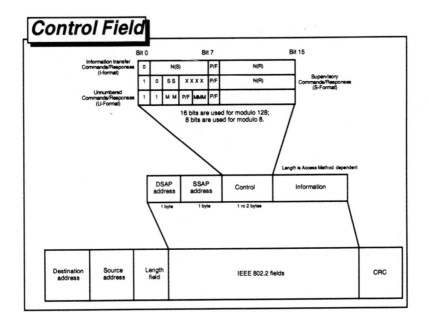

• The control field is used for supervisory and control of a session

• The first two bits indicate the type of frame that has arrived.

• These can be an information frame, a supervisory frame, or an unnumbered frame

• Poll and final bits are used to solicit a status response or to indicate a response to a previous request.
  These bits are set to demand immediate response or to indicate an immediate response.
  — The P bit is set by the requester.
  — The F bit is set by the responder.
  — The F bit does not indicate the end of a transmission.

• The N(R) and N(S) fields are used for the sequencing of data.

• Information and supervisory frames are used with LLC2 only.

• Unnumbered frames can be used with LLC1 or LLC2.

• The SS and the MMM bits are defined as follows:

SS bits	Unnumbered frame types including M bits
00=RR	1111P110=SABME Command
01=REJ	1100P010=DISC Command
10=RNR	1100F110=UA Response
	1111F000=DM Response
	1110F001=Frame Reject Response

SEQUENCING OF DATA (LLC2)

Transferring information between two stations requires that reliability be established. Sequencing allows for some of this reliability. Sequencing assigns a number to each packet to indicate the order of transmission to the receiver of frame. Upon receipt of a frame, the receiver will compare the sequence number of the received frame to the sequence number it expected. A receiver can receive multiple frame before it will send an acknowledgment back to the transmitter.

Sequencing of transmitted data ensures that when the data is received, it will be presented to the receiver in good condition and in the same order that it was sent. Imagine sending data between a PC and a host. During transfer, the data was mixed up and was received at the host in the wrong order. Without sequencing, the host's application would receive the data as it was presented by the LAN software. It would then process the data, incorrectly perhaps by saving the file incorrectly. Needless to say, in any application, misordering LAN data can have catastrophic effects.

Most network protocols offer some type of sequencing for data delivery, whether simple, as in Novell's stop-and-wait method, or complex, as used with LLC2 and TCP/IP.

Perhaps the most emulated method of sequencing used by many LAN architectures is automatic return request (ARQ). With ARQ, once a connection is established, two communicating stations will establish which type of sequencing numbering to use and what is the starting sequence number which is then incremented by 1 for each packet that is sent. The sequence number is embedded into each frame. Upon receipt of the frame, the receiver has the option to acknowledge the frame or to wait for more frames before acknowledging a group of frames. ARQ is balanced in that each side of the connection maintains its own sequence numbers for frames received and frames sent.

Sequencing of Data (LLC2)

- Transferring data between two stations requires that reliability be built in.
- Sequencing permits this.
  - Upon connection, a starting sequence number is assigned by both ends of the connection.
    - » Each end keeps its own set of sequence numbers.
    - » One set of sequence numbers for data that it is transmitting and
    - » one set for incoming data from a remote station.
  - A number is assigned to every packet sent by a transmitting station
  - Upon receipt of the packet, the receiver compares the sequence number to the number it expected to receive.
    - » If the number matches:
      - An acknowledgment may be sent.
      - The station may receive multiple packets before an acknowledgment is sent for all.
    - » If the sequence number does not match a reject message is sent.
      - Inside the reject packet will be the expected sequence number.
      - The originator will then re-transmit the expected sequence number packet.

Sequence Numbering

Sequence numbers can start and stop at any number. It is protocol dependent. Not all protocols operate the same. For LLC2, upon connection establishment, the sequence number starts at 0 and may go as high as 127. For now we'll stick with LLC2 sequence numbers that comply to modulo 8. Modulo 8 means that sequence numbers start at 0 and may go as high as 7 but then must return (wrap around) to 0. This permits seven frames to be outstanding (0 through 6 not acknowledged). It does not permit eight frames to be outstanding. It also guards against wrapping for if a station has eight outstanding frames (0–7), a sending station may not use 0 again until it has been acknowledged. This is highly unlikely. Most frames will be acknowledged within two to three sequence numbers.

Frames are lined up for transmission and each is given a unique sequence number. These sequence numbers are also kept track of as a separate entity. As packets are transmitted, a logical box called a *window* is placed over the sequence numbers. For the sender, this window will indicate the three-part combination of packets that have been transmitted, the packets that have been acknowledged, and the packets that are waiting to be transmitted. The receiver of packets will also establish a sequence number window. This two-part window will indicate which packets have been received and acknowledged, packet received but not acknowledged. One important consideration is the actual size of the window. While having a modulo of eight is nice in that seven frames may be transmitted with one acknowledgment; however, it is also a resource constraint. No transmitted frame may be erased by the sender until it has been acknowledged by the recipient. This means that a network station should have enough memory to keep a copy of the data sent until it is acknowledged.

The window slides—opens and closes. For the sender, as transmitted frames are acknowledged, the window slides giving a new three-part combination of sequence numbers. If the window closes, all frames that can be transmitted have been and no more will be transmitted. For the receiver of frames, as frames are received, the window will slide over the sequence numbers indicating a new three-part combination. If the window is closed, it cannot receive any more frames and it will indicate this condition to the transmitter with an RNR frame. This allows for efficient use of resources and also allows a network station to deal with other stations on the network. In other words, it eliminates the possibility of one station hogging another station's time.

Inclusive acknowledgments are one advantage of a windowing system. This means that if a network station has five outstanding (unacknowledged) frames (frames 0–4), and it receives one acknowledgment frame of 5, the recipient has received frames 0 through 4 and the sender can now send new frames starting with the sequence number of 5. This has many advantages. For one, it keeps the receiving station from transmitting five acknowledgment frames.

Sequence Numbering

- Two types for LLC2:
  - Modulo 8 which uses 8 sequence numbers (0 - 7).
  - Modulo 128 which uses 128 sequence numbers (0 - 127).

- When frames are transmitted a logical window is placed over the sequence numbers.
  - Indicates which frames have been transmitted and acknowledged.
  - Indicates which frames have been transmitted but not acknowledged.
  - Indicates which frames are waiting to be transmitted.

- The window slides over as each group of frames sent are acknowledged by the other end of the connection.

- With modulo 8, up to 7 frames may be transmitted without an acknowledgment.
  - After 7 are transmitted, the network station must wait for an acknowledgment.
    » If it receives an acknowledgment of 0, it may transmit more frames.
    » 0 is a higher sequence number than 7.

- Stations may not discard any frames until they have acknowledged.

SEQUENCING TYPES

This ability to detect and correct sequence errors is basically characterized by three types of retransmissions: go back to N, selective reject, and stop and wait. All three types have their merits.

The go-back-to-N method specifies not only that a specific sequence number is to be retransmitted but that any frames before that up to the last acknowledged sequence number. Go-back-to-N is a simpler method, but it uses more network bandwidth and is generally slower than the selective reject. It states that when an acknowledgment is received, all frames up to but not including that sequence number were received in good condition. Negative acknowledgment means that not all frames sent were received in good condition and to repeat the transmission of those frames starting with the acknowledgment number in this packet. This the same method used by LLC2 REJ packets.

With selective reject, only the frame indicated needs to be retransmitted. This method offers better bandwidth utilization because only one frame needs to be retransmitted. But the receiving network station must wait for that frame and when it does arrive, it must reorder the data in the correct sequence before presenting it to the next layer. This consumes memory and CPU utilization.

Stop and wait means send a packet and do not transmit another until that frame has been acknowledged. This is said to have a window size of 1, for only one frame may be outstanding at a time. With stop and wait a transmitting station transmits a frame and waits for an acknowledgment; it cannot transmit any more frames until it has received the acknowledgment. The sequence numbers used can be of two types. One can be a incrementing number and the other can be a 0 to 1 exchange. With the 0 to 1 exchange, a starting number is established—say a zero—between the two stations. When the transmitting station transmits a frame, it sets the sequence number to a 0. When the receiver receives the packet, it sets its received sequence number to a 0 and then acknowledges the packet. When the response packet is received, the original station notices the zero sequence number and sets the next transmit sequence number to 1. This sequence number will flip-flop throughout the length of the data transfers. Zero and one are the only two sequence numbers used. The other method is to start with a sequence number—say a 0—and continually increment the number from there. There will be an upper limit on the sequence numbers at which the sequence numbers will return to 0. Each frame transmitted must be acknowledged even though different sequence numbers are used. Novell NetWare uses this and the REJ methods of sequencing.

Sequencing Types

- Three types of sequence protocols:

  - Go back to N

    » This is also called inclusive acknowledgment.

    » The acknowledgment frame will contain the next expected sequence number.

      • If the acknowledgment number indicates frames that have already been sent, frames starting with the indicated sequence number are to be retransmitted (an error occurred forcing a retransmission or certain frames).

      • If frames have not already been transmitted, the network station will continue transmitting normally (no error occurred and the remote is waiting for more data).

  - Selective reject

    » States that a network station received all frames but the one indicated in the reject frame.

      • The station will resend the frame indicated by the sequence number in the reject.

  - Stop and wait

    » Every frame transmitted will be acknowledged before another is sent.

SEQUENCE FIELDS

In order for sequencing to work properly, the following elements are used to keep track of the sequence operation. They are:

V(R)	Receive state variable. Located as a counter in the network station. It indicates the sequence number of the next in-sequence I frame, to be received on a connection. It is maintained in the network station and not the frame.
N(S)	Sequence number of the transmitted frame (called the send sequence number) and is located in the transmitted frame's control field. This field will only be placed in Information frames.
V(S)	Send state variable. This number indicates the next sequence number to send. It is incremented by one for each successive I-frame transmission. It is maintained in the network station as a counter and is not located the frame. Before sending an I-frame, a network station will read this counter. The value of this counter is placed in the N(S) field of a transmitted packet.
N(R)	Receive sequence number. This is an acknowledgment of previous frames and it is located in the control field of the transmitted frame. All I-frames and S-frames will contain this. This field is set to the value of the receive state variable V(R) before a network station transmits a frame. Upon receiving this frame a network station will know that the destination station accepts all frames up to N(R) minus 1. If this field equals a 5, the recipient of this frame knows the destination accepts frames 0 through 4. The next frame to send should have a sequence number of 5.

Sequence Fields

- V(R)
  - This is called the receive state variable.
  - It is located in the network station counters .
  - Indicates the next expected receive sequence number.

- N(S)
  - This indicates the sequence number of the transmitted frame.
  - It is located in the transmitted frame.
  - It is known as the send sequence number.

- V(S)
  - Indicates the next sequence number transmit.
  - It is kept in the network station's counter.
- N(R)
  - This is called the receive sequence number.
  - It is an acknowledgment of a previously transmitted frame or frames.
  - Located in the received frame. It is the next expected sequence number that the remote station is expecting. All previously transmitted frames, but not including this sequence number, are said to be acknowledged.

SEQUENCE OPERATION

Windows are maintained by the state variables. Each end of a connection will maintain its own sequence numbers for the connection. N(S) and N(R) are located in the packet and V(S) and V(R) are counters that are located in the network stations.

V(S) is incremented with each frame that is successfully transmitted by a network station. V(R) contains the sequence number that is expected to be the next frame received. N(S) is the sequence number assigned to a packet and N(R) is the next expected sequence number.

When a network station receives a frame, it looks for the sequence number, N(S), in the received frame. If N(S) matches the receiving station's V(R), the station increments its V(R) by one, and may place the number located in V(R) in the N(R) of an acknowledgment packet that will be transmitted back to the originator of the received frame. In building the frame, the station will set N(R) to one sequence number ahead of the sequence number located in the last packet it received. When the intended recipient of this acknowledgment frame receives it, N(R) indicates the packets that are being acknowledged. Remember, not every packet transmitted must immediately be acknowledged. A receiver may receive many packets before transmitting an acknowledgment.

If, during the matching of V(R) to the received sequence number N(S), there is a mismatch, and usually after a wait timer expires, the receiving station sends a negative acknowledgment packet to the originator. In the N(R) of this packet is the sequence number the receiving station was looking for. In LLC2, this type of frame is a REJ frame. In other words, the station expected one sequence number but received another; the number it expected is transmitted back to the sender in hopes of receiving the correct packet.

When the REJ is received by the originating station, it will look at the received sequence number N(R). It will also know that it has already sent this frame, but something went wrong in the process. If the station can it will retransmit the frame and any frames after this sequence number.

This is a confusing subject, but real examples are shown in the back of this section.

Sequence Operation

- Sequence numbers are maintained by network stations through the use of state variables.
    - These are also known as simply as counters.
    - They are kept in the network station.

- Once a session is set up between two stations each keeps its own sequence number counters.
    - Data flows bi-directionally in LLC2.

- Each side maintains V(S) for the frames that it has transmitted.
    - The station will increment V(S) by one for every frame transmitted.

- Each side will maintain a V(R) that indicates the next expected receive sequence number.
    - For each frame that is received, the V(R) will be incremented.

• When a network station receives a frame, it extracts N(S) from the received frame, and
   if N(S) matches V(R) the station increments V(R) and sends back an acknowledgment with N(R) set to its V(R).
   if N(S) does not match its V(R), the station sends a reject message with N(R) set to its V(R).

• When a network station sends a frame it places the value of its V(S) into the N(S) field of the frame and sends the frame and increments the V(S).

TIMER FUNCTIONS

Timers are used extensively throughout the operation of LLC2. Their purpose is part of the control functions of LLC and they control the amount of time that any LLC2 function is allowed to have. There are four types of timers:

1. Acknowledgment Timer. This is a data link connection timer that is used to define the time interval during which a network station is expecting to see a response to one or more information frames or to one unnumbered frame.

2. P-bit Timer. This is the amount of time that a network station waits for a response frame in regard to a frame that was sent with the P bit set.

3. Reject Timer. This is the amount of time that a network station waits for a response to a REJ frame sent.

4. Busy State Timer. This is the amount of time that a network station waits for a remote network station to exit the busy state.

When an LLC2 timer expires, the LLC2 function trying to be performed is started over. To prevent LLC2 functions from being endlessly restarted, a counter is used to indicate when an LLC2 function should be discontinued. The N2 counter indicates the maximum number of times that a frame is resent following the expiration of the P-bit timer, the acknowledgment-timer, or the reject-timer.

The N1 parameter is a user-settable parameter that sets the maximum number of bytes allowed in an I-frame.

The counter k indicates the maximum number of outstanding I frames (those which have not been acknowledged). For example, this can be set from 1 to 7 for modulo 8 (a 1 indicates every transmitted packet should be acknowledged and 7 means that seven frames may be outstanding waiting for an acknowledgment.

Timer Functions

- Acknowledgment timer - is a timer that is used to time an expected response.

- P-bit timer - is the amount of time that a network station waits for a response to a P-bit frame.

- Reject timer - is the amount of time that a network station waits for a response to an REJ.

- Busy state timer - is the amount of time that a network station will wait for a remote station to exit the busy state.
  - Station received a RNR from its remote end of the connection.

- N2 - is the maximum number of times that a frame is sent following the expiration of the above timers (except busy state timer).

- N1 - is the maximum number of bytes allowed in a frame.

- k - is the maximum number of outstanding, unacknowledged frames.

ASYNCHRONOUS BALANCE MODE (ABM)

LLC2 is known as a peer-to-peer service, as opposed to a master/slave service. Any LLC2 station is allowed to request a session to be established of another LLC2 network station. Likewise, once a connection is set up, either end can request information about a session or disconnect from a session. This is known as Asynchronous Balance Mode (ABM).

ABM means that a connection at the data link layer has been established between two SAPs. Each end of the connection can send commands and responses at any time without receiving permission for the station.

ABM has four phases of operation:

1. Data link connection phase

2. Information transfer phase

3. Data link resetting phase

4. Data link disconnecting phase

Asynchronous Balance Mode

- ABM has four phases of operation:

  - data link connection,

  - information transfer,

  - data link reset, and

  - data link disconnection phase

CONNECTION-ORIENTED SERVICES OF THE IEEE 802.2 PROTOCOL

There are two modes of operation for LLC2: operational mode and non-operational mode.

Non-operational mode will not be completely discussed in this text. It is used to indicate that a network station is logically (not physically) disconnected from the physical cable plant. No information is accepted when a network station has entered into this stage. Examples of possible causes for a network station to enter this mode are:

1. The power is turned on but the receiver is not active.

2. The data link has been reset.

3. The data link connection is switched from a local condition to a connected on the data link (on-line) condition.

Operational mode means that a network station is attached to the LAN and is an active participant. There are three primary functions:

- *Link establishment*
  A source station sends a U-frame to a destination, indicating that it wants a connection. The destination station responds to the requesting station with an acceptance or rejection to that attempt. Once a connection is established, the two network stations provide each other with a series of handshaking protocols to ensure that each is ready to receive information.

- *Information transfer*
  Sequenced data is transferred from the originating station to the destination station, and checked for possible transmission errors. The remote station sends acknowledgments back to the transmitting station. During this phase the two network stations may send control information to each other indicating flow control, missing frames, and so forth.

- *Link termination*
  Two stations are disconnected, ending the transfer of data until a session is re-established. Usually, the link between two stations remains intact as long as there is data to send. Once all the data is sent, a session is not necessarily disconnected. A session may be maintained even when there is no data to send. If all the data is sent between two stations, the connection may be maintained by each side of the connection sending RR frames to each other, indicating that the connection is still needed but there is no data to send.

Connection Oriented Services

- Two modes of operation:
  - Operational
  - Non-operational

- Operational mode incorporates three functions:
  - Link establishment.
    - » A source station sends a packet to a destination station requesting a connection.
    - » The destination station may accept or reject the connection request.
  - Information transfer.
    - » Allows information to be transferred after a connection is set up and the required handshaking has taken place.
    - » Reliable information is transferred between the two stations.
  - Link termination.
    - » Either side of the connection may terminate the connection at any time.

DATA LINK CONNECTION PHASE

Any network station may enter into the data link connection phase with the intention of establishing a reliable session with another network station. Network stations use the U-frame SABM. When the SABM frame is sent, an acknowledgment timer is set. If the frame is not responded to, it will be resent up to N2 times. If the frame is not responded to in that amount of time, the connection attempt is aborted. This type of frame has the P-bit set.

In response to the connection request, there are two responses that may be received. They are:

- *DM frame*

    DM stands for *disconnect mode*. This allows a destination network station to indicate to the requester that no connection is allowed. With the receipt of the DM frame, the acknowledgment timer is stopped and the requesting network station will not enter into the information transfer stage. The connection attempt is aborted. If a connection is already established and a network station received this frame type, the connection would be disconnected. The station will respond to the DM request frame with a UA frame. The DM frame has the P-bit set and the UA frame has the F-bit set.

- *UA frame*

    When the requesting station receives a UA response frame, the connection is established and the two stations enter into the information transfer phase. This type of response frame will also have the F-bit set.

Data Link Connection Phase

- Any station may enter this state with the intention of establishing a reliable session to another station.

    - Transmits the U frame SABM with P-bit set and sets a timer.
        - » If there is no response, the SABM will be sent up to N2 more times.
        - » If there is no response after N2 times, the connection attempt is aborted.

    - Two responses may be received:
        - » DM received
            - Indicates to the source station that the destination station will not allow a connection.
        - » UA received
            - Indicates to the source station that the destination station accepted to the connection request.
        - » F bit will be set with either response.

    - If a UA frame is received, a connection is established and sequence numbers are set to start at 0 on both ends of the connection.

    - Enters into the information transfer phase.

INFORMATION TRANSFER AND DATA LINK RESET PHASE

When a network station has sent or received a UA frame, a network station and its partner immediately enter the information transfer phase; a session is established. Information is sent over the connection using I-frames, and the connection is maintained using S-frames. Sequence numbers are placed in the frames. All I-frames are sequenced using the N(R) and N(S) control fields. These fields have already been explained and another explanation is given momentarily.

This is an upper limit to the number of outstanding frames that may be un-acknowledged, and when this limit has been reached, the sending station will not send any more frames, but it can still resend an old frame. I-frames not only contain information for the destination but I-frames can also contain acknowledgments for previous frames a station has received.. This allows for an efficient use of network bandwidth.

If the transmitting station enters into the busy state, it can still transmit I-frames, it just cannot receive any. If the source receives an indication that the destination is busy (RNR frame received from the remote station) then it will not send any more I-frames until it receives a receive ready (RR) frame from the remote station.

A station may send a FRMR (Frame Reject) frame. In this state a station will not transmit any more information for that particular link. Inside this frame is any explanation of why the transmitting station sent the FRMR frame. The link is disconnected when this frame is sent. When the sending station transmits the FRMR frame, it will start an acknowledgment timer in anticipation of receiving a response frame back for its transmission. The recipient of the FRMR frame should acknowledge it and the connection between the two stations is disabled.

Data Link Reset Phase. If a network station receives an SABM (or SABME) frame while in the information transfer phase, it will reset, not disconnect, the connection. It is used to return the connection to a known state. All outstanding frames are lost and sequence numbers are reset to 0. Retransmission of any outstanding frames occurs between the two network stations and are acknowledged at this time.

Information Transfer / Data Reset Phase

- After a session has been established, the information transfer phase is entered.

- Information is sent using the I-frames.

  - Inside the I-frames are sequence numbers.
  - Acknowledgments can be embedded in an Information frame or a RR frame.

    » If the destination station has information to transmit back to the source, it may do so using the I-frame, which can also be used to acknowledge previous frames to the source.

      - This feature conserves bandwidth.

- The connection is maintained using the S (supervisory) frames.

- If a station receives a SABM during this phase, the recipient will return to a known state.

  - All unacknowledged data is lost.

  - The session does not disconnect.

DATA LINK DISCONNECTION PHASE

While in the information transfer phase, either network station involved in the session may disconnect the session by transmitting a disconnect (DISC) frame to its partner. The DISC frame will have the P-bit set and the UA response will have the F-bit set. This phase can be entered when a normal disconnection is wanted or when an abnormal disconnection is wanted. A normal disconnection means that all information has been transferred successfully and there is no need to continue the connection. Abnormal disconnection means that the link is still needed but there have been too many errors that have occurred to continue it.

When one side of the connection sends this frame, the sending station starts an acknowledgment timer and waits for a response. When it receives a UA or DM response frame, the timer stops and the station enters into the disconnected mode.

If the acknowledgment timer expires before it receives a response frame, the originator will again send the DISC packet and restart the timer. When this station hits an upper limit of resends, it enters into the disconnection phase but informs its upper layer protocols that an error occurred when it attempted to disconnect from the remote station.

Normally, when a network station receives a DISC frame, it responds with UA frame and enters into the data link disconnection phase.

Data Link Disconnection Phase

- Either side of the connection may terminate the session by sending the DISC frame.

  – After sending it, the disconnecting station sets an acknowledgment timer.

  – A UA response is expected to the DISC frame within the acknowledgment timer.

  – If no UA frame is received,

    » at expiration of each acknowledgment timer a DISC frame will be re-sent up to N2 times.

LLC2 Frame Reception

Frame reception for LLC2 has many more functions than frame transmission. When a network station is not in the busy condition and receives an I-frame that contains the sequence number $N(R)$ equal to its $V(R)$ variable, it accepts the frame, increments its $V(R)$ by one, and then does one of three things:

1. If it has its own I-frame to transmit, it transmits the frame as discussed previously but sets the $N(R)$ field in the transmitted packet to its $V(R)$ and transmits the packet. This combines two functions into one frame; a I-frame for data and an acknowledgment for the data received. Again, this allows for better utilization of network bandwidth. LLC2 does not use separate packets to indicate an acknowledgment unless there are no more I-frames to be sent.

2. If there are no more I-frames to be sent, the station sends a RR frame with $N(R)$ set to its $V(R)$. RR frames are also transmitted to each other periodically to keep the session alive. In other words, the stations have no data to send to each other but they want to keep the connection alive. The sequence numbers in these RR frames will remain the same until an I-frame is received by either end.

3. The station may also send a receive not ready (RNR) frame back, indicating that it is now busy, and tells the remote end of the connection not to send any more data but it does acknowledge the previous frame is sent as indicated by $N(R)$.

Any frames received as invalid frames (containing wrong SAPs, for instance) are discarded.

LLC2 Frame Reception

- Frame reception is more complicated than frame transmission.

- If a network station is not busy and receives an I frame with N(S) = V(R), it:
  - increments V(R) by 1. Then,
    » if the station has an I frame to send back to the source,
      - set N(R) in transmit frame to its V(R) and transmits the I frame.
      - set N(S) in transmit frame to its V(S), and transmits the frame.
    » if there are no I frames to transmit back to the source, then
      - send a RR frame with N(R) set to its V(R).

- The station may send a RNR frame to:
    » indicates that it cannot accept any more data.
    » acknowledge the just received frame using the RNR N(R) field.

- Invalid frames are discarded.

eXchange IDentification Frame (XID)

The exchange identification frame, or XID frame, is used for the following functions:

1. A XID frame with a null SAP is used to retrieve information from a remote network station to request microcode levels, software release levels, and so forth. It is also used to test the presence of the remote station. This is an "Are you there?" packet.

2. With a group SAP (DSAP or SSAP), the XID frame can be used to determine group membership.

3. To test for duplicate MAC addresses.

4. If the link between the two stations is operating in LLC2 mode, this frame can be used to request a receiver's window size.

5. To request or identify a service class (Type 1 or Type 2 LLC operation).

6. Permits a station the ability to announce its presence on the LAN.

7. Permits a station the ability to announce the SAPs that it supports.

eXchange IDentification Frame (XID)

- XID frame is used by LLC1 for the following operations:
    - Retrieve information from a remote network station.
        » Request microcode levels, software release levels, or "Are you there?"
    - Determine group membership.
    - Test for a duplicate MAC address on the LAN.
    - Request receive window sizes (used in LLC2 mode).
    - Identify whether a remote station can support LLC2 mode.
    - Announce a network station presence on the network.
    - Allow a station to announce the SAPs it supports.
- This type of frame can be used with LLC2 or LLC1.

TEST FRAME

The primary use of the TEST frame is for loop back and locating and testing the validity of a path to a destination. The TEST frame is transmitted on a certain data path with the information field set to a specific entry. The network station then waits for a response to the frame. The information field in the response frame will be checked for errors. It should be exactly as it was sent.

A very common use of this frame is when a network station attempts to connect to a destination station on a source route Token Ring network (source routing is detailed in Part 3). To find the destination, the source transmits the TEST frame, on the local ring first. If the destination station does not respond, the source station will transmit the packet to all rings on the network. Information about the path is placed in this frame, and upon returning to the source station, the TEST frame will indicate the path to take to the destination. Once this frame returns, the source station will transmit an XID frame and then LLC1 I-frames will follow.

Although LLC1 operation does not require a LLC1 response frame to any LLC1 command frame during information transfer, the TEST and XID do require a response. The TEST command frame is not a requirement in LLC1 operation but the ability to respond to one is.

TEST Frame

- Used primarily for loop-back testing and checking the validity of a path to a destination.
  - Data portion of the frame is set to a certain value.
    - » Upon return of the frame it is checked for errors.

- Commonly used to find a destination station before session is established.
  - Transmitted on the local ring first.
  - Transmitted to all rings if there was no response on the local ring.
  - This frame should return with routing information in it so the source station will know the path to the destination.
    - » This is the frame used with the Token Ring source routing algorithm.
- This type of frame can be used with LLC2 or LLC1.

A Live LLC2 Connection

Prior to establishing a session LLC2 will transmit TEST and XID (exchange identification) frames which are not shown here. They are used before the SABME frame to test or find a path to the destination. Once the path is found (using the TEST frame), an XID frame is transmitted to exchange certain parameters between the two. It is assumed that each connection attempt issues these packets. After the connection is established, these frames will not be used unless the connection needs to be re-established. The event numbers are shown in the diagram on the following page.

Event	Operation
1–2	Station A requests a link to be established to station B by sending station B a SABME. Station B responds with a UA. Both the Poll and Final Bits are set to 1.
3	Station A sends an I-frame and sequences the frame with N(R) = 0, which means the starting sequence number expected is 0. The P-bit is set to 0.
4–6	Station B sends frame numbers N(S) = 0 through N(S) = 2. Its N(R) field is set to 1, which acknowledges station A's frame which had an N(S) value of 0 and was sent in event 1. Remember, the N(R) value states that the receiving station acknowledges all previously transmitted frames and also identifies the N(S) value that is expected from the other station.
7	Station A sends an I-frame sequenced with N(S) = 1, which is the value station B expects next. Station A also sets the N(R) field to 3, which inclusively acknowledges station B's previously transmitted frames numbered N(S) = 0, 1, 2.
8	Station B has no data to transmit. However, to prevent station A from "timing-out" and resending data, station B sends a receiver ready (RR) frame with the N(R) = 2 to acknowledge station A's frame with N(S) = 1 (sent in event 6).
9–10	The arrows depicting the I-frame flow from the stations are aligned horizontally with each other. This depiction means the two frames are transmitted from each station at about the same time and are exchanged almost simultaneously. The values of the N(R) and the N(S) fields reflect the sequencing and acknowledgment frames of the previous events.
11–12	Stations A and B send RR frames to acknowledge the frames transmitted in event 9–10. If neither side has data to send, each continues to send these frames to ensure that the other side is active. The sequence numbers in N(R) remain the same throughout the RRs transmitted.

A Live LLC2 Connection

Station A sends to station B — Station B sends to station A

Events — Events

1 SABME, P = 1
UA, F = 1   2
3 N(S) = 0, N(R) = 0, P = 0, I
N(S), = 0, N(R) = 1, P=0, I   4
N(S), = 1, N(R) = 1, P=0, I   5
N(S), = 2, N(R) = 1, P=0, I   6
7 N(S) = 1, N(R) = 3, P = 0, I
RR, N(R) = 2, P=0   8
9 N(S) = 2, N(R) = 3, P = 0, I   N(S) = 3, N(R) = 2, P=0, I   10
11 RR, N(R) = 04 P = 0,
RR, N(R) = 3, P=0   12

- The above illustration shows how all the previous (very complicated) text all plays together.

- TEST or XID frames have been used prior to the session set up.
  They are used to find or test a path to a destination station or to exchange operational parameters with the
  destination station; the XID frame is used.

- The illustration shows how the state variables are used to control the session.

T1 Timer Example

This figure shows how LLC2 uses timers. A session has already been established and data has previously been transferred. The frame also depicts how the P/F bits can be utilized to manage the flow of traffic between two network stations.

Event	Operation
1	Station A sends an I–frame and sequences it with N(S) = 3.
2	Station B does not respond within the bound of the timer. Station A times out and sends a receiver ready (RR) command frame indicated by the P-bit set to 1.
3	Station B responds with F-bit set to a 1 and acknowledges station A's frame by setting N(R) = 4.
4	Station A resets its timer and sends another I–frame, keeping the P-bit set to 1 to force station B to immediately respond to this frame.
5	Station B responds with an RR frame where N(R) = 5 and the F-bit set to 1.

T1 Timer Example

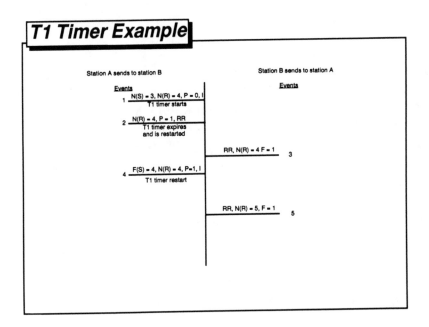

• The connection has been previously set up.

• The illustration shows how a timer can expire and the session is maintained.

SELECTIVE REJECT EXAMPLE

The following text explains how most transport level protocols work. They do not follow this exact interpretation of LLC2, but the functions are basically the same. LLC2 is primarily used when transporting SNA traffic across Token Ring, when the IBM LAN Server is being used, and with LANs that are implementing serial lines (bridges or routers that are using a telephone line to connect to a remote network). Serial lines are usually conditioned to handle the digital traffic, but there may be instances in which the serial line is not conditioned and the LLC protocol ensures that data is reliably transferred across these lines.

Event	Operation
1	Station A sets up a connection with station B by sending a SABME. Station B accepts this request by sending back a UA. P- and F-bits are set accordingly.
2	Station A sends an I-frame and sequences it with $N(S) = 0$. The $N(R) = 0$ means that station A expects station B to send an I-frame with a send sequence number of 0.
3–6	Station B sends four frames numbered $N(S) = 0$, 1, 2, and 3. The $N(R)$ value is set to 1 to acknowledge station A's previous frame. Notice that the $N(R)$ value does not change in any of these frames, because station B is indicating that is still expecting a frame from station A with a send sequence number of 1. During these transmissions, we may assume that the frame with $N(S) = 1$ is distorted.
7	Station A issues a REJ frame where $N(R) = 1$ and $P = 1$. This means that it is rejecting station B's frame that was sequenced with the $N(S) = 1$, as well as all succeeding frames.
8	Station B must first clear the P-bit condition by sending a non–I frame (RR frame) with the F-bit set to 1.
9–12	Station B then retransmits frames 1 through 3. During this time (in event 9), station A sends an I-frame where $N(S) = 1$. This frame has its $N(R) = 2$ to acknowledge the frame transmitted by station B in event 8.
13	Station A completes the recovery operations by acknowledging the remainder of station B's transmissions.

Selective Reject Example

Station A sends to Station B		Station B sends to Station A	
Events		**Events**	
1	SABME, P = 1		
		UA, F = 1	
2	N(S) = 0, N(R) = 0, P = 0, I		
		N(S) = 0, N(R) = 1, P = 0, I	3
		N(S) = 1, N(R) = 1, P = 0, I	4
		N(S) = 2, N(R) = 1, P = 0, I	5
		N(S) = 3, N(R) = 1, P = 0, I	6
7	N(R) = 1, P = 1, REJ		
		RR, N(R) = 1 F = 1	8
		N(S) = 1, N(R) = 1, P = 0, I	9
10	N(S) = 1, N(R) = 2, P = 0, I		
		N(S) = 2, N(R) = 2, P = 0, I	11
		N(S) = 3, N(R) = 2, P = 0, I	12
13	RR, N(R) = 4, P = 0,		

• The connection has been previously set up.

• This example shows how a frame is rejected and retransmitted.

LLC Type 1

LLC2 is a very difficult topic. The LLC1 protocol is much easier than LLC2. It has one frame type and one mode. With the exception of SNA and the IBM LAN Server Program, Type 1 is the most commonly used class of LLC. It is used by Novell NetWare, TCP/IP, OSI, and most other network protocols. There are no specific subsets for the operation of LLC Type 1. Type 1 operation consists of only one mode: information transfer.

Most network protocols do not need the overhead provided by the LLC2 operation. A LAN provides a media type that is highly reliable when compared to serial lines. Error rates on serial lines tend to be in the 1 in 10^3 range while errors on a LAN tend to be in the 1 in 10^8 range. Therefore, it does not make a lot of sense to provide for connection-oriented services for a LAN. Error control is usually provided for by the application as well as the upper-layer software of a LAN (the OSI transport layer). Today with LAN network protocols handling the connection-oriented services, connectionless methods are the most common.

LLC2 has its origins in HDLC, which is a protocol that was developed for data transmission across serial lines. The lines tended to be an unreliable media source so the reliability for data transfer was built into the protocol itself.

Type 1 operation does not require that prior connection be made between the source and destination network stations before data is transferred between them. Once the SAP information field has been set, information may be transferred between two network stations.

There are three types of frames that may be used with LLC1: the information frame, the exchange identification (XID) frame, and the TEST frame. XID and TEST frames are used in LLC2 to perform the same functions. The TEST and XID frames were explained previously.

LLC Type 1

- LLC1 primarily uses one frame type and one mode of operation: information transfer.

- LLC1 is used by LAN protocols that are robust and reliable.
  - Most LAN protocols do not need the overhead associated with LLC2.

- LLC1 was adopted to allow existing network protocols to operate with the IEEE 802.2 protocol.

- LLC1 does not require a connection to be set up before data is transmitted.

- LLC1 can make use of the XID and TEST frames.

SubNetwork Access Protocol (SNAP)

The most common implementation of LLC1 operation is through a special subsection of the IEEE 802.2 specification known as SubNetwork Access Protocol (SNAP). Most LAN network protocols supported the Ethernet frame format at the introduction of the IEEE 802 protocols in 1984. To allow for the migration of protocols written for Ethernet to the IEEE 802.x LAN types, SNAP was introduced to allow an easy transition to the new frame formats. It basically allows any protocol to run over any of the IEEE 802 LANs, including 802.3, 802.4, and 802.5, SNAP is supported by NetWare, TCP/IP, OSI, AppleTalk, and many other full OSI stack protocols. Any protocol may use it and become a pseudo-IEEE-compliant protocol.

Another purpose of SNAP is to allow those protocols that do not support IEEE 802.x to at least be able to traverse an IEEE 802 LAN. For example, if a packet needs to traverse from an Ethernet LAN over a Token Ring and then back to an Ethernet LAN (through some type of forwarding device such as a router or bridge), SNAP encapsulation allows the frame to traverse the Token Ring LAN.

As stated previously, IEEE 802.2 defined two fields known as the destination and source service access point (DSAP and SSAP respectively). For the most part, the SAP fields are reserved for those protocols that implemented the IEEE 802.x protocols. One SAP that has been reserved for all non-IEEE standard protocols. To enable SNAP, the SAP value in both the DSAP and SSAP fields are set to AA (hex). The control field is set to 03 (hex) to indicate a UI LLC1 frame. Having the DSAP, SSAP, and CTRL fields set to this combination indicates the frame is using SNAP encapsulation. Many different protocols may be run using this one SAP. Therefore, to differentiate between the protocols, any packet with the AA SAP address also has a 5-byte protocol discriminator following the control field. This identifies the protocol family to which the packet belongs. It truly imitates the Type field of an Ethernet packet.

The SNAP header contains two distinct parts: the 3-byte 802.2 headers (DSAP and SSAP set to AA, AA and the control field set to 03) and the 5-byte protocol descriptor.

Let's take a look at how Novell NetWare implements the SNAP protocol. Novell NetWare has the capability of using SNAP. An Ethernet packet using Novell NetWare simply has the destination and source address, the Type field, set to 8137 (hex), the data field, and the CRC. To convert this to a SNAP packet, the format for the DSAP, SSAP, Control fields reads AA-AA-03-AA. The SNAP header contains three bytes of zeros to indicate an encapsulated Ethernet packet and then the Ethernet Type field assigned to Novell: 8137. Altogether the IEEE 802.2 and SNAP fields read AA-AA-03-00-00-00-81-37.

SubNetwork Access Protocol (SNAP)

- Most common implementation of LLC1 is from a subsection of the IEEE 802.2 standard known as SNAP.

- At the time of IEEE 802.2's introduction, most network protocols were designed to use the Ethernet packet format.

- SNAP allows for the migration of the standard network protocols to the IEEE 802.2 format.

- Supported by TCP/IP, NetWare, OSI, AppleTalk, and many other protocols.

- The second purpose for the SNAP protocol is to allow those protocols that do not support the IEEE 802 standard to be able to traverse IEEE 802 LANs.

- SNAP uses a reserved SAP: AA (for both the DSAP and SSAP).

  - It uses the unnumbered frame format: control field equal to 03.

  - Actual SNAP header consumes 5 bytes:

    » Three bytes for the Organizationally Unique Identifier (OUI) field, and

    » Two bytes for an Ethernet Type field.

PROTOCOL DISCRIMINATOR

For SNAP, the important field to notice is the 5-byte protocol discriminator. The first three bytes of this field are the organizationally unique identifier or OUI, which is actually a vendor ID. There is one exception to this, if the field is set to 00-00-00, then it represents a generic Ethernet encapsulated packet not assigned to any particular vendor. If it is set to anything else (08-00-07 indicates Apple Computer, for example), it indicates that the packet is using the appropriate IEEE 802.x packet format for the LAN that it is transmitted on. It acts much like the vendor ID of a MAC address. This becomes important in bridging and routing and is in more detail in Part 3.

AppleTalk is the protocol that Apple Computer uses to converse on a network. AppleTalk originally used the Ethernet V2.0 packet format. AppleTalk Phase 2 has switched to the IEEE 802.x packet format. To accomplish this, AppleTalk packets use SNAP encapsulation. The OUI is set to 08-00-07 and the Type field is set to 80-9B. This indicates an AppleTalk packet running on an IEEE 802.x LAN using SNAP encapsulation.

Another use for SNAP is when TCP/IP packet that has been sent from a network station in Ethernet packet format and is destined for a station on FDDI. FDDI uses a different packet format than Ethernet. In order to go from Ethernet to FDDI, the packet must traverse a forwarding device such as a bridge or a router. It is that device that would use SNAP on the FDDI LAN. The DSAP, SSAP, and Control fields will be set to AA, AA, and 03, respectively. Since the originating packet was received with the Ethernet packet format, the OUI is set to 00-00-00, and not to a specific vendor ID, indicating an encapsulated Ethernet packet. The last two bytes will be set to 08-00. This is the registered Type field for TCP/IP. The packet will then be transmitted to the FDDI LAN. It is received by the FDDI station and processed. If a response packet is transmitted, it uses the same SNAP header. When the response packet is received by the forwarding device, it will know that the destination station on the Ethernet uses the Ethernet packet format (00-00-00 in the OUI field).

What is important here is the first three bytes of 00-00-00 indicating an encapsulated Ethernet packet. If another forwarding device received this packet and needed to forward it to an Ethernet LAN, which packet type should it use: Ethernet, or IEEE 802.3? With the three bytes 00-00-00, there is no question. The forwarding device would use the Ethernet packet format. If the three bytes had been filled in with a unique identifier—08-00-07 for example—it would use the IEEE 802.3 format.

SNAP can also be used for packets that are destined for network stations on the same cable plant. AppleTalk Phase 2 is a perfect example of this.

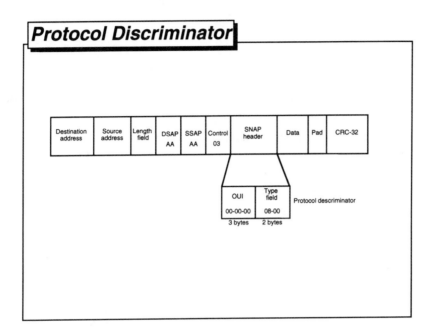

- The five byte protocol discriminator contains:
    three bytes of the organizationally unique identifier, and
    two bytes of Ethernet Type field.

- If the OUI is set to 00-00-00, it indicates the packet is encapsulated Ethernet packet.

- If the OUI is set to a numeric value (other than 00-00-00), the packet is emulating an Ethernet packet on an IEEE 802 LAN.
    A non-zero OUI indicates the vendor assigned ID.
        — This is important when translating through a bridge or a router.
        — To traverse different media types (Ethernet to FDDI), the originating packet type must be known (Ethernet or IEEE 802.3).
    With the OUI set to 00-00-00, this means to format the packet as an Ethernet frame when transmitting on an Ethernet network.
    If the OUI is set to a numeric value, the packet is to be transmitted on the Ethernet with an IEEE 802.3 header.

- The above example shows how an TCP/IP packet would look in a IEEE 802.3 frame using SNAP.
    Since TCP/IP primarily uses the Ethernet packet format, the OUI is set to 00-00-00.

- AppleTalk Phase 2 uses the SNAP header for its protocol. The OUI is set to 08-00-07 to indicate that it is an IEEE 802.3 packet format and the OUI is Apple.

TOKEN RING HISTORY

The emergence of this technology was precipitated by IBM's move to use the technology as its Local Area Network. Initial work was presented to the IEEE committee in 1982 and the first prototype was demonstrated in 1983 in Geneva, Switzerland.

The IBM cabling system for Token Ring was announced in 1984. It used only shielded and unshielded twisted pair wire. IBM officially announced the product in 1985. It was also standardized by the IEEE 802.5 committee in 1985 and it is the only ring access method accepted by the IEEE committee. For many years, it was the only access method supported by IBM. IBM was late delivering its implementation and therefore Ethernet gained a stronger hold on the market when a company named Synoptics delivered a physical star wired topology for the trusted Ethernet standard. This allowed Ethernet to retain its stronghold on the LAN marketplace. IBM is supporting the IEEE 802.3, FDDI, and IEEE 802.5 LAN access methods as well as TCP/IP, as a network protocol for terminal access (PC) to their hosts.

Token Ring History

- Presented by IBM in 1982 to IEEE 802 committee.

- First prototype developed in 1983 in Geneva, Switzerland.

- Cabling System was announced in 1984.

- Officially announced in 1985.

- Standardized by IEEE in 1985.

- Only one adopted by the IEEE 802.5 committee.

Token Ring Technology Summary

Token Ring is an access method by which network attachments on a physical star topology gain transmission access to the cable plant. The right to transmit is granted by converting a token into a data frame. The token is a special 24-bit pattern that continuously circulates the ring granting access to those stations wanting to transmit. There is only one token on any single ring.

A station needing to transmit waits for the token to arrive. When the token does arrive, if it is not already reserved for another network station, it is converted into a data packet. The network station places its information into the data packet and this packet is transmitted onto the ring. When the network station is finished transmitting, the station waits for its transmitted frame to return before releasing the token (true only for 4-Mbps rings).

Token Ring is a broadcast medium and every station can see every transmission that occurs on the ring. In order to correctly receive the data, a Token Ring controller compares the destination address in the received packet with its own address (MAC address). If there is a match, the controller copies the frame as it repeats it back to the ring. It also sets certain bits in the packet to indicate to the source station that it recognized its address and was able to copy the whole packet.

When the data frame arrives back at the source station, the source station strips the packet from the ring and releases the token back to the ring. With the token released, another station may follow the same process to transmit onto the ring.

The original Token Ring ran at 4 Mbps; in 1989, it was upgraded to 16 Mbps. The Token Ring standard does not specify speed or frame length. It does specify how long a station may hold the token—0.010 milliseconds. This translates to a 4,472-byte maximum packet size for 4 Mbps and a 17,800-byte maximum frame size for 16 Mbps. The only speeds for IBM's Token Ring are 4 and 16 Mbps. It is currently rumored that a faster Token Ring is forthcoming from IBM.

For IBM protocols that operate over the ring, such as NetBIOS and SNA, the link layer supported is the IEEE 802.2 connection-oriented LLC2 protocol. IBM protocols do not support the LLC1 connectionless protocol. Other protocols, such as NetWare, TCP/IP, etc., that run over Token Ring do support LLC1 operation.

Token Ring Technology Summary

- Access method by which network attachments gain access to the cable plant by acquiring acquiring a special frame called the token.
  - Token is a special 24-bit pattern that continuously circulates the ring.

- Token Ring is a broadcast medium.
  - To receive data, a destination station performs an address match.

- The destination station merely copies the frame as it repeats it back to the ring.

- When the frame arrives back to the source station, it strips the frame from the ring and then
  - releases the token (4 megabit operation only).
    » The token is allowed to be released prior to frame reception on 16-megabit rings.

- Token Ring originally ran at 4 Mbps.
  - Upgraded in 1989 to 16 Mbps

- Maximum frame size for 4 Mbps is 4472.
  - This is based only on the fact a station cannot hold the token longer than 0.010 milliseconds.
- Maximum frame size for 16 Mbps is 17,800.

CONTROLLER OPERATION—THE ATTACHMENT PROCESS

Token Ring operation is quite complex when compared to Ethernet. The frame format is complex, the operation of the ring is complex, and the controller itself is complex. Let's start with the controller.

There are many types of Token Ring controller cards but all of them possess the Token Ring access method controller chips. The ring protocol is loaded into PROMs on the controller card. This ensures that all the ring controllers operate the same way on the ring no matter what vendor the controller card came from.

Management of a Token Ring is very structured. It starts when the controller is initialized. Before the controller card may become an active participant on the ring, there is a five-phase initialization procedure that the controller card must go through before it is considered an active participant on the ring. Any error during this procedure takes the controller card off the ring.

Phase 0 is the lobe test and is accomplished before the controller logically attaches to the ring. The lobe is the section of cable that attaches the controller to the MAU. The test consists of sending a series of specially formatted lobe test MAC frames between the controller and the MAU. The relay in the MAU is not flipped in this operation; therefore, the controller is active on the ring at this time. The frames are transmitted and looped at the MAU to return immediately to the controller. If these frames return without error, the test will check the receive logic of the controller by transmitting duplicate address test MAC frames. If these frames are received without error, the controller attaches to the ring by flipping the relay in the MAU, and proceeds to phase 1. Otherwise, further tests are disabled and an error is reported.

Phase 1 is a monitor check. This is the process by which the controller waits for certain MAC frames—the active monitor present, standby monitor present, or ring purge MAC frames (all to be explained later)—to pass by. If it receives any of the above frames it will proceed to phase 2. If the controller does not see these frames, it assumes it is the first station on the ring, that no active monitor is present, or that inserting has disabled the ring. The controller enacts the token-claiming process (explained later). If it is the first station on the ring, it will become the active monitor.

Controller Operation - Phases 0 and 1

- Five-phase initialization
  - Phase 0 - Lobe test
    - » The controller transmits frames between the controller card and the cable attached between the controller card and the MAU.
    - » The controller tests to ensure that the lobe cable can successfully transmit and receive frames.
  - Phase 1 - Monitor Check
    - » Station inserts into the ring (flips the relay in the MAU) and looks for special frames that are transmitted by the monitors.
    - » Sets a timer to wait for these frames.
    - » If the station does not receive any of the frames, the controller assumes:
      - ✧ it is the first ring station on the network,
      - ✧ there is not an Active Monitor present, or
      - ✧ inserting into the ring disrupted the ring.
      - ✧ The controller may initiate the token claim process.

CONTROLLER INITIALIZATION (CONT.)

Phase 2 is the duplicate address check which checks to make sure other stations do not have the same MAC address at itself. Since Token Ring controllers possess the ability to assign their own addresses (through network administration intervention) the controller issues duplicate address MAC frames during this phase to ensure that its MAC address is not already being used on the network. If a duplicate address is found, the controller removes itself from the ring.

Phase 3 is neighbor notification. In Token Ring, all data flows on the ring in a counter-clockwise direction. This allows for neighbor notification, which occurs when a network station finds out the station address of the controller card upstream of it. The NAUN is defined as the nearest active upstream neighbor. This also allows the controller card to identify itself to its downstream neighbor. This is a continual process and will be examined in detail later.

Phase 4 is the request initialization phase. This is the controller's request for changed operational parameters from a special server on the ring known as the *ring parameter server*. This server need not be present on the ring for the initializing controller to become active; it is usually present in the source route bridge (discussed later).

   If any of this information is incorrect or a threat to ring integrity or if too many stations are already attached to the ring, the ring parameter server notifies the LAN Network Manager (explained later) which will request that a station be removed from the ring.

   If the controller passes all the phases, it will become a participating member of the ring adhering to all the rules of the ring.

Controller Initialization Phases 2, 3, and 4

- Phase 2 - Duplicate address check.
  - Checks to ensure that it can successfully transmit and receive a frame and to detect other stations that might have the same MAC address.
    » The controller transmits a frame to itself.
    » If the frame returns with the address recognized bit set, it notifies one of the monitors and removes itself from the ring.

- Phase 3 - Participation in neighbor notification.
  - The station transmits a special frame that will identify itself to its downstream neighbor.
  - The station should receive a similar frame for its upstream neighbor.

- Phase 4 - Lan Network Manager Notification
  - Notifies LAN Network Manager about its presence on the ring

IEEE 802.5 FRAME FORMAT

Once a controller is active on the ring, it is able to transmit frames onto the ring. There are multiple frame types that may be transmitted. First, a generic explanation of the Token Ring frame format. The Token Ring frame format is quite different from the Ethernet frame format; most of the field definitions will be saved until the discussion on Token Ring functions. The points we'll discuss here are the address fields, IEEE 802.2 fields, and the bit transmission order.

The address scheme uses 6 bytes. The Token Ring specification allows for a 2-byte address field, but this is not commonly used. Two-byte addresses and 6-byte addresses may not be intermixed on the same LAN. Anyway, 2-byte address are not commonly used in commercial networks.

Like the Ethernet frame, the Token Ring frames uses the I/G bit to indicate whether the frame is addressed by a universal authority (the IEEE) or is locally assigned (known as a locally assigned address or LAA). If the bit is set, it is locally assigned. If it is set to a 0, it is a universally administered address. Either way, all addresses must be unique. A network administrator at the customer's site should be tasked with the responsibility of assigning unique LAAs. Again there are many benefits to this. The address can be customized to indicate a building, floor, user, file server, workstation, computer type, etc. The conventions used for LAA's are virtually limitless. The main idea to keep in mind is consistency and uniqueness.

At the data link level, an important difference between the Token Ring and Ethernet frame is the bit-order transmission. Both the Ethernet and IEEE 802.5 frames always transmit bit 0 first. The difference is that bit 0 is the rightmost bit on an Ethernet byte and it is the leftmost bit of an IEEE 802.3 byte on Token Ring packets. This is very important when trying to negotiate packets between Ethernet networks and IEEE 802.5 networks. If the MAC portion of the frame is not translated correctly, the frame will not be addressed correctly when traversing different network types.

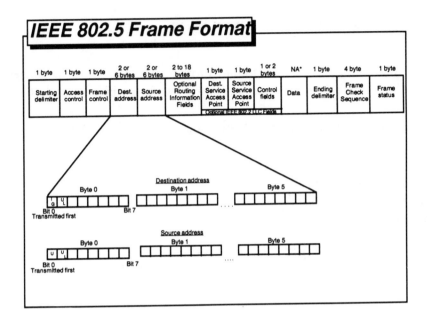

- The source and destination addresses used are 6 bytes long.

- The destination address has I/G and the U/L bits.
    The I/G bit is the individual/group address.
    The U/L bit indicates whether the address is universally (UAA) or a locally administered address (LAA).
        — In the source address, if the U bit is set, this indicates that the frame contains source routing information.
        — This is commonly called the Routing Information Indicator or RII bit.
        — If it is not set, there is no source routing information in the frame.

- Bit 0 is transmitted first.
    Bit 0 is now the leftmost bit of the byte.

- In a Token Ring network there are no limitations on the size of the data field.

Bit Order Transmission for Token Ring

Again, though Token Ring packets are transmitted with bit 0 of byte 0 first, the difference is that bit 0 is the leftmost bit of a byte. Therefore it is the leftmost bit of every byte in Token Ring that is transmitted first.

A packet with the first three bytes of the MAC address header of 40-00-12... is transmitted as follows:

        40 (hex) = 0100 0000 (binary)
        00 (hex) = 0000 0000 (binary)
        12 (hex) = 0001 0010 (binary)

Therefore the transmission on the ring would be:
                        0100 0000 0000 0000 0001 0010 ...

Compare this same frame as received on Ethernet LANs:
                        0000 0010 0000 0000 0100 1000 ...

If a Token Ring controller received the Ethernet transmission, it would incorrectly determine the first three bytes to read 02 00 48. Obviously, the transmission differences between Ethernet and Token Ring can cause problems when two stations are communicating with each other on a different medium type. The problems occur only at the MAC header of a frame; this is fully discussed under the IBM 8209 bridge section of Part 3.

Bit Order Transmission for Token Ring

- Bit 0 is the first bit transmitted.
    - Bit 0 is the left most bit of the byte.
        - » Unlike Ethernet, the bits in the bytes are not reversed as they are transmitted.

- Example:
    - 40-00-12 are the first three bytes of a MAC address.
        - » Translated to binary:
            01000000-00000000-00010010
        - » As transmitted on a Token Ring:
            01000000-00000000-00010010
        - » Compared to Ethernet transmission:
            00000010-00000000-01001000

FUNCTIONAL ADDRESSES OF TOKEN RING

There truly is no practical way to provide for multicast addressing on Token Ring networks. Remember that multicast packets are addressed to a specific group of stations attached to a network. It is different than a broadcast packet in that not all active stations receive and process a multicast packet. Stations will be assigned a multicast address upon their initialization. Transparent bridges are example of devices that can receive multicast packets. Multicast packets are efficient in that only one packet has to be sent but this one packet can be processed by multiple stations. A broadcast packet is received and processed by every station even though the packet was not meant for all stations. Routing updates (the Routing Information Protocol, or RIP, to be explained in the routing section) are examples of broadcast packets not meant for everyone.

Functional addresses are reserved for entities on the Token Ring network that are running certain functions—ring parameter server, active monitor, and so forth. They are similar yet different from multicast addresses. The first two bits of the destination address must be set to 11 (C in hex). This will indicate an LAA group address. Then bit 0 in byte 2 of the destination address is the functional address indicator, or FAI. If it set to a 1, it is a group functional address; set to a 0 it is a unique functional address. Stations on the ring will have a mask set in their drivers so that when a packet is received with the first two bits set, they will apply this 48-bit mask to the destination address. Any bits that are still set after the mask indicate the type of multicast packet. Using a 48-bit mask allows one station to be able to receive many different types of functionally addressed packets.

The remaining 7 bits in byte 2 and the 8 bits each in bytes 3, 4, and 5 allow for up to 31 functional addresses to be defined. These bits are not counted in binary. They are bit-specific. Each bit has a meaning and bits are not combined to give one meaning. Usually multiple bits are not set in the destination address.

Certain functional addresses are reserved. They are primarily used for the management servers of Token Ring. The remaining addresses may be user-defined. These addresses and definitions are shown on the next page.

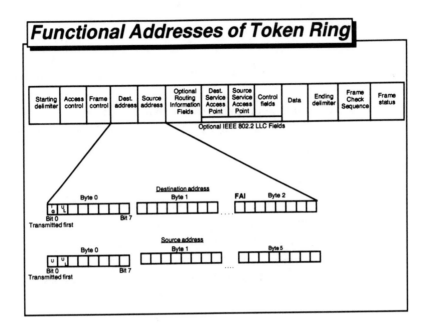

• Token Ring possesses no way to perform a multicast so it uses functional addresses.

• Functional addresses are used for common functions on Token Ring.

• Bits 0 and 1 of byte 0 must be set to a 1 (C in hex)

• The functional address bit (bit 0 of byte 2) is set to a 0 to indicate a unique functional address.
    Set to a 1 indicates a group functional address.

• The remaining 7 bits in byte 2 and the 8 bits each in bytes 3, 4, and 5 allow up to 31 functional addresses to be defined.
    Addresses are bit specific, 31 bits yields 31 functional addresses.

• Certain functional addresses are reserved:
    Active Monitor   C00000000001
    Ringer Parameter Server   C00000000002
    Ring Error Monitor   C00000000008
    Configuration Report Server   C00000000010
    NetBIOS   C00000000080
    Lan Network Manager   C00000002000
    All Bridges Broadcast   C00000000100
    User defined   C00000080000 through
                                            C00040000000

TOKEN RING FRAMES

There are four types of Token Ring frames that may traverse the ring. These are the LLC, MAC, Token, and abort frames.

The LLC is the frame that is used by controllers to distribute user data.

The MAC frame is used by the controllers to carry certain "housekeeping" information on the ring. This "housekeeping" helps to maintain the proper operation of the ring. This type of frame is not used to carry user data. It is a local frame in that it stays on the ring on which it was transmitted. It cannot be forwarded by bridges or routers.

The Token frame is a 3-byte frame that is commonly called *the Token*. This frame continuously circles the ring "polling" controllers for transmit requests. If a controller needs to transmit, it must wait for the Token. If the Token frame arrives at a controller, the controller converts the Token and, with few exceptions, starts to transmit its data. The controller card changes a bit in the Token frame which converts it to a start-of-data frame header. The controller then appends destination and source address information and data to the frame and transmits it to the ring. Once the data has been transmitted, the controller waits for its transmission to return and then it releases the Token. With Token Ring, there will be only one Token that traverses a single ring.

The abort frame is used by a controller to indicate that a transmitted frame should be ignored. It may be transmitted due to an internal error on the controller that is not severe enough to force the controller to remove itself from the ring. After transmitting the abort frame, the controller continues to participate on the ring.

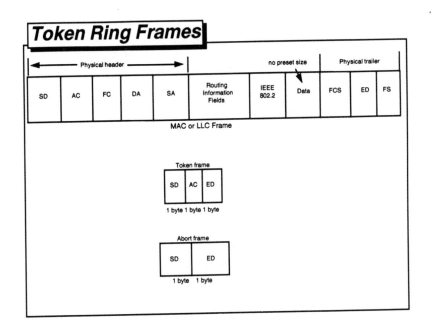

• There are four frames that may traverse the Token Ring.

• The MAC/LLC frames are standard frames that serve two functions.
     The FC field controls which frame type it is.
     The LLC frame is used to carry normal user commands or user data.
     The MAC frame is used to perform "housekeeping" chores.
         — Housekeeping is the ability to maintain the ring integrity.

• The Token frame is a 3-byte frame commonly called the token.
     The token permits access to the ring by "polling" the network attachments.

• The abort frame is used by a ring station that wishes to abort a previously transmitted frame.

TOKEN RING FRAME FIELD DEFINITIONS

1. The Starting Delimiter (SD) is the first byte of a frame. It indicates to a controller that a frame (Token, LLC, or MAC) is about to arrive.

2. The Access Control (AC) indicates whether the frame is a Token or a data frame. This byte contains reservation and priority bits that allow a station to capture the Token or to reserve it. It also contains a monitor bit (explained later).

3. The Frame Control field (FC) indicates whether a frame is an LLC or MAC frame. LLC frames usually contain user data, but MAC frames have special purposes on the ring that have nothing to do with user data; they maintain and report errors on the ring.

4. The Destination Address (DA) is the address of the intended destination station.

5. The Source Address (SA) is the address of the controller that transmitted the packet.

6. The Routing Information Field (RIF) indicates the path a packet should take when traversing a network of source route bridges, which are explained in more detail in the bridge section of this book.

7. IEEE 802.2 field—previously explained.

8. The data field.

9. The Frame Control Sequence (FCS) is a 32-bit field used for bit-level error detection.

10. The Ending Delimiter (ED) indicates the end of the frame. Contains the I (intermediate) bit and the E (error) bit.

11. The Frame Status field (FS) is used by the controller to indicate whether the destination station saw the packet and was able to copy its contents. This field is not covered by the FCS because it is changed by the destination and not the source station.

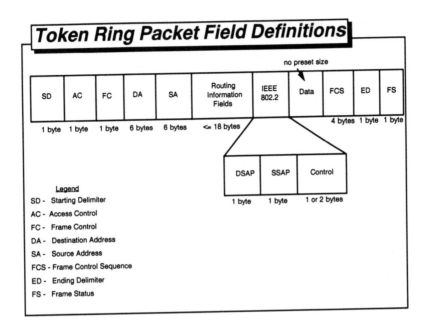

- The address fields were explained previously.

- The starting delimiter is preset and indicates the arrival of a frame.

- The access control field indicates whether the frame is a Token or data frame and contains the reservation and priority bits and the monitor bit.

- The frame control field indicates whether the frame is a MAC or LLC frame.

- The IEEE 802.2 field was previously explained.

- FCS—is a 32-bit CRC similar in function to Ethernet's CRC.
    The FCS does not cover the FS field.
       — This field is set by the destination station.

- The ending delimiter indicates the end of a frame and also contains the I (intermediate) and E (error) bits.
    Setting the I bit was a way of transmitting multiple frames while holding the token.
    It is not usually implemented in most Token Ring environments.

- The frame status field contains the A (address recognized) and C (frame copied bits).
    These bits indicate whether the destination station recognized its address and whether the frame was copied or not.

THE STARTING DELIMITER AND THE ACCESS CONTROL FIELDS

Each frame field contains bit-level information. A field is not simply read as a single 8-bit (byte level) indicator; each bit or a group of bits represents an indication by itself.

The 8-bit SD field has the following format: JK0JK000. If a controller reads this bit pattern it knows that some type of frame is about to enter the controller card. When there is no activity on the ring, a controller repeats idle characters which originate from one station that is providing the master clock to a single ring (clocking is used to synchronize the bit pattern in the packet). Idle characters are clock signals to which all stations synchronize their receive clocks. In this way, all stations will transmit and receive with a synchronized clock pattern. At this time, the controller card will not know what type of frame, but simply that a frame is about to enter the controller. When information is transmitted on the cable, the electrical signal should be a specific wave form. If there is a deviation from this wave form, it may be an error. If it is a known deviation (having a specific wave form) it may be a J or K symbol. These symbols are known as *phase violations* and are beyond the scope of this book. For the purposes of this book, it will be assumed that the controller recognizes certain electrical wave forms; if there is a recognizable deviation of this wave form, it can be classified as a J or K symbol. Otherwise, the controller will report a problem on the cable plant.

The access control field (AC) is the next field read by the controller. This field contains three priority bits, one Token bit, one Monitor bit, and three reservation bits. The term of priority indicates access priority. The priority bits indicate the priority of the incoming frame. A ring station can use a token whose priority is equal to or less than that of the ring station. There are eight priority levels, with all zeros being the lowest. If the received token's priority bits are higher than the controller's, the controller must wait for the next time the token returns.

The Token bit indicates whether the frame is a token or a data frame. If the bit is a 0, it is a token frame. When a station captures the token, it simply flips this bit to become a 1; appends its data to the frame; applies the ED, FCS, and FS fields; and transmits this to the ring.

The monitor bit is used by a special station on the ring known as the active monitor (AM). This bit allows the AM to control how many times a data frame has circulated the ring. It is the transmitting station that must remove its frame from the ring. If, for some reason, the source station cannot remove its frame, the active monitor removes the frame. The first time the frame passes the AM, this bit is set. If the frame passes by the AM and this bit is already set, the AM removes the frame. The AM is discussed in detail in the monitors section of this chapter.

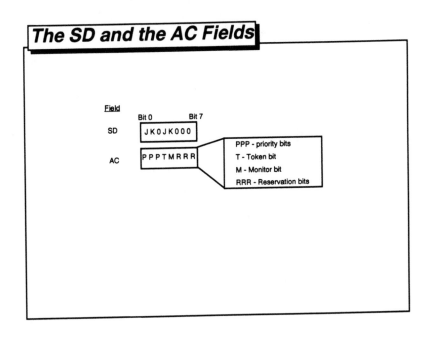

- The individual bits within each field are shown above.

- The J and K bits are known phase violation bits and will be recognized by the controller card as non-data bits and will only be recognized as symbols J and K.

- The access control field contains the reservation bits, the token bit, the monitor bit, and the priority bits.

TOKEN RING FRAME FIELDS—THE RESERVATION BITS, THE FC, ED, AND FS FIELDS

The reservation bits are used by a controller to reserve the next token. When it has priority data to send, a ring station will set these bits to its given priority for the frame to be transmitted; the next token that is generated should have its priority bits set to the previously set reservation bits. A ring station does not always have priority data to send and does not always set these bits. Normally, these bits are set to normal user priority allowing every station equal access.

Next the controller reads the 8-bit FC field. In this field, two bits indicating the frame type, two reserved bits and 4 bits used only for MAC frames. If the frame type is LLC data (01 are the first two bits) then the Z bits are ignored. If the frame type is a MAC frame (00 are the first two bits), then the Z bits indicate what type of MAC frame it is.

The ending delimiter (ED) contains the J and K bits, which indicate to a controller that this is the end of the frame. This field also contains two other bits: the intermediate frame and the error detection bits. When set to a 1, the intermediate frame bit indicates to the destination that more packets are to immediately follow. The I bit is not implemented in most Token Ring Controllers. The error detection bit indicates that some station of the ring detected an error in the frame. A transmission passes through every active controller on the ring, and any controller may be able to detect an error in the frame. These errors are limited to electrical signalling errors (code violations) between the SD and ED fields (the SD and ED fields are the only fields that should have J and K code violations), a frame contained a nonintegral number of bytes, or a frame has a CRC error. Again, any station can set this bit.

The frame status field contains the bits ACrrACrr. The r bit indicates reserved and is ignored by a controller. The A bit is the address-recognized bit. If a destination station received a packet and the destination address in the packet is its own, it will set the A bits before repeating the frame back to the originator. The C bits are the frame copied bits. If the destination station is able to copy the frame, it sets the C bits. There are two A bits and two C bits, and the reason behind this is that this single field is not covered by the FCS. Therefore, to ensure that no corruption in the packet has taken place, two bits were placed in the field. When a controller receives its transmission back, both bits (either the A or C bits) must be set to the same value.

The A bits may be set without the C bits being set. This indicates that the controller recognized its address and/or it was too busy to copy the frame. The C bits cannot be set without the A bits being set, since a controller cannot copy a frame without recognizing its own address. Naturally, neither bit is set if the frame was received with the E bit set, indicating an error. If neither bit is set and the E bit is a zero, then no station recognized the destination address of the packet.

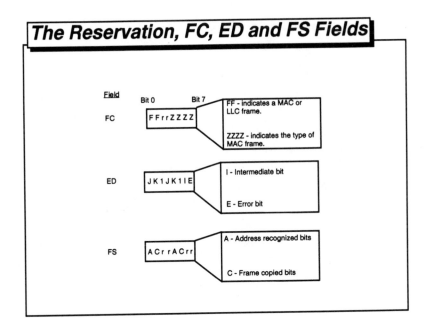

- The FF bits indicate whether the frame is a LLC or MAC frame
    If it is a MAC frame (FF=00).
        — The ZZZZ bits indicate the type of MAC frame.

- The I bit was implemented as a method to transmit multiple frames while holding the token.
    It is not usually implemented in most Token Ring environments.

- The E bit of the ED field indicates whether some station on the ring found a problem with the quality of the signal (the electrical signals used on the wire). If set, no station will copy the frame.

- The A bit of the Frame Status field indicates whether the destination station was able to recognize its own address. Also used during initialization of controller.

- The C bit of the Frame Status field indicates to the source station whether the destination station was able to copy the frame before repeating it back to the originating station

- The A and C bits are duplicated because the FCS does not compute its frame checking on these fields.
    The A bit can be set without the C bit being set.
    The C bit cannot be set without the A bit being set.
    Neither the A nor C bits should be set if the E bit is set.

EXAMPLES OF HARD AND SOFT ERRORS

Token Ring error conditions are classified as soft and hard errors. A soft error is a condition that is easily recoverable. This means that the ring is continuing to operate normally but there are errors occurring that need monitoring. Soft error reporting is accomplished through the MAC frames which are sent to the monitors on the ring.

A hard error is a permanent fault from which the ring cannot recover by itself. Hard errors are often caused by faulty equipment. All data operations on the ring cease, until the error is corrected. Examples are faulty lobe cables, an intializing station entering the ring at the wrong ring speed (16 and 4 Mbps stations cannot exist on the same ring). When a hard error condition exists, the ring will start to beacon. A beacon is a MAC frame that indicates who is beaconing the ring and what is its Next Available Upstream Neighbor (NAUN). In this way, the station causing the problem should be able to be found.

Example

When a ring station downstream (the next station in the path of the token) of the faulty ring station detects a hard error on its receive logic, the token claiming process by the Active Monitor (discussed on the next text page) should take effect. If this procedure fails to correct the problem, a beacon condition exists. A beacon is a MAC frame that indicates that the normal Token operation of the ring has been disrupted and needs to be corrected. Hard errors are detected, isolated, and bypassed through the use of a beacon MAC frame. All data transmissions halt until the condition is corrected. For example, when a downstream ring station detects a hard error on the receive side of its attachment, it will start to transmit beacon frames. Inside of this frame is the address of its upstream neighbor and the type of hard error detected. Other stations on the ring will simply repeat the frame to their downstream neighbor. The NAUN (indicated in the beacon frame) should pick up these packets and test itself. If the hard error persists, the beaconing station and its NAUN deinsert from the ring and test themselves. If the beaconing station and the NAUN do not recover, manual intervention is needed to recover.

Soft errors do not fully affect the operation of the ring; for example a bad CRC (data integrity checker) or receiver congestion. (Receiver congestion means that the ring station receive buffers are full. These receive buffers are located on the controller card's memory.) With these types of errors, the ring can continue to operate. If too many soft errors happen, they will be reported to one of the monitors and further action may take place. This will not affect the proper operation of the ring, only one or two workstations.

Examples of Soft and Hard Errors

- Soft errors are errors that are recoverable. Examples are:
  - a CRC error,
  - temporary loss of the token.
  - These errors will be reported by using the MAC frame, but the ring should remain operational.
- Hard errors are faults that break the ring.
  - Downstream neighbor will detect a hard error on its receive logic. Examples are:
    » the loss of the token, or
    » loss of the clock signal.
- Hard errors are detected, isolated and bypassed through the use of a beacon frame.
  - A station receiving a hard error will immediately issue beacon frames.
  - Contained in the beacon frame is the address of its upstream neighbor.
  - Eventually the station indicated in the frame should receive this frame and test itself.
  - The beaconing station tests itself.
    » Any errors found keep the station from inserting into the ring.
- The ring should eventually recover.

THE TOKEN CLAIM PROCESS

Before a Token Ring network can operate there must be a token on the network for ring stations to convert. If a ring station does not have the token it cannot transmit.

The Token-Claiming process serves two purposes. First, it elects the Active Monitor (AM), which controls the operation of the ring. After the AM is elected, it purges the ring; that is, it "cleans" the ring to ensure that it can transmit a packet on the ring and receive that packet back in good condition. The AM is the only station that can place a token on ring.

The Token-Claiming process is started when one of the following conditions occur for the AM:

1. It detects the loss of its clock signal.

2. A timer expires and it has not received its active monitor present MAC frame.

3. It cannot receive enough of its Purge Ring MAC frames.

The Token-Claiming process is started when one of the following conditions occur for the standby monitor:

1. It detects loss of signal.

2. It detects expiration of its timer for receiving its standby monitor frames or its timer for receiving a token.

This process will occur when something as simple as a ring station inserts into the ring. The AM will detect a loss of clock signal (the relay on the MAU causes the error), and it will start the Token-Claiming Process.

Claim Token Process

- A ring cannot operate without a token circulating on the ring.
  - There is only one token per ring.

- The token-claiming process allows one station to insert the token onto the ring.
  - This station will be elected as the AM.
    » It will purge the ring (ability to transmit a frame to itself).
    » After purging the ring, it will insert a new token on the ring.

- The Token-Claim process can be started when the AM
  - detects a loss of signal,
  - a timer expires and it has not yet received its AM frame back, or the AM
  - cannot receive enough of its own Purge Ring MAC frames.

- It can be started when the SM
  - detects loss of signal or
  - detects expiration of its timer for receiving SM frames.

DETAILS OF THE TOKEN-CLAIMING PROCESS

Without a Token on the ring, no ring station has the ability to transmit to the ring. As mentioned previously, there are certain conditions that may occur that stop the ring from operating correctly. The Active Monitor should be able to restart the ring if any of these conditions occur. It may also be assumed by any ring station that the AM is not running (the AM broadcasts identification notices on the ring every five seconds), then any station on the ring has the right to become the AM. If this is the case, ring stations bid against each other for this right. The ring station that wins the right to become the AM will be the only station that can insert a Token onto the ring.

The ring station that detected any of the previous Token-Claiming conditions will insert its master clock and a 24-bit delay. It will then start to transmit Token Claim MAC frames which are received by all stations on the ring. This ring station will broadcast the frames without waiting for a token to transmit. Following the frames are idle characters to maintain the clock on the ring (idles are used to keep a constant signal on the ring).

After transmitting the Token-Claim MAC frames the ring station will start a timer. If it does not receive its own frames back or it does not receive a frame indicating another station should be the active monitor by the time this timer expires, it will start to beacon the ring. If the ring station is not attached to the ring, it will stop the attachment process and remove itself from the ring.

Once a station has started this process, other stations will either repeat the ring station's frames or become involved in the process. It is a very simple process based on priority. If a ring station received a Claim Token MAC frame, it will compare its priority (not be confused with the priority bits in the AC field) to the received MAC frame. If its priority is higher, the ring station will not repeat the received frame. It transmits its own Claim Token MAC frame. When the original workstation receives this new frame, it will stop transmitting its own Claim Token MAC frames and repeat the higher priority frames. Any station that is participating in this process will perform the same comparison. The priority is usually based on the MAC address of the ring station. The higher the MAC address the better the chances are for the ring station to become the active monitor.

Not only can any station on the ring start the Token-Claiming Process, they contain the option to not participate in the Token-Claiming Process. If they choose not become involved, those ring stations will simply repeat any Token Claim MAC frames. The only way a non-participating station can participate is when it detects a condition that necessitated the Token-Claim Process, i.e., it had to start the Token Claim process itself. It did not receive a Token Claim MAC frame from another station.

Details of the Claim Token Process

- If there is no token on the ring, all activity will cease on the ring.
  - The Active Monitor should be able to recover by purging the ring and issuing a new Token.
  - If the Active Monitor cannot recover, the token-claim process will begin.

- Any station will insert its master clock, a 24-bit delay, and start to transmit Token-Claim frames.
  - These frames are received by all stations on the ring.
  - The station will follow these frames with idle (clock) signals.
  - After transmitting the Token Claim frames, the station starts a timer.
    » If it does not receive its frames or someone else's claim frames, it will beacon the ring.
- Once the process is started other stations may participate.
  - Stations bid for the right to become the AM.
  - The station with the highest priority (MAC address) wins.
  - That station becomes the AM.
    » It will purge the ring and insert a new token.

TOKEN-CLAIMING PROCESS EXAMPLE

Say, for example, there are four stations on a ring, each identified with a unique MAC address used to determine the active monitor. Once the active monitor is elected, it will purge the ring and issue a new token to the ring.

The four stations are MAC addressed A, B, C, and D. For now, assume the priority that B > A > C, and D is not participating. If C were to detect a condition that would cause it to start the Claim Token process, it would issue these frames at timed intervals followed by idles between the frames. Station D receives these frames but since it is not participating in the process it simply repeats the frame to the ring. Station A receives station C's frame and compares its address to the received MAC frame address. It has a higher address and does not repeat station C's Token-Claim MAC frame. Instead, it transmits its own. Station B receives this frame and does a compare on the MAC addresses. If it finds that its address is higher, it therefore does not repeat station A's MAC frame but instead transmits its own Token-Claim MAC frame.

Station C receives station B's MAC frame and compares the addresses. Its address is lower in priority and it quits transmitting its Token-Claim MAC frame. It repeats station B's MAC frame to the ring. Station A receives this frame and it too stops transmitting its own MAC frame and repeats station B's MAC frame. When B has received three of its own Claim Token MAC frames, it knows that it has won the right to become the AM.

Station B purges the ring and issues a new token. It sends a Report New Active Monitor MAC frame to the configuration report server. The ring is considered operational at this point and normal data operations may now start.

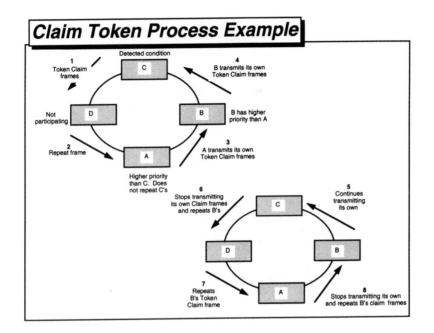

- Assume B> A> C in priority, and D is not participating.

- D is upstream of A. B is downstream of A.

- C detects a hard error and starts to transmit Claim Token frames.

- D is not participating and repeats C's frames.

- A has a higher priority than C, so it transmits its own Claim Token frame.

- B has a higher priority than A, so it transmits its own Claim Token frame.

- C receives B's Claim Token frame; stops transmitting its own.
    Station C repeats station B's Claim Token frame.

- D repeats B's Claim Token frame.

- A receives B's Claim Token frame and stops transmitting its own.
    Station A repeats station B's Claim Token frame.

- B is successful when it receives three of its Claim Token frames.
    Station B becomes the Active Monitor.
    Station B purges and inserts a token on the ring.

NEIGHBOR NOTIFICATION PROCESS

One of the more important housekeeping functions of the ring is the *neighbor notification process*. Since data travels on the ring in one direction only, a ring station receives frames only from its upstream neighbor and gives frames only to its downstream neighbor. Thus, a ring station monitors who its upstream neighbor is but has no idea of its downstream neighbor. If a ring station acquires a new upstream neighbor, it notifies one of the monitors. This process occurs every five seconds.

Neighbor notification is a very important part of the management of a ring. The process starts when the active monitor transmits an active monitor present MAC frame. The first station to receive this frame copies it and sets the A (address recognized) and C (frame copied) bits in the frame status field (set to a binary 1) as it repeats it. It knows that it is the first station to receive this frame because the A and C bits are set to 0, meaning that no other station has received the frame before it. This ring station saves the source address of the received frame as the NAUN, which in this case is the active monitor. After copying the frame it sets a timer. When this timer expires, it will send a standby monitor present MAC frame.

The next station to receive this active monitor present MAC frame will ignore it because the A and C bits have already been set, indicating there is one or more stations between it and the active monitor. It sets a timer expecting to receive a Standby Monitor MAC frame from its NAUN. When it receives this frame, a standby monitor present frame, (the A and C bits are set to binary 0), it copies and records the source address as its NAUN and sets the A and C bits in the FS field to a 1. It repeats this frame back to the ring. This station sets a timer and transmits its own standby monitor present frame to be copied and recorded by its downstream neighbor.

Each station repeats the above process. Eventually, all stations are notified of their NAUNs and the process is stopped when the active monitor receives a standby active monitor frame from its upstream neighbor. The active monitor knows this because in the received MAC frame, the A and C bits are set to zero. The active monitor sets these bits and repeats back to the ring. Once this has happened, the neighbor notification process is complete and will be restarted by the active monitor when its neighbor notification timer has expired.

If the active monitor receives its MAC frame back with the A and C bits set to a 0, it assumes that it is the only ring station active, and the ring considers the process complete.

Neighbor Notification Process

- Data travels in one direction only on the ring (counter-clockwise).
  - Because of this, stations can find out who is upstream but not downstream from them.

- This process starts when the Active Monitor transmits a special MAC frame called the Active Monitor present MAC frame.
  - » First station to receive this will set the A and C bits, note its upstream neighbor address (MAC address).
    - ✧ Knows that it is the first station to receive this for the A and C bits were set to 0.
  - » Sets a timer to transmit its standby monitor present frame.

- The frame will return to the AM and it strips the frame off the ring.

- The timer expires and the standby station transmits its standby monitor present frame.
  - The station downstream of it will receive the frame.
    - » Sets the A and C bits and notes the MAC address of its upstream neighbor.
    - » Sets a timer to transmit its own Standby Monitor present frame.

- All stations do this and the process will end when the AM receives a standby monitor present frame with the A and C bits set to a 0.
  - Sets a timer to start the process again (usually about every five seconds)

TOKEN RING TRANSMIT MODE

Now that all functions and ring operations have been explained, it should be easier to understand how ring stations operate in a normally functioning ring. In normal transmit mode, the controller has already captured and converted the token. It sets the Token bit in the AC field to 1 to indicate a data frame. It then transmits the rest of the AC field and FC field. The Token Ring controller then checks for the presence of the ED field. If the controller cannot find the ED field, it assumed that it has incorrectly identified the received frame as a token, and immediately transmits the abort frame. If it does find the ED field, it inserts the rest of its information into the frame; places the ED, CRC, and FS fields on the end of the frame; and transmit the rest of the frame.

If the controller finds the ED field, the rest of the frame includes the destination and source addresses, the optional source routing field, the information field, and the CRC field. It will then append the ED and FS fields. This completes packet transmission.

With the completion of the transmission, the controller waits for the frame to return, looking for its physical header. If the controller does not receive the physical header by the time it transmits the frame status field, it transmits binary zeros (idle characters) until the frame does return. If the physical header does not return, the controller returns to normal repeat mode without initiating a token.

When the physical header returns, the controller strips its frame from the ring and releases the token. After taking its packet off the ring, the controller enters normal repeat mode.

Token Ring Transmit Mode

- A station that needs to transmit receives the SD of approaching frame. This station quits transmitting idles (clock signals).

- Checks for priority.
  - If the priority in the frame is greater than the station's priority, then
    - » the station sets reservation bits and awaits new token.

- If the priority in the frame is less than or equal to the station's priority then
  - the station changes the T bit in the AC field from a 0 to a 1,
  - appends its information to the rest of the frame and transmits the frame.
  - If the end of its transmission is reached and it has not received its current transmission back, the station
    - » transmits idle characters and awaits current transmission.

- When the station receives its frame back it will strip the frame and release the token.

- The station enters normal repeat mode.

TOKEN RING COPY MODE

A station will copy a frame that matches its unique address, or is a multicast or broadcast packet. In copy mode, if the controller finds one of the three conditions exist, it will start to copy a frame into its buffer.

If at any time an error is detected in the frame, the controller sets the two A bits and the one E bit and repeats the frame onto the ring. If no errors are found, the controller will set the two A and the two C bits, indicating to the source that it received the frame, (recognized its address), and was able to copy the frame without an error. The station accomplishes this as it repeats the frame onto the ring.

The station that originally transmitted the packet onto the ring then pulls the packet off the ring. The destination station is not the one that takes the packet off the ring. There is too much information collected along the way that the originator is interested in.

Token Ring Copy Mode

- The destination Token Ring controller recognizes its address in the destination field of a received packet and copies the packet into its buffer.

- If at any time an error is detected, the copy phase ends and the controller sets the A and E bits and repeats the frame back to the ring.

- If no errors are found, the destination sets the A and C bits and repeats the frame back to the ring.

- The destination station enters Normal Repeat mode.

- The frame travels on the ring until it reaches the originator and that station strips the frame off of the ring and submits the token to the ring.

TOKEN RING REPEAT MODE

If the station does not copy a frame (that is, if the frame is not intended for this ring station), the controller card simply repeats the frame to its downstream neighbor, checking the data in the tokens and frames it receives for errors. The station will set the error-detected bit upon recognition of an error.

Normal Repeat Mode

- A station in normal repeat mode checks current frames and token for signalling errors.
  - If any errors are found the station sets the E bit and repeats the packet back to the ring.
- A station in this mode also checks every packet for its address.
  - A duplicate address could be found.
  - If a duplicate address is found, the station will transmit a soft error MAC frame to one of the monitors.

TOKEN RING MONITORS

The management functions of a Token Ring network are an underlying protocol that makes the Token Ring network more reliable by continually monitoring for errors. To allow for this, there are many built-in network management functions. Any error condition on a ring is reported by any ring station. Depending on the error condition, dynamic actions by the ring stations themselves may take place to correct this condition. The components that are used to manage a Token Ring network are:

- Ring stations

- Management Servers, including the:
  - LAN Reporting Mechanism (LRM)
  - Ring Error Monitor (REM)
  - Configuration Report Server (CRS)
  - Ring Parameter Server (RPS)
  - LAN Bridge Server (LBS)

- LAN Network Manager

- SNA Control Point

The purpose of the management servers is to collect data from the ring stations, analyze it, and forward it to one or more LAN Network Managers. Most of the server functions are in a source route bridge. The LAN Network Manager stores and analyzes the data sent to it by the servers. The ring stations sent error condition statements to the servers which send it to the LAN Network Manager. It is up to the LAN Network Manager to report any conditions indicated by received data to the SNA control point (NetView).

To identify any of the servers on the network, each server is assigned a reserved functional address.

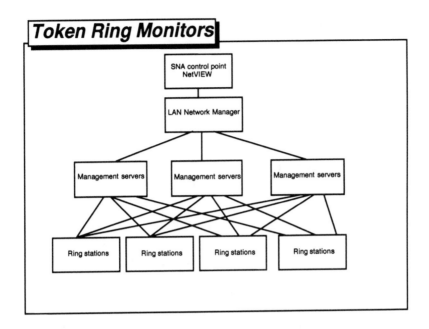

- As part of the network management scheme for a Token Ring network, all stations participate as monitors that provide special functions to the operation of the ring network.

- The management servers collect data from individual ring stations in the network, analyze it, and forward the information to one or more management servers on the network.

- The LAN Network Manager is a software program that collects its data from each of the servers and analyzes it. Further actions may be taken.

- Any of these monitors may or may not be present on the network.
   With the exception of the Active Monitor, these monitors need not be present for the ring to function properly.

- Most of the monitor functions are implemented on the source route bridge (explained later).

RING PARAMETER SERVER (RPS)

The ring parameter server is a network management function that can be available on each and every ring. This server usually runs in a source route bridge, but it need not be present on the ring in order for the ring to function correctly.

The ring parameter server basically serves two functions:

1. It is the destination station that receives all Request Initialization MAC frames that are sent by any ring station during initialization to the ring. When a ring station successfully inserts into the ring, it requests values for the ring's operational parameters from the RPS. With this it passes information about itself (its own configuration parameters, micro code level, and so on) to the RPS. The RPS responds to a station's request with the ring number of the ring and the soft error report timer. The RPS should then report to the LAN network manager that a new station has entered the ring.

2. It is a parameter response server to any ring station on a ring (in response to a Request Initialization frame). Any ring station that has inserted into a ring will request parameters using a specially addressed packet (function address C00000000002). Since this is a MAC frame, it does not traverse any bridges or routers but stays on the local ring. The ring parameter server will send this registration information to the LAN network manager. A second function is to forward to the registering ring station a ring number, a ring station soft error report timer value, and a physical location. This guarantees that the ring number and the ring station soft error report timer value are the same for all ring stations on a ring.

Ring Parameter Server (RPS)

- Functional address is C00000000002.

- It sends initialization information to new stations that are attaching to the ring.

- It ensures that stations on the ring have consistent values for operational parameters.

- Forwards registration information to LAN Network Managers from stations attaching to the ring.

RING ERROR MONITOR (REM)

The ring error monitor provides three functions:

1. It collects error reports from ring stations on the attached ring.

2. It analyzes information based on soft error reports.

3. It forwards other information to the LAN Network Manager.

This monitor collects all soft errors, since this information is functionally addressed to it. Hard error information is sent as an all stations broadcast, and the REM simply monitors for hard error frames. Since all hard errors are reported by the beacon frame, the REM sets a timer based on the first beacon MAC frame. If the condition is not corrected in a certain period of time, the REM reports to LAN Network Manager this information including the *fault domain,* which is the beaconing station's address and its NAUN address. If the condition corrects itself, the REM will report this to LAN Network Manager also.

Soft errors are reported a little differently. The REM analyzes the soft error MAC frames as they arrive and determines whether soft errors are occurring at a rate that will significantly affect the operation of the ring. If this condition exists, the REM reports this to the LAN network manager, trying to pinpoint the problem.

Common errors monitored by the REM:

Lost Frames	Receiver congestion errors
Frame Copied Errors	Token errors
Beacons	Beacon condition recovered
Ring Recovery	

Ring Error Monitor (REM)

- Functional address is C00000000008.

- Collects error reports from the ring stations.

- Analyzes information based on soft error reports.

- Forwards information to LAN Network Manager.

- Errors monitored:
  - lost frames,
  - frame copied errors,
  - beacons,
  - receiver congestion errors and recovery,
  - token errors, and
  - beacon condition recovered.

CONFIGURATION REPORT SERVER (CRS)

The configuration report server contains four functions:

1. It collects unsolicited configuration information from the ring (when a new station attaches to the ring or when there is a new active monitor, for example) and it reports this information to the LAN Network Manager.

2. When requested to do so by the LAN Network Manager program, it collects information from the ring stations.

3. When asked to do so by LAN Network Manager program, the CRS can set operational values for ring stations on its local ring.

4. When asked to do so by the LAN Network Manager program, it can also request a station to remove itself from its local ring.

A CRS accepts commands from the LAN Network Manager to get station information, set station parameters, and remove stations from the ring.

Some of the information that the CRS contains about a station is:

Ring Station Address	Ring Number
NAUN Address	Ring Station Micro Code Level
Product Instance ID	Enable Function Classes
Report New Active Monitor	Report NAUN Change

Configuration Report Server (CRS)

- Functional address is C00000000010.

- Collects unsolicited configuration information from the ring.

- When requested by LAN Network Manager, it can
  - collect information from the ring stations.
  - set operational values for ring stations on its local ring.
  - request a station to remove itself from its ring.

- The information that is maintained about a station is:
  - a ring station address,
  - a NAUN address,
  - a Product Instance ID,
  - a ring number,
  - to report a NAUN change,
  - the ring station microcode level, and to
  - report new active monitor.

THE ACTIVE MONITOR (AM)

One station on each ring must be the Active Monitor (AM), as determined by a bidding process. Any station (host, routers, a user's PCs) can acquire this right. The end user does not know that his or her station is the AM. All other stations on the ring will become standby monitors, prepared to assume the duties of the Active Monitor should it fail.

The Active Monitor ensures that only one token exists on its ring. Upon receipt of the token, the AM transmits it and starts a timer. If this timer expires before the token returns, the AM assumes that the token is lost and purges the ring. Purging is a special MAC frame that is transmitted by the AM to ensure that a packet can traverse the ring reliably. Upon return receipt of this frame, it issues a new token.

The AM ensures that each frame transmitted traverses the ring only once. Inside the AC field of the Token Ring frame is the M bit. This is set by the AM when the AM repeats a packet. Should the AM receive a packet with the M bit set, it strips that frame off the ring assuming that the ring station that originated it cannot remove it from the ring. The AM then purges the ring and issues a new token.

The AM initiates neighbor notification. This was explained previously. Briefly, this allows the AM to identify itself to all ring stations and also allows other ring stations to identify their NAUNs. Periodically, the AM will transmit a frame called the active monitor present MAC frame. During the process the standby monitors transmit a standby monitor present MAC frame. This is important for network management. New neighbors can be reported and management actions can take place based on NAUN and NADN (Next Available Downstream Neighbor). Second, it ensures that no station falsely assumes that it is the AM.

The AM also ensures that the ring is large enough that at least one token can be transmitted to the ring. To do this, the AM presents a 24-bit transmission delay onto the ring. A Token Ring may be simply two ring stations hooked back-to-back (through a MAU) on a short piece of cable. The ring must be large enough that at least one token is on the cable plant at a time.

The AM also provides the master clock to the ring. All stations transmit and receive using the master clock. The clock allows for the bits to be synchronized in the packet so that a 1 can be differentiated from a 0 (binary). Having a master clock ensures that all stations are synchronized to the receive clock's waveform.

The Active Monitor (AM)

- Functional address is C00000000001.

- It must be present in order for the ring to function properly.

- The AM is the kingpin of the ring.

- The AM:
  - tracks lost tokens and ensures that only one token exists on a single ring.
  - monitors frames and priority tokens that circulate the ring more than once.
  - initiates neighbor notification,
  - provides a latency buffer to recover the clock signal and so that at least 24 bits (the size of the token) can be transmitted on the ring, and
  - supplies the master clocking .

OPTIONS FOR TOKEN RING

The 16 Mbps Token Ring network controller cards can operate in either of two modes:

1. 16 Mbps

2. 16 Mbps Early Token Release (ETR)

A controller card operating at 16 Mbps is simply the network operating as stated previously. A controller waits for the Token and upon capturing it, transmits its data then idle characters (binary zeros) until it receives the physical header of its packet back.

A controller card operating at 16 Mbps ETR allows a controller to release the token even if it has not received the physical header of its packet back. This still allows only for one token to exist on the network but allows a data frame and a token to exist on the same network. This speeds up a Token Ring network.

As of this writing, Token Ring operates at two speeds, 16 and 4 Mbps. A 16 Mbps controller cannot operate on a 4 Mbps ring and a 16 Mbps controller card cannot operate on a 4 Mbps Token Ring. Sixteen Mbps and 4 Mbps rings may communicate with each other through a bridge or a router, which are explained in Part 3 of this book. A concentrator MAU may house 16- and 4-Mbps ring cards, but these cards are separated from each other through a management card that will not allow them to see each other. The two rings may then be connected together through a source route bridge or a router.

IBM is currently experimenting with a new Token Ring controller that will operate at 52–100 Mbps, but as of this writing it has not been released.

Options for Token Ring

- For 16 megabit rings, early token release allows a ring station to release the token before receiving its original frame back.
    - It is based on the ring length
        » A station will not release the token when it is still transmitting its frame and it has started to receive its frame back.
    - Allows greater use of Token Ring bandwidth.
- Token Ring operates at 4 and 16 Mbps.
    - 4 and 16 Mbps controllers are not allowed on the same ring.
        » Ring will beacon when this condition occurs.
    - To have 4 and 16 Mbps ring interoperate, you must use a data forwarding device such as a bridge or a router.
- IBM is currently experimental with a new Token Ring controller which allow it to operate between 52 - 100 Mbps.

• The early release option allows for greater bandwidth utilization.

• It allows a station to release the token before it has received its own physical header back.

• The controller releases the token, setting the priority and reservation bits to the same bits as when the controller originally captured the token.

FDDI Ring Operation

FDDI allows stations to communicate over a dual ring topology by guaranteeing access to the cable plant at timed intervals, using a Token. A token is a special bit pattern that continuously flows on the ring, and any station that captures this token may then transmit onto the network. This may seem similar to the Token Ring architecture but the operation of FDDI is different from Token Ring. Both are ring architectures but the algorithms for the access methods are different.

A network station must wait for the arrival of the token before transmission may begin. Upon arrival of the Token, the network station captures the token and this stops the token repeat process (no token will now be on the ring, guaranteeing no other station access to the cable plant). A station transmits a series of symbols combined into frames to the next active station on the network (data flows in one direction only). Frame transmission will continue (meaning multiple frames may be transmitted, not just one) until the token holding timer expires, or the station has no more frames to transmit. The station then releases the Token to the ring.

The downstream neighbor will receive these symbols, regenerate them, and repeat them to its downstream neighbor. When the frame returns to the originator, it will "strip" the frame from the ring. The intended destination station will not strip the frame. Only the originator of a frame may take it back off the ring.

FDDI is a dual counter-rotating ring topology; that is, the network consists of a primary and a secondary ring. Although both rings are allowed to carry data, the primary ring is used for data and the secondary ring is used for backup. To use both rings requires more hardware and is an unnecessary cost.

FDDI Ring Operation

- FDDI allows stations to communicate over a dual ring topology by guaranteeing access to the cable plant at timed intervals using a Token to control access.

- Network stations must wait for the Token before transmitting.

- A network station will capture the Token and transmits a series of symbols (data) to the ring.
    - The station may transmit as many frames as it can until a timer expires.

- Downstream neighbors of the transmitting station will receive and retransmit the symbols.

- The destination as indicated in the FDDI frame copies the frame and repeats it to the ring.

- The originating station strips the frame from the ring when it returns.

FDDI Ring Timers

Proper ring operation requires: physical connection establishment between two network stations, ring initialization (the ability of the ring to continuously, without error, circulate a Token), steady-state operation (the ring is in normal operation), and ring maintenance (the ring can be dynamically managed by the stations on the ring).

Stations are locally administered by each station on the ring, that is, each station has management capabilities built into itself, which dynamically enables the network station to manage the ring. Various timers in an FDDI network are used to regulate the operation of the ring. These timers are:

1. Target Token Rotational Timer (TTRT)—A ring latency parameter which sets the latency for the ring. During ring initialization, MAC frames are passed between the network stations called T_Req, which is a network station requesting a Token Rotation Time Request value. Each station submits a request for how fast it wants the Token to rotate. That is, if a station wants to see the token once in x milliseconds, it will put a request in for T-Req = x ms. The station requesting the fastest T_Req will win, as it satisfies all other stations. The TTRT will be set to whatever that station's T_Req is.

2. Token Rotational Timer (TRT)—This timer measures the time between successive arrivals of the token. It is set to the TTRT value. If the token arrives within the TRT time, this timer is reset back to the TTRT. If the token does not arrive within the TRT time, the network station increments a late counter and reloads TRT with the value of the TTRT. If this timer expires twice, the network station tries to initialize the ring.

3. Token Holding Timer (THT)—This timer determines the amount of time that a station may hold the token after capturing it. When a station is holding the token, the network station may transmit as many frames as it can without letting the THT expire. The station must release the token before the expiration of this timer. The THT is loaded to the time remaining in the TRT every time the token arrives. Therefore, if a station receives a token with 10 ms left in the THT, it may transmit data for 10 ms.

4. Valid Transmission Timer (TVX)—This timer allows an FDDI ring to recover more quickly from the loss of a token. Normally, when 2*TTRT time occurs, the ring should initialize itself. Since the TTRT maximum value is 165 ms, in the worst case, this could take up to 330 ms. This timer times the duration between valid frames and is reset upon receipt of a valid frame. This time is calculated from the time it would take to transmit a 4,500 byte frame around a maximum-sized ring, 200 km. This equals 3.4 ms.

FDDI Timers

- Proper ring operation requires connection establishment, ring initialization, steady-state operation, and ring maintenance.

- A series of timers play a very important part for proper ring operation.

- These timers are:
  - Token Rotational Timer (TRT) - used to time the duration of operations in a station.
  - Token Holding Timer (THT) - determines the amount of time a station may hold the token.
  - Valid Transmission Timer (TVX) - detects excessive ring noise, loss of a token and other faults.

- Another parameter that is not a timer but is a parameter used by the timers is the:
  - Target Token Rotational Timer (TTRT) - a ring latency parameter which sets the latency for the ring.

FDDI FRAMES

Since there is not a master clock on the FDDI ring, each station produces its own clock when transmitting frames. Each station's clock is independently generated and each station's clock has the possibility of being slightly different. FDDI frames use a preamble so that receiving stations may synchronize their clocks to the received clock signal of the packet being transmitted.

The starting delimiter (SD) is a specially formatted frame that contains phase violations in the signal. These phase violations are signals that would normally cause an error. But the FDDI chip set has been programmed to recognize two special patterns and to read them as so. Therefore, the SD indicates the presence of a frame approaching.

The frame control (FC) indicates what kind of frame is approaching. For instance, it could be a Token frame, an SMT frame, beacon, claim-Token, or an LLC (data frame).

The destination (DA) and source addresses (SA) can be set to 16 or 48 bits. This is indicated by the L (address length) bits in the FC field. All stations on the ring must be set to 16 or 48. Most FDDI implementations use 48-bit addresses.

The ending delimiter (ED) indicates the end of a frame. Like the starting delimiter it has signal phase violations placed at certain locations in the ED so that the controller will recognize this field as the end of the frame.

The frame status (FS) field contains three important bits that are set by other stations on the ring. They are the address recognized, frame copied, and the error bits. The address recognized bit is set by a station for one of two reasons: it recognized its address in a duplication address SMT frame or it recognized its address in an LLC frame. But just because a station recognized its address does not mean that it copied the frame—it could have been too busy. The C bit indicates that a destination station was able to copy the frame. The E bit indicates that some station (not necessarily the destination station) found a signaling error in the frame. If this bit is set, the C bit can never be set, for any frame found in error will not be copied.

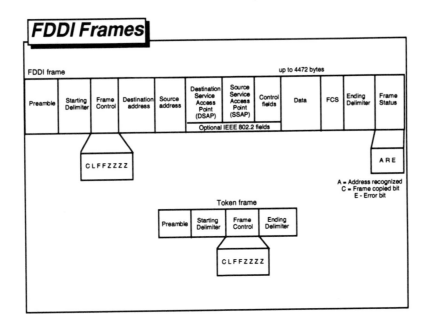

- These are two items that can traverse a FDDI LAN:
    A token, which gives a station the right to access the cable plant.
        — It is not needed for receiving data.
    Frames, which are used for information transfer.
        — Frames are used for management purposes to maintain the integrity of the ring.

- At the beginning of the frame, the preamble is used to maintain the clock.
    These is not master clock on FDDI and each transmitter uses it own clock.

- The starting delimiter indicates the presence of a Token or Frame.

- Frame Control indicates:
    Non-restricted Token   LLC (data) frame
    Restricted Token   Reserved for implementor
    SMT frame   Reserved for future implementation

- The source and destination addresses indicate the sender and recipient of the frame.

- The IEEE 802.2 fields have been previously discussed.

- The data field is used to hold data.

- The ending delimiter indicates the end of the frame.

- The frame status has three bits, one each for address recognized and frame copied and an error bit to detect signaling errors.

FDDI Addressing and Bit Order Transmission

The addressing for FDDI is similar to the IEEE 802 MAC addressing. The addresses may be 16 or 48 bits long. If 16-bit addressing is used, all stations on the ring must be set to 16-bit addressing; 48-bit and 16-bit addresses cannot be mixed on the same ring.

For 48-bit addresses the first two bits of each address are important. For the destination address, bits 0 and 1 of the first byte are the I/G bit and the U/L bit. The I/G bit indicates whether the address is an individual (unique) address or a group (multicast) address. The next bit, U/L, indicates whether the address is universally administered (assigned by the IEEE to a vendor, called the PROM address) or a locally administered address (LAA).

In the source address there are also two bits of importance. The first is the Routing Information Indicator or RII bit (this displaces the I/G bit, since all source addresses are individual addresses). This bit indicates whether there is source route information in the field. Source routing generally is not used with FDDI, but the option is there. Bridges that encapsulate frames onto FDDI will use source routing if the received packet was originally a source route packet (meaning the bridge was forwarded to FDDI from a Token Ring network). The second important source address bit indicates whether the address is universally or locally administered, as explained above.

Bit order for FDDI transmission is the same as for Token Ring. Bit 0 of any byte is always transmitted first and is the leftmost bit. Since this is opposite of Ethernet packets, a bridge that interconnects FDDI and Ethernet must bit-swap the MAC addresses before transmission.

For example, if the first three bytes of the FDDI MAC address were 02-60-8C, this would translate to binary as 00000010-01100000-10001100, and would be transmitted on the FDDI exactly as shown (remember Ethernet reverses the bits as it transmits them. The receiving station reverses the bits again as it receives them off the medium).

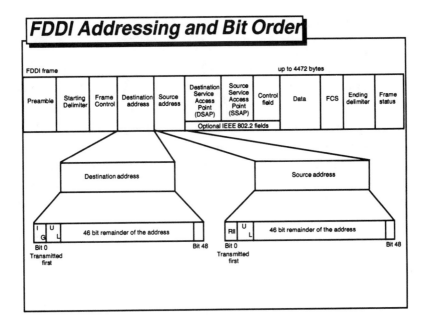

- An FDDI destination address contains two significant bits:
    the I/G bit indicates whether the address in individual (unique) or group (multicast/broadcast).
    the U/L bit indicates whether the address is universally assigned (by the IEEE) or locally assigned (by the network administrator of the LAN)

- An FDDI source address also contains two other significant bits:
    the RII bit indicates whether source route information is included in the frame.
        — RII = 1 indicates source route information is present.
    the U/L bit indicates whether the address is universally or locally assigned (by the network administrator of the LAN).

- Bit 0 is the leftmost bit of a byte and it is transmitted first.
    This is similar to the Token Ring transmission.
    It is the exact of opposite of Ethernet transmission.

CONNECTION ESTABLISHMENT

The Connection Management (CMT) portion of Station Management (SMT), explained at the end of this section) controls the physical connection process by which stations find out about their neighbors. This is accomplished by stations transmitting and acknowledging defined line state sequences. During this process, network stations exchange information about port types and connection rules and determine the quality of the link between them. If the connection type is accepted by each end of the link and the quality link test passes, the physical connection is considered established. This connection test is accomplished by each point-to-point connection on the FDDI ring. Each station on the ring is considered to have a point-to-point connection with its directly connected neighbor.

Connection Establishment

- When a network attachment is initialized, it must find out about its neighbors.
  - Used for management purposes of the ring.

- The connection management (CMT) portion of Station Management (SMT) control the physical connection process.

- Adjacent stations exchange information about port types, connection rules, and determine the quality of the link.

- If the connection type is accepted and the link quality test passes, the physical connection is considered established,

- This test is accomplished between each point-to-point connection on the ring.

RING INITIALIZATION

After the station attachments have achieved a physical connection, the ring must be initialized. Since FDDI uses a token for stations to be granted access to the ring, one of the stations must place the token onto the ring. This process is known as the claim process and may be accomplished when a new station attaches to the ring, when there are no other active stations on the ring, or when the token gets lost for some reason. Any station on the ring has the capability to initialize the ring but there is a bidding process so that only one station at a time initializes the ring. The station with the lowest TTRT wins the right to initialize the ring.

This process starts when the MAC entity in one or more stations enters into the claim state, in which it continually transmits MAC claim frames that contain the station's MAC address and its TTRT bid. When another station on the ring compares a received claim frame with its own bid for TTRT, it may take either of the following actions:

1. Shorter time bid for TTRT in the received frame, the station quits transmitting its own claim frames and starts repeating the received claim frame.

2. Longer time bid for TTRT in the received frame, the station continues transmitting its own claim rather than repeating the received claim frame.

The process stops when a station receives its own claim frame back. This means that all other stations on the ring have conceded their rights to initialize the ring. The station that won issues a new Token to the ring.

If two stations bid the same TTRT, the tie breaker becomes the station's MAC address. The station with the highest address wins. The first time a new token circulates the ring, it cannot be captured by any station. Instead, each station that receives the token will set its own TTRT to match the TTRT of the winning station. On the second pass of the token, network stations may transmit synchronous traffic. On the third pass of the token, stations may pass asynchronous traffic.

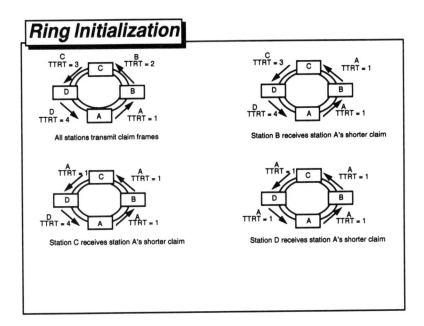

- All stations start the claim process.

- When station B receives A's claim and notices that its TTRT is larger than A's, it quits sending its own claim frame and starts repeating A's claim frame.

- When station C receives station B's claim frame, it quits transmitting its claim frame and starts repeating B's claim frame.

- When station C receives station B's frame, it quits transmitting its own and repeats B's.

- When station D receives stations C's frame, its quits transmitting its own and repeats C's.

- Station A receives station D's frame but does not repeat it. It continues to repeat its own frame. It does not repeat any claim frame that has a higher TTRT than its own.

- When station C receives station A's claim from B it repeats A's claim frame.

- When station D receives station A's frame from C it repeats A's claim frame.

- When station A receives its own claim frame it sets the TTRT and issues a token to initialize the ring.

- Any ties will be broken by the station that has the highest MAC address.

- On the first pass of the new token, no data will pass. Instead, each station will set its TTRT to that of the station that won the right to initialize the ring.

- Synchronous traffic (voice or video) may pass on the second pass of the token.
- Asynchronous traffic (data) will pass on the third pass of the token.

SYNCHRONOUS AND ASYNCHRONOUS DATA TRANSMISSION

There are two types of transmission on FDDI: synchronous and asynchronous.

Synchronous traffic is reserved bandwidth that is guaranteed to a network station that holds the token. This service is used primarily for voice and video applications. It is bound on an access delay. Its support is optional.

Asynchronous traffic is a service class in which unreserved bandwidth is available to the station that has captured the token. This is the most common mode of operation available to network stations. Asynchronous traffic can be classified as restricted and non-restricted. Non-restricted asynchronous allocation supports eight priority levels. Asynchronous transmission allows a station to use the FDDI ring using a time token protocol. This allows for dynamic bandwidth allocation. Restricted asynchronous transmission allows for extended transmissions to exist between two or more stations on the FDDI ring. It allows ring stations to "hog" the cable for their transmissions. This requires a station to set the token as restricted for its use. Restricted asynchronous mode is optionally supported on FDDI.

These two service classes, synchronous and asynchronous, should not be confused with the asynchronous and synchronous services that mainframe (or mini) computers and their terminals use to communicate.

Synchronous and Asynchronous

- There are two types of transmission on FDDI:
  - synchronous and asynchronous.

- Synchronous traffic is reserved bandwitdth that is guaranteed to a network station that holds the token.
  - It is is used for voice and video applications.

- Asynchronous traffic is a service class in which unreserved bandwidth is available to the station that has captured the token
  - This is the most common mode of FDDI operation.
  - There are two modes of asynchronous traffic
    » Restricted and non restricted.

- The two service classes should not be confused with the serial transmission standard used in terminal to computer communications.

Neighbor Notification and Duplicate Address Check

When an FDDI controller is initialized or the port on the concentrator is started or restarted, each network station must find out about its next available upstream neighbor (NAUN). This process, called the neighbor notification protocol (NNP), is similar to the active monitor present and standby monitor present algorithms used in Token Ring. There are two times when this algorithm is invoked: when a station first becomes operational on the ring and on a periodic process every thirty seconds. A station transmits a management frame called a neighborhood information frame, or NIF. Among other fields, inside of the NIF are two fields: the upstream neighbor address (UNA) and the downstream neighbor address (DNA). Using these frames a network station not only can find the ad-dresses of the stations on its ring but can check for an address duplicate to its own.

Say, for example, there are three stations on a ring, X, Y, and Z. The first time station X enters the ring, it transmits the NIF request with the UNA and DNA fields set to unknown. Station X's downstream neighbor, station Y, receives this NIF request and sets the UNA field to X and transmits a NIF response; station Y now knows its upstream neighbor is X. Immediately, station Y transmits a NIF request with UNA set to X and DNA set to unknown. Station Z receives station Y's request and sets the UNA to Y and DNA to unknown and transmits it as a response; station Z now knows its UNA is Y. Immediately, station Z transmits a NIF request with UNA set to Y and DNA set to unknown.

Station X receives station Y's response and now knows its downstream neighbor is Y. Station X also receives station Z's NIF request and now knows its UNA is Z. Station X transmits a NIF response to station Z with the DNA field set to Y and the UNA field set to Z. Station Y receives station Z's NIF response and now knows its DNA is Z. Station Z receives station X's NIF response and now knows its DNA is station X. At this point all stations know their UNA and DNA.

Neighbor Notification and Duplicate Check

- When an FDDI controller is initialized, it must find its next available upstream neighbor (NAUN).

- The process to determine a NAUN is called the neighbor notification process (NNP).
  - Activated when a FDDI controller is initialized and on a periodic basis every thirty seconds.

- A station transmits a management frame called a neighborhood information frame, or NIF.
  - There are two fields in this frame:
    » the upstream neighbor address (UNA) and the downstream neighbor address (DNA).

- Using these frames a network station not only can find the addresses of the station on its ring but can check for a duplicate address.

NORMAL OPERATION

Once all the verifications and tests have been successfully completed, an FDDI ring may start normal data transmission or the *steady state operation*. With this network stations may transmit frames to each other using the rules of the FDDI ring. The ring will remain in this state until a new claim process is initiated.

Frames are transmitted on a ring using the timed token protocol. The timed token protocol is a series of steps that the network station must perform before data transmission is allowed on the ring. A network station wishing to transmit must wait for the arrival of the token. Upon token arrival, the network station will capture the token, stopping the token repeat process. A station transmits a series of symbols (bytes), which when combined form frames, to the next active station on the network. Frame transmission will continue until the THT expires, or the station has no more frames to transmit. For example, if a station receives the token and its THT has 10 ms left, the station starts to transmit asynchronous frames, in order of priority, until the THT expires. The station then releases the token to the ring and resets the THT.

Every other active station on the ring receives the frame and checks it for the destination address. If the destination address of the received frame is not its own, it will check for signal or FCS errors and repeat the frame to its downstream neighbor. If the destination address is its own, it will copy the frame into its receive buffer, set certain control bits in the frame to indicate to the sender that it has copied the frame (the A and C bits in the FS field), and repeat the frame to its downstream neighbor.

Any other downstream station that receives this frame will check the frame for errors and repeat the frame. If any station detects an error (usually a signal or framing error), it can set the error bits (E bit in the FS field) in the frame. If the destination station has not copied the frame and detects the error bit set it may set the address recognized bit and the E bit and repeat the frame.

This process continues until the frame circles the ring and the station that originally transmitted the frame removes the frame from the ring. This is a process known as *stripping*.

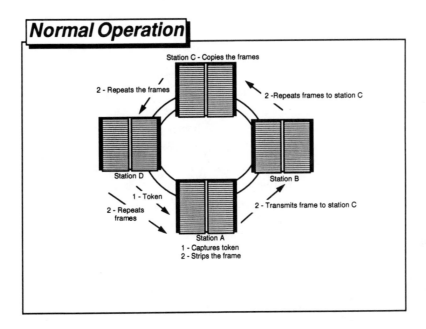

- A station wishing to transmit captures the token.

- A station that has captured the token immediately begins transmitting frames until the THT expires.

- After finishing transmitting frames that station releases the token.

- With the previously transmitted frame, any other station that is not the indicated destination checks the received frame for signaling errors and repeats the frame to its downstream neighbor.

- The destination station copies the received frame, sets control bits to indicate that it copied the frame, and repeats the frame to its downstream neighbor.
     It will not copy a frame that has the error bit set.

- After the frame circles the ring and returns to the source station, the source station will strip the frame from the ring.

STRIPPING AND SCRUBBING FDDI

To minimize delays for data to pass through the controllers, each network station reads and repeats each frame, bit by bit, as it receives the frame. As shown before, the frame contains destination and source MAC addresses to determine what station sent the frame and what station the frame is intended for. Under normal circumstances the station that transmits a frame is the only one that is allowed to remove the frame from the ring through a process called *stripping*. The source station reads each frame on the network as if to repeat the frame immediately to its downstream neighbor. When a station recognizes its own address in the source address of the frame, it knows that it must strip the frame from the ring. But by the time it recognizes the frame as its own, the frame header and destination address have already been repeated to its downstream neighbor, thus leaving a fragment of the original packet on the ring.

To ensure that the ring does not deteriorate, each FDDI station contains the ability to remove these fragments from the ring. They are either removed by the downstream neighbor or by the operations of each repeat filter in each active stations PHY. This process is called *scrubbing*.

The process of scrubbing is enacted to keep the ring from deteriorating due to stray frames. This can happen when a new station inserts into the ring or leaves the ring. If a station transmitted a frame and leaves the ring before it can strip it, it is the responsibility of another station to remove this stray frame. To remove the stray frame, a station will send a series of idle frames to the ring. At the same time, the MAC entity of the FDDI controller card will strip the ring of frames and tokens. This will force other stations to enter into the claim process. The scrubbing process ensures that any frames on the ring occurred after the ring was scubbed. It eliminates the possibility of stray frames continually circulating the ring.

Stripping and Scrubbing

- To minimize delays in the ring, each station repeats each frame bit by bit as it receives the frame.
  - A station does not buffer any part of the packet.

- Each frame contains a source and destination address and only the intended destination copies the frame.

- As each frame is received by the source station, it must decide whether to take the frame off the ring.
  - This process is known as *stripping*

- By the time a source station recognizes its own frame, some of the frame has already been repeated to its downstream neighbor.
  - This leaves incomplete frames on the network.
  - Can also happen when a station inserts onto the ring creating incomplete frames

- Each station has the ability to remove the stray frames from the ring.
  - This process is known as *scrubbing*.

- The scrubbing process eliminates the possibility of stray frames from continually circulating the ring.

FDDI Station Management (SMT)

FDDI provides for standardized management functions that are present in every network attachment on a ring. These cover a broad range of items, from signaling errors to lost tokens. The paramount idea behind the management functions is to force a standard FDDI management platform. All FDDI controllers contain the same management entities, and each FDDI controller will function the same (with respect to management). The current version of this standard is SMT 7.2. SMT is used only on a ring-by-ring basis. That is, the management functions are performed locally. The management frames do not cross bridges or routers. Management within FDDI is called station management (SMT). SMT provides for the integrity of the ring as well as access to the network management services. We will not discuss all components of FDDI SMT, but only the pertinent ones.

SMT not only manages an network attachment internally but produces frames on the network as necessary. Neighbor notification, duplicate address, and invalid port type connections are examples of the SMT frames that may be generated on an FDDI network.

SMT provides management in four areas:

1. Connection management (CMT) which operates at the link level (the physical link between two stations) and consists of three components:
   • Physical Connection Management (PCM)
   • Configuration Management (CFM)
   • Link Error Monitoring (LEM)

2. Network attachment level consists of two components:
   • Configuration Management (CFM)
   • Entity Coordination Management (ECM)

3. Ring Level Management consists only of:
   • Ring Management (RMT).

4. Frame Based Management consists of a series of frames that allow remote management of the ring stations over the network.

FDDI Station Management (SMT)

- FDDI provides for a standardized mechanism for managing FDDI rings
  - SMT provides management in four areas:
    - » Connection Management (CMT)
      - ✧ Operates at the physical link level
      - ✧ Physical Connection Management (PCM)
      - ✧ Configuration Management (CFM)
      - ✧ Link Error Monitoring (LEM)
    - » Network attachment level:
      - ✧ Configuration Management (CFM)
      - ✧ Entity Coordination Management (ECM)
    - » Ring level management
      - ✧ Ring Management (RMT)
    - » Frame Based Management
      - ✧ Consists of a series of frames that allow management of the ring stations over the ring.

PHYSICAL CONNECTION MANAGEMENT (PCM)

PCM initializes the duplex connection between two stations. Each side negotiates with the other until both ports agree that a connection be allowed. PCM has four functions:

1. It performs synchronization of the link between two stations. Certain signals are passed between each end of the connection and are used to ensure that each end is willing to have a connection established based on a negotiated sequence of requests.

2. One of these requests is to identify the port types on each end of the connection. Stations, through PCM, identify the port types on the physical connection. This is useful to remove undesirable links. For example, port A to port A is allowed but it can produce unknown results in the ring.

3. Another request is to perform a *link confidence test* and ask for the time period of this test. The two points of the connection pass a series of frames between each other and monitor the results. This test is performed prior to connection establishment to isolate faulty physical links. This test is also accomplished after the connection has been established as a post-connection test to ensure the connection does not degrade over time. A faulty link could be a link that, when tested, produced too many errors (line type of errors).

4. PCM finds the identity of the downstream and upstream neighbor (identify the MAC address of each end of the link). The two sides of the connection will pass tokens and neighborhood identification frames (NIF) before the port is placed onto the operational ring. By finding the MAC addresses of the UNA and DNA, this test can be used for security reasons, allowing only certain stations to enter the ring.

Physical Connection Management

- Link level management monitor the physical link between stations is provided by PCM.
  - Performs synchronization of the link between stations.
  - Identifies port types.
  - Performs a link confidence test (LCT).
  - Find the identity of upstream and downstream neighbors.

CONFIGURATION MANAGEMENT (CFM)

CFM is used for the monitoring of the port or the MAC. Each port contains a configuration control element that controls the state of its port. It controls the insertion or removal of a port or MAC on the active ring. It not only monitors the link at initialization, but provides continuous monitoring during port operation. It performs the interconnection of the PHYs and the MACs within a node. Remember that FDDI contains a primary and secondary ring and also a mode known as local (basically, a port in loopback that is used for diagnostics and monitoring of the port before it is placed on the active ring). The CFM is the entity that places a station on a requested path. CFM also configures the node in the event of a fault, and can place a port in the wrap state.

Configuration Management

- Configuration Management
  - Monitor the port of the MAC.
  - Controls the insertion and removal of a port or MAC.
  - Allows for the interconnection of the PHYs and MACs within a ring station.
  - Places a station on the requested path.
    - » Puts the ring station on the requested port.
  - Configures the ring station in the event of a fault.
    - » Enables wrapping.

LINK ERROR MONITORING (LEM)

Link Error Monitoring is part of the PCM and its functions are spread throughout the PMD, PHY, MAC, and the SMT in an FDDI network attachment. It is provided by the FDDI hardware. For example, the PMD detects a loss of electrical signal, the PHY detects and accumulates line-state violations and clock rate problems, the MAC detects FCS errors. Each entity of the FDDI station has the responsibility to monitor and detect errors on its active links. Information gathered by these monitors are compared to set thresholds.

Depending on the accumulated information and when the errors occur (for example, during initialization or when the ring is considered up and running) the link may be determined to be faulty and could be disabled, causing a wrapped condition. The accumulated information might not take a link down but would consider it marginal and the notify the ring of this network station's condition through the use of SMT MAC frames.

Link Error Monitoring

- Link Error Monitoring
    - is spread throughout the PMD, PHY, MAC, and the SMT.
    - is provided for in the FDDI hardware.
        - » The PMD detects a loss of signal.
        - » The PHY detects and accumulates line state violations and clock problems.
        - » The MAC detects FCS errors.
    - Accumulated information could allow the ring station to determine whether or not it should be taken off the ring or just reported to a management station.

ENTITY COORDINATION MANAGEMENT (ECM)

The Entity Coordination Management function does very little. It controls the optical bypass switch, which is used when the network station's ports are shut down for any reason. Since the node is not inserted as an active repeater in the ring, the optical bypass is functionally a mirror that reflects an incoming signal to the disabled network station's downstream neighbor without disrupting the dual ring. ECM can start and stop any or all of the PCMs. For example, it is this entity that will allow a PCM to initialize a connection setup between two stations. Its purpose is to act as an interface to SMT requests of the individual PCMs.

In the event of a beacon condition, ECM on a network station stops all activity to the PCMs and activates the trace signal to detect errors. An internal test occurs on this network station and if this station passes its test, after the trace signal is sent, the ECM reinitializes all other SMT components in the network station.

Entity Coordination Management

- Entity Coordination Management (ECM) performs only a few functions:
  - Controls the optical bypass switch
  - Can start or stop any of the PCMs
  - In the event of a beacon condition
    - » ECM stops all PCMs.
    - » It may activate the trace signal or
    - » Reinitialize the PCMs.

Ring Management (RMT)

The purpose of ring management is to control the MAC chip. It is designed to control initialization, error detection and recovery, and the duplicate address detection. RMT receives signals for the MAC chip indicating a condition change. RMT has four functions:

1. Upon receiving a signal from the CEM (which controls the state of the port) that a port has inserted into the ring, RMT causes the MAC chip to start the claim service, or if inserting caused the ring break, to beacon the ring.

2. After this, RMT checks for a duplicate address on the ring. MAC addressing on FDDI allows the MAC address to be supplied by a management function of the network station. Normally, the FDDI controller will use the PROM address. To detect any other station that may be using the same address, this function is performed using the SMT NIF (neighbor information frame). This process was discussed earlier under neighborhood notification.

3. During a hard error on the ring (an error that causes the ring to become disabled), stations send out beacon frames. This helps stations determine where the fault is (the MAC address of the station that is transmitting the beacon and its UNA are embedded into the beacon frame). If a station becomes stuck in this condition, it is RMT that tries to recover from this condition. RMT notifies the ring network manager, using a special multicast address, of the condition, using the trace feature.

4. Monitoring of restricted tokens. The token may be set to restricted use so that only certain stations may use it. This effectively stops all normal transmission of data. This option is rarely used but the possibility exists. When the MAC on a network attachment receives a restricted token, it notifies RMT of this. RMT knows that a token can only be restricted for a certain amount of time. If this time limit is exceeded, RMT transmits claim-token beacon SMT frames, which interrupts the restricted token and forces the ring back to normal service. The default for the restricted token timer is 0. This means that no restricted token is allowed on the ring.

Ring Management

- Purpose is to control the MAC chip.

  - After ring insertion it starts the token claim or beacon service.

  - It checks for duplicate addresses.

  - It sends beacon frames.

  - It monitors the restricted token.

FRAME BASED MANAGEMENT

The beforementioned management entities are primarily for point-to-point management of the network attachments. Some portions of the FDDI management scheme can be performed either locally on the network attachment, or remotely, through the use of MAC frames to control the management entities. Not only do these SMT entities control the FDDI network, a network administrator can control an FDDI network. For example, a network administrator can force a port to insert into the ring or remove a port from the ring. A network administrator can query for statistical information from the network attachment. This type of remote management is caused by passing SMT frames across the ring from the network administrator's network terminal.

Frame based management (local or remote) requires the use of the FDDI network and special MAC frames to perform the management. There are many network management types available. In order to prevent any one nonstandard network management protocol to take over the management procedures of FDDI, a standardized remote management scheme was developed. This can be used in conjunction with a popular standard known as Simple Network Management Protocol (SNMP).

There is a process on every FDDI network attachment called the SMT agent. Like the name states, it acts as an agent for SMT. The SMT agent provides for SMT frame services. When an SMT MAC frame is received and the FC field is set to 41 (hex) or 4f (hex), the frame is handed to the SMT agent. The SMT agent reads the frame and generates a response if needed. There are eight frame types supported:

- Neighborhood Information Frames (NIF)

- Status Information Frames (SIF)

- Request Denied Frames (RDF)

- Echo Frames

- Status Report Frames (SRF)

- Parameter Management Frames (PMF)

- Extended Service Frames (ESF)

- Resource Allocation Frames (RAF)

Frame Based Management

- This is the ability to control the ring through the use of SMT MAC frames.
- These frames include:

  - Neighborhood Information Frames (NIF)
  - Status Information Frames (SIF)
  - Request Denied Frames (RDF)
  - Echo Frames
  - Status Report Frames (SRF)
  - Parameter Management Frames (PMF)
  - Extended Service Frames (ESF)
  - Resource Allocation Frames (RAF)

FRAME BASED MANAGEMENT FRAME TYPES

Neighbor Information Frames (NIF)

These frames perform a "keep alive" function. Inside this frame is a description of the station, the state of the station, and the capabilities of the MAC. NIF allows a station to send a frame out to notify its downstream neighbor of its existence. The downstream neighbor's response is addressed directly to its upstream neighbor. All stations attached to the ring perform this operation every thirty seconds. Through this process, each station knows who its upstream neighbor and downstream neighbor is (this type of frame is discussed fully under the heading of Neighborhood Notification and Duplicate Addresses).

Status Information Frames (SIF)

These frames are used to request more information about a station, such as the number of ports, the number of MACs, the neighbors of each MAC, and how the station is connected to the ring (DAS, SAS, and so forth). Also included in these frames could be the LEM or any of the frame counters in the MAC.

Request Denied Frames (RDF)

These frames are used to deny requests received from the ring. An example could be an SMT request from an unsupported SMT version.

NIF, SIF, and RDF

- Neighbor Information Frames (NIF)
  - Frames that are transmitted to a ring station's directly connected neighbors
    » The neighbor notification process is an example of use for this frame.

- Status Information Frame (SIF)
  - Requests information from a station.

- Request Denied Frame (RDF)
  - This frame is used to deny requests from the ring.
    » For example, to deny a request from an unsupported version of SMT.

MORE FRAME BASED MANAGEMENT FRAME TYPES

Echo Frame

These frames are used to test a path to a ring station using a simple echo request/response protocol. A ring station will send a request to another ring station, which should respond with an echo response frame. The information in the echo frame's information field is copied by the recipient and echoed back to the requester.

Status Report Frame (SRF)

A management station must have a reliable image of the network so it may properly perform management functions. This frame is sent with a special (reserved) multicast address that allows stations to report their status to the management station. Status report frames are used to indicate that certain events or conditions have taken place, such as the ring has wrapped, a duplicate address was detected, the LEM thresholds have been exceeded (because of excessive line errors, for example), or an illegal configuration (port type mismatch) has been found.

Parameter Management Frame (PMF)

The PMF protocol allows a network manager to query information from SMT on a ring station or make changes to any of the entities in SMT. There are four types of PMF frames: get information from a remote ring station, change an attribute value, delete an attribute value, add an attribute value, and retrieve information.

Extended Service Frame (ESF)

These frames are used to allow FDDI vendors to define their own SMT frames and services as an addendum to the established one. They can be used by an FDDI vendor to place vendor-specific information in the SMT that is not supplied by the standard SMT.

Resource Allocation Frame (RAF)

These frames are used to request FDDI allocations from a network resource. They are not implemented in version 6.2 of SMT.

Echo, SRF, PMF, ESF, and RAF

- Echo Frame
  - Tests a path between two stations.

- Status Report Frame (SRF)
  - Enables stations to report their status to a management station.

- Parameter Management Frame (PMF)
  - Allows a network manager to query or send information to or from a ring station.

- Extended Service Frame (ESF)
  - Allows FDDI vendors to define their own SMT frames and services.

- Resource Allocation Frame (RAF)
  - Requests allocations from a network resource .
    » It is not implemented in version 6.2 of SMT.

FDDI Faults

Each station on the ring has the responsibility for ensuring proper ring operation. Each station continually monitors the ring for any condition that may force the ring to be initialized, for instance there has been no ring activity for a certain period of time or there is a break of some type in the ring.

The valid transmission timer (TVX) is a timer used by each network station to detect an absence of network activity. It continually times the duration between receptions of valid frames by a network station. If a certain interval is exceeded, a possible error condition exists on the ring. Stations whose timer expires enter the token-claim process. If the token-claim process fails to correct the error condition—that is, a new token cannot circulate the ring—the ring enters a beacon state. This is a serious error condition indicating that the ring is completely inoperable.

The beacon frame is a special error frame to indicate that something serious is wrong with the ring. In the beacon frame is the transmitting MAC address of the station and its UNA. Any station may initiate this frame, which does not indicate exactly what is wrong with the ring. A station continues to transmit a beacon frame until:

1. It receives a beacon frame from its upstream neighbor that indicates that the cable segment is good, at least between itself and its upstream neighbor. In this case, the station will stop transmitting its own beacon frame and repeats the beacon frame it received from its upstream neighbor.

2. It receives its own beacon frame, indicating the problem has been fixed.

If the ring stays in the beacon condition for more than ten seconds, the ring management (RMT) function of SMT begins stuck beacon recovery procedures, which attempt to return the ring to normal operation. The stuck beacon process begins with the transmission of a special frame called *directed beacon*. A directed beacon informs the ring of the stuck beacon condition, forcing Ring Management into the trace function.

The trace function uses PHY signaling to recover the ring. The fault is localized to two stations: the beaconing MAC and its nearest upstream neighbor. A station transmits a trace message on the secondary ring to the beaconing station, causing both stations to leave the ring and perform self-tests. If both stations fail, both stay off the ring. Either station may enter the ring, assuming it has passed the self-test.

FDDI Faults

- Maintaining the ring is the responsibility of each active station on the ring.

- A timer known as the TVX timer is used to detect the absence of network activity.

- When the timer expires a station tries to intialize the ring.
  - Failure of the claim process will cause stations to *beacon* the ring.

- A beacon frame is a special MAC frame that is used to indicate that a serious error has occurred.

BEACON CONDITION

The following page shows the series of events that will take place for a beacon condition.

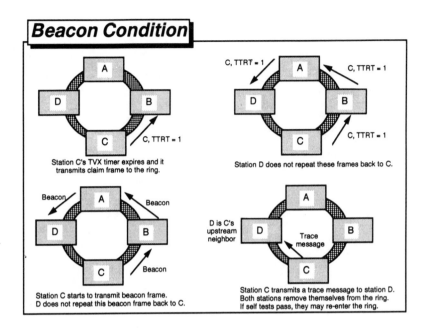

Beacon Condition

Station C's TVX timer expires and it transmits claim frame to the ring.

Station D does not repeat these frames back to C.

Station C starts to transmit beacon frame. D does not repeat this beacon frame back to C.

Station C transmits a trace message to station D. Both stations remove themselves from the ring. If self tests pass, they may re-enter the ring.

- Station C's TVX timer expires and station C tries to initialize the ring.

- Station D does not repeat station C's claim frame and station C starts to transmit beacons.

- Station B receives station C's beacons and repeats them to station A.

- Station A receives station C's beacons and sends them to station D.

- If station D repeats station C's beacon, station C receives its own beacon back and station C tries to initialize the ring.

- If station C does not receive its own beacon frame back, it continues to transmit beacon frames for ten seconds.

- After this period of time, a trace function is enabled.
  The trace function includes only that station that initiates it and its nearest upstream neighbor.

- Station C sends a trace message to station D on the secondary ring.
  This causes both station C and D to leave the ring and run self-tests.
  If the fault is in D, it remains off the ring and station C rejoins the ring.
  If station D passes its self tests, it too rejoins the ring.

FDDI TOPOLOGIES

Like any other LAN, FDDI has topologies that simplify the network and make it more efficient. There are basically five types of FDDI topologies:

1. Standalone concentrator

2. Dual Ring

3. Tree of Concentrators

4. Dual Ring of Trees

5. Dual Homing

FDDI Topologies

- Like any LAN, FDDI topologies play a large role in planning an efficient network.

- The recommended topologies for FDDI are:
    - Standalone concentrator
    - Dual Ring
    - Tree of Concentrators
    - Dual Ring of Trees
    - Dual Homing

STANDALONE CONCENTRATOR

This topology is the simplest in design. It is a single concentrator with all stations attached to it. The concentrator is at the root of the topology; it acts like the backbone. All attachments to this concentrator stations are single attached stations (SAS). Any station type may be connected to the concentrator but they function as SAS.

This is a good design for small sites that need little network management and have a lot of reliability. Any station may power off and the other stations on the ring are unaffected. The concentrator provides for fault isolation.

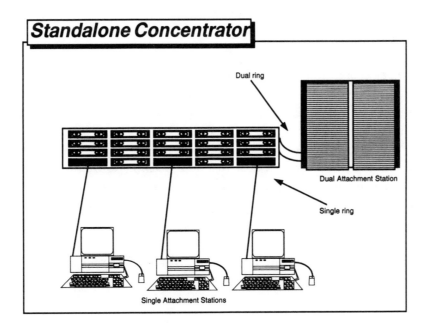

Standalone Concentrator

Dual ring

Dual Attachment Station

Single ring

Single Attachment Stations

• The standalone concentrator:

    is the simplest topology.

    contains a single concentrator with all stations attached to it.

    is a concentrator that acts like the backbone.

    allows single or dual attachment stations to connect to it but forces the attachments to operate as single
        attachment stations.

    is a good design for small sites.

    is easy to manage and reliable.

DUAL RING

This type of topology consists of dual attachment stations (DAS) attached directly to a dual ring—users' workstations, bridges, or routers. This is a fault-tolerant topology that is designed primarily for small sites (if the DAS are user workstations). It may act as a backbone for medium to large sites using routers and bridges in their networks.

This design does have its drawbacks. It does not work well with station attachments that physically move, turn off, or have additions made to them. Each station is attached to the backbone and it is up to each station to ensure the reliability of the ring. Something as simple as a user powering off a workstation will break the ring and cause it to wrap. Worse, multiple failures may cause the ring to wrap more times, thereby creating two or more separate FDDI rings. Wrapping is an inherent design of FDDI, but it can cause connectivity loss between workstations.

This type of design should be employed when there is little risk of ring interruption.

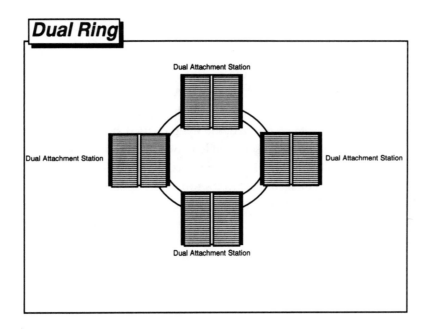

• Consists of dual attachment stations directly attached to a dual ring.

• Designed for fault tolerance, for small sites, or for use as a backbone to a network.

• Dual ring topologies have drawbacks:
  Does not work well for those stations that may be powered on and off or if there are additions constantly made to the ring.
  Something as simple as powering off a station will cause a disruption on the ring.
  It is up to a single attachment to guarantee the reliability of the ring.
  Multiple failures may cause the ring to segment into multiple autonomous rings.

• This design should be used when there is little risk of ring interruption.

TREE OF CONCENTRATORS

With this design, a concentrator is used as the root of the tree to which network attachments are connected. Attachments may be user workstations (DAS or SAS), other concentrators (DAC or SAC), bridges, and routers. Every attachment will branch from the root.

A better design than the last two mentioned, this design is used in medium to large networks that tie together different groups of network users, and lends well to building environments. With a root concentrator, a second tier of concentrators can be placed for multiple floor connections. This second tier of concentrators would then connect to the root concentrator.

This type of design allows for fault isolation to a single station. It also allows for greater flexibility in network management, in that individual network attachments or groups of attachments can be singled out for management purposes.

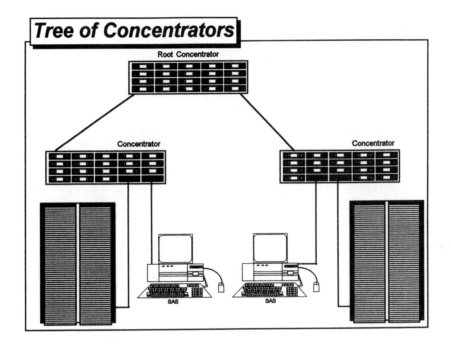

• The tree of concentrators topology:
    allows for a better design for end station attachment.
    is used in medium to large environments.
    allows for one concentrator that is used as the root concentrator.
    works well in multistory buildings.
    allows for fault isolation to single attachments for management purposes.

• Other concentrators connect to the root concentrator mainly for floor and station connection.

• Network attachments and concentrators are allowed to connect to the root.

• The root concentrator may connect single or dual attachment stations or concentrators.

DUAL RING OF TREES

This is the most structured and most popular type of topology. A dual ring backbone is the root of the tree. From here, a second tier of concentrators is placed with direct attachment to the root concentrators. All further network attachments—including user workstations, other concentrators, bridges, or routers—are placed on the second tier of concentrators.

The root is fault-tolerant. Concentrators are simple, passive devices that tend to operate for a long time before failing. Usually a cable will fail before the concentrator will. This ensures good connectivity no matter how many branches are added to the root. This topology provides fault isolation at any layer of the topology. It also allows for easy expansion at any branch of the tree, since network stations should be added to the ends of the branches.

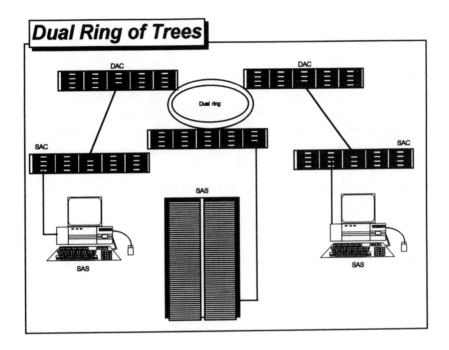

- The dual ring of trees topology:
    is the most popular of FDDI topologies.
    is a dual ring used to build the backbone of the topology.
    allows for a second tier of concentrators to be placed in direct attachment to the root concentrators which
        constitute the backbone.
        — Second level concentrators are usually Single Attachment Stations.
    provides for fault isolation at any level of the topology.
    allows for easy expansion from any level of the tree.

- Concentrators have few electrical parts and therefore are less likely to segment the ring.

DUAL HOMING

Dual homing is actually an FDDI topology. A topology that contains DACs connected to a dual ring topology may have an outside DAS with one port connected to one concentrator and the other port connected to a different concentrator. This is a dual homing topology

With it, a DAS is allowed to connect to two DACs. The A port of the DAS is connected to the first concentrator's M port and the B port of the DAS is connected to the second concentrator's B port. With this topology, the DAS is not considered part of a dual ring. The only active port on the DAS is the B port (by FDDI rules, the B port has precedence over the A port). If port B fails, the A port becomes inserted on the other concentrator. This is a dynamic process by which the DAS can identify the B port failure and knows that it can insert its A port. No outside management function is needed.

This is known as a *redundant topology* and is used in environments where uptime is critical and is useful in the event of a station or cable failure.

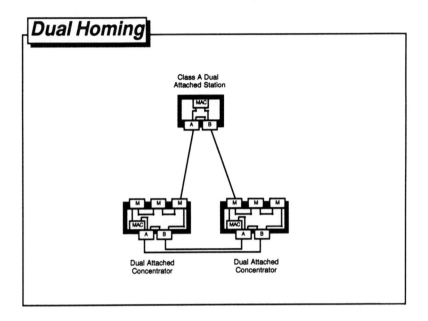

- This allows a DAS to connect to two concentrators to add redundancy.
    If one path fails or a concentrator fails, the other path may take over.

- The B port of the DAS is attached to one of the concentrator's M ports.

- The A port of the DAS is attached to one of the second concentrator's M ports.
    Precedence is given to the B port.
        — If everything is working, data passes on the B port and the A port stays idle.
        — If the B port fails, the A port becomes attached and data flows over the A port.

COMPARISON OF ETHERNET, TOKEN RING, AND FDDI

The following chart is a comparison of Ethernet, Token Ring, and FDDI.

Ethernet, Token Ring, and FDDI

	FDDI	IEEE 802.3	IEEE 802.5
Bandwidth	100 Mbps	10 Mbps	4 or 16 Mbps
Number of stations	500	1024	250
Maximum distance between stations	2 km (1.2 mi) with MMF 20 km (12.4 mi) with SMF	2.8 km (1.7 mi)	300 m (984 ft) station to wiring closet (4 Mbps); recommended standard is 100 m (330 ft) for 16/4 Mbps
Maximum network extent	100 km (62 miles)	2.8 km	300 / 100 m
Logical topology	Dual ring, dual ring of trees	Bus	Single ring
Physical topology	Ring, Star, Hierarchical star	Star, bus Hierarchical star	Ring, star Hierarchical star
Media	Optical fiber	Optical fiber Unshielded twisted pair Coaxial Cable	Shielded or unshielded twisted pair Optical fiber
Access method	Timed token passing	CSMA/CD	Token passing
Token acquisition	Captures the token	N/A	Sets a bit converting token into a frame
Token Release	After transmit	N/A	After stripping (4) or after transmit (16)
Frames on a LAN	Multiple	Single	1 (4) or multiple(16)
Frames transmitted per access	Multiple	Single	Single
Maximum frame size	4500 bytes	1518 bytes	4,500 bytes (4) or 17,800 (16)

MMF = Multimode fiber, SMF = Single Mode Fiber

Data Link Encapsulation Types

Now that all three access method types have been discussed, their formats may be shown. A compilation of the packet formats is shown on the next page. Packet formats are often called *encapsulation methods*.

Data Link Encapsulation Types

6 bytes	6 bytes	2 bytes	Up to 1500 bytes	4 bytes	
Destination address	Source address	Type field	Data field	CRC	Ethernet V2.0

6 bytes	6 bytes	2 bytes	Up to 1500 bytes	4 bytes	
Destination address	Source address	Length field	Data field	CRC	IEEE 802.3

6 bytes	6 bytes	2 bytes	1 byte	1 byte	*		4 bytes	
Destination address	Source address	Length field	DSAP	SSAP	CTRL	Data field	CRC	IEEE 802.3 with IEEE 802.2

6 bytes	6 bytes	2 bytes	1 byte	1 byte		3 bytes	2 bytes	1492 bytes	4 bytes	
Destination address	Source address	Length field	DSAP	SSAP	CTRL	OUI	EtherType	Data field	CRC	IEEE 802.3 SNAP

SNAP header

6 bytes	6 bytes	2 bytes		Up to 1500 bytes	4 bytes	
Destination address	Source address	Length field	FFFF	Data field	CRC	Novell proprietary

Token Ring

			6 bytes	6 bytes		1 byte	1 byte		4472 (4 Mbps or 17800 (16 Mbps) bytes	4 bytes	
SD	AC	FC	Destination address	Source address	RIF	DSAP	SSAP	CTRL	Data field	CRC	FS

			6 bytes	6 bytes	2 bytes	1 byte	1 byte		4472 bytes	4 bytes	1 byte	1 byte
Preamble	SD	FC	Destination address	Source address	Length field	DSAP	SSAP	CTRL	Data field	FCS	ED	FS

FDDI

* - This field may be 1 or type bytes depending on the type of LLC frame

EXTENDING THE NETWORK THROUGH BRIDGES AND ROUTERS

LAN Traffic

When Ethernet entered the commercial marketplace there were very few attachments for it. One of the first attachments to the Ethernet LAN was the communications server, more commonly called the terminal server. This allowed asynchronous devices such as terminals, modems, printers, and host ports to attach to the LAN. The personal computer was also in its infancy and was not commonly found on desktops as it is today.

With very little traffic on the Ethernet most companies expanded by designing their network around repeaters. Separate devices known as routers were used but this was only for networks that were geographically separate. Networks were extended without concern and the only design consideration was the four-repeater limit.

As the connections to Ethernet networks expanded, everything that could be placed on the LAN was placed on the repeated network. Simple terminal traffic became host traffic, which included distributed computing devices, graphics devices, file servers, and such. The amount of traffic was greatly increased, and it was soon found that single strands of Ethernet cable could not handle the load. Extending a network through repeaters only made the problem worse.

Another problem occurred because LANs are usually broadcast-oriented, which does not mean that all traffic is a broadcast packet; this means that all traffic is seen by all stations. It is up to the Ethernet controller card to determine whether the packet should be discarded or it should be processed further by its host. Most of this traffic does not need to be seen by everyone on the network, and it does lead to security problems. It also leads to inefficient use of the cable plant. If the network is designed correctly only stations that communicate the most with each other are placed on the same network; otherwise some network workstations hog the cable plant while others do not get access to it. A bridge is the device that allows a network to be more efficiently utilized.

It is most efficient for network traffic to be separated into separate LANs, but if needed these separate LANs can communicate like one network through the use of bridges.

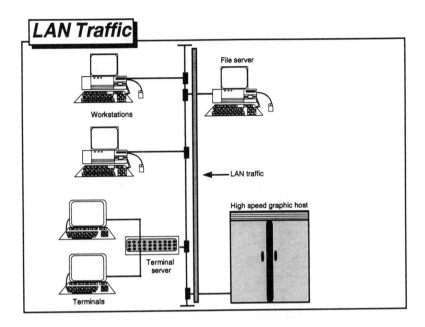

- LANs in the commercial marketplace initially produced very few traffic concerns.
  Companies expanded their networks by designing them around simple bit-level repeaters.

- As networks proliferated, all computing devices were attached to the LAN without consideration of design.
  Graphics workstations, producing heavy amounts of LAN traffic, were on the same cable segment that is being used for terminal emulation, causing potential bottlenecks (slowdowns) for other network stations.

- Ethernet is a broadcast-oriented network.
  All traffic is seen by all stations on the cable segment or segments.
  Not all packets *need* to be seen by all stations on the single cable plant.

- Designing a network this way produced an inefficient utilization of the cable plant.

AN INTRODUCTION TO FORWARDING DEVICES

LANs do have their restrictions. For example, for thick coaxial cable, the longest segment allowed is 500 meters; to extend beyond this requires the use of a repeater, which simply repeats any signals to the next cable plant. Although today's repeaters (hub or concentrator) are sophisticated in that they can restrict errors, they have many other limitations too—mainly that they do not have the sophistication to allow for a network to scale well as it grows larger.

Properly extending a LAN requires the use of special devices known as bridges and routers. When a LAN is extended though the use of a bridge, it is known as an *extended LAN.* When a LAN is extended though the use of a router, it is known as *internetworking.* There are major differences between these devices and they are the subject of this chapter.

Bridges and routers do not simply repeat any signal that is present on a LAN. They literally separate a LAN into multiple segments that look like one network. Bridges separate LANs at the data link layer. Routers operate at the network layer (although they incorporate the use of the data link layer but not for routing purposes). These data-forwarding devices allow for better network design, congestion control, and manageability; they gracefully allow a network to grow by increasing the performance and throughput.

Bridges and routers operate at or close to what is known as *wire speed.* This is the capability of a device to decide whether to discard or forward the packet at the same rate as the maximum capability of the LAN. This means that a bridge can make a filter/forward decision on a received packet at the rate of 14,880 packets per second (pps), which is the maximum transmission rate of Ethernet (64-byte packets). The larger the packet size, the lower the pps speed.

Bridges and routers provide for a more efficient network. Network and traffic management are easily accomplished using these devices.

An Introduction to Forwarding Devices

- Networks have their restrictions.
  - Thick coaxial cable maximum length is 500 meters.
  - LANs are broadcast-oriented.
  - Proper network design is impossible using repeaters.
- Properly extending the LAN requires special devices known as bridges and routers.
  - A LAN that uses bridges is called an extended LAN.
  - A LAN that uses routers is called an internet or internetwork.
- Bridges and routers are data-forwarding devices that forward packets to one or more LANs.
  - They operate at or close to the theoretical access method speed, or wire speed which is:
    - » 14,880 pps for Ethernet.
    - » 32,000 pps for 16 Mb Token Ring
  - They allow for more efficient networks to be designed.

INTERNETWORKING CATEGORIES

There are four distinct categories of forwarding devices for networks (including internetworks). These are:

1. *Repeaters* operate the physical layer. The physical layer is concerned with the electrical (including the signal), wiring, and connectors of a specification. It is here that a repeater receives a signal, regenerates it, and transmits it to the next cable segment. Remember that repeaters do not care about the type of packet, the type of protocol used, or any other thing associated with a particular protocol. They are concerned only with the electrical and physical components of their specific media type. Repeaters are not truly forwarding devices but they do provide the capability to extend networks beyond a single-segment implementation. They were covered in chapter 1 and will be briefly discussed in this section.

2. *Bridges* operate at the data link level, specifically, at the MAC sublayer of the data link layer, which is concerned with packet formatting, packet addressing, and packet validity. Bridges operate based on the MAC address, so it is in the MAC sublayer that bridges operate in the OSI model. Bridges use the physical layer for data transmission and to regenerate a packet before it is forwarded to the next cable segment. But the core of the bridge operation takes place at the data link layer.

3. *Routers* operate at the network layer through they use the data link and physical layer also. Routing is performed based on network numbers. These network numbers are analogous to the area code of a phone system; they group individual hosts into one network number, thereby allowing routers to forward packets based on network numbers and not on individual host numbers.

4. *Gateways* operate at the session layer, the presentation layer, and the application layer. They use the network, data link, and physical layers for data flow.

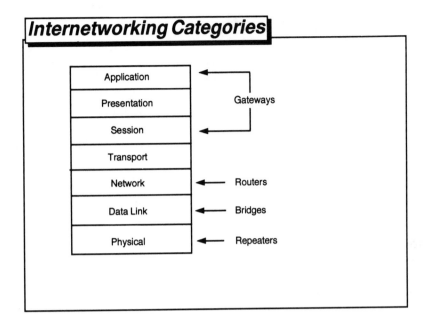

• Repeaters work at the physical layer.

    They simply repeat any signal from one cable plant to the next.

    Concentrators are repeaters but offer more fault isolation than normal repeaters.

• Bridges work at the data link layer.

    Specifically, they forward based on the MAC address of the packet.

• Routers work at the network layer.

    They forward based on network identification inside the packet, not on the MAC address.

• Gateways operate the session, presentation, and application layers.

    They provide protocol translation between different communication types.

INTERNETWORKING HISTORY

There is plenty of history behind internetworking. The following text deals primarily with the commercial introduction of LANs. Remember that LANs were designed so that any protocol could run on top of them. There are network protocols such as TCP/IP, X.25, and others that allowed host computers to communicate without the use of a LAN. The development of these protocols incorporated network layer schemes and therefore, routers were actually used many years before LAN repeaters were.

Gateways were also used many years before the advent of LANs. Their use included protocol conversion between asynchronous and synchronous devices, protocols such as X.25 and SNA, and so forth.

But our history starts around 1980. Repeaters were the primary unit used to extend LANs in the early eighties. Networks were not heavily utilized at this time. Most connections were through hosts using terminal servers, and allowing a network to expand through the use of repeaters did not pose any network problems.

As customer networks expanded and other protocols were ported to run on LANs, the routing scheme used for each protocol was also ported to the LAN. LAN based routers were introduced with the introduction of the Ethernet LAN. In the beginning routers were extremely slow (300 to 1000 pps) and operated at far less the wire speed of Ethernet (14,880 pps). Routers could not easily update themselves (learn where other networks are), and were hard to manage. But they were the first devices used for extending networks beyond a repeater.

Bridges were introduced around 1985 and represented a breakthrough not only in speed, but in network extension technology. At first, bridges offered many advantages over routers and they were installed by the millions. It was around 1986 that the disadvantages of bridges started to be noticed. This was due to the rapid expansion of networks that incorporated many different protocols.

Routers have since made a comeback but in a truly different form. They are now known as *multiprotocol routers*. Advances in hardware and software made it possible for one unit to handle multiple protocols (including routing and bridging). Most multiprotocol routers can operate near or at the wire speed of a LAN.

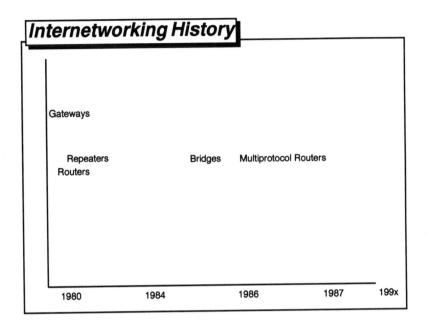

- Routers were present well before the advent of the commercial LAN.
    Routers are used with network protocols that did not require a LAN.

- Gateways were also around before routers and repeaters.
    They provide protocol translation such as asynchronous to synchronous conversion, SNA to X.25, and so
        forth.

- Repeaters were actually around well before the LAN.
    They are used as part of the telephone network.
    They are used with LANs to provide cable extension similar in function to that of the telephone network.

- Routers were implemented on LANs in 1980 but they were big, slow, and expensive.
    Routers were hard to manage and configure and caused a lot of frustration in medium to small networks.

- Bridges came along around 1985–86.
    They provided traffic isolation, were easy to use, and breathed life into the Ethernet standard.

- Multiprotocol routers entered the marketplace around 1986.
    They were slower than the bridges at that time, faster than the older routers, easier to manage than the
        older routers, and are able to route multiple protocols in a single box.

REPEATERS

Repeaters were covered in depth in chapter 1. A synopsis is given here.

Repeaters

- Extend the network by interconnecting multiple segments:
  - Extend 10BASE2 networks to 1000 meters.
  - Extend 10BASE5 networks to 2500 meters.
  - Extend the physical topology of the network.

- Governed by the IEEE 802.3c working group standard.
  - This governs the electrical specifications of a repeater.
  - The physical configurations of a repeater varied from vendor to vendor.

- Some repeaters contain the intelligence to:
  - detect collisions per cable plant (will not repeat collision fragments to other cable plants).
  - de-insert themselves from a wiring concentrator (when there are excessive errors on the cable plant).
  - submit network management information to a central controller.

- Repeaters have transformed into wiring concentrators or hubs.

- Repeaters are low in cost.

- Repeaters can be used to interconnect different wiring types but not different access methods (i.e., Token Ring to Ethernet).

SEGMENTING TRAFFIC

It became clear that to speed things up and cause fewer errors, traffic needed to be segmented. This meant implementing routers—but at this time, routers were big, slow, and expensive. Another solution was needed. This solution was implemented around 1985 and it is called a bridge. Bridging allows a cable plant to be segmented similar to the way a repeater segments a cable plant. The main difference is that when a bridge segments a cable plant, the packets that traverse one cable plant do not necessarily traverse any other cable plants.

Bridges allowed for more efficient design of a network. Network stations that communicated with one another most could reside on the same cable segment. Only when a packet needed to be forwarded to another cable segment would the bridge allow the packet to be forwarded to that cable plant. Otherwise, the packet stayed on the same cable segment that it was transmitted on.

Early bridges could forward packets from one LAN to another at 10,000 pps (packets per second). This was a dramatic increase in performance over the router. Not only were bridges able to configure themselves but early bridges were able to converge the network when a link became disabled. They implemented proprietary loop detection algorithms prior to a standardized algorithm to allow for this.

Moreover, bridges allowed for a more efficient network design. Network stations that most communicated with one another could be placed on the same LAN. When a station needed to communicate with another station across the bridge, the bridge would forward the packet to that station's LAN. The packet would not be forwarded to any other cable plant, unless the bridge did not know the destination address. In this case, it forwarded the packet to all LANs attached to the bridge. But once the address is learned, packets will only be forwarded to that particular cable plant.

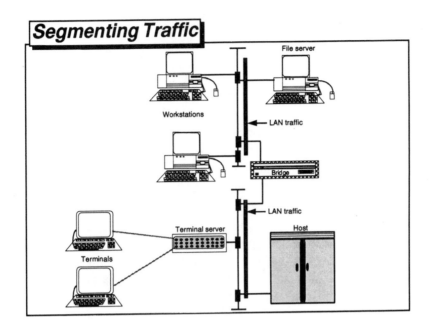

Segmenting Traffic

- Routers could have been used to separate the cable plants.
  At the time routers were big, slow, and expensive.

- Before Ethernet became a bottleneck, bridges were introduced.
  Bridges were a technical advancement at the time, could operate at 10,000 pps at their introduction, could configure themselves, and allowed for a more efficient network design.

- A bridge is installed to segment the cable plant, isolate stations to their own cable plants, and provide security.

- Using the before-and-after approach, there are now two cable plants separated by a bridge.

- Bridges allow packets to traverse other cable plants only when they need to except when the packets are multicast or, broadcast or contain unknown addresses.

An Introduction to Transparent Bridges

The following pertains mainly to the protocol of transparent bridges. This protocol deals with Ethernet/IEEE 802.3 networks. Source Route (Token Ring) bridges will be covered shortly.

Beyond segmenting a network, bridging allows for the proper extension and design of a network. This means that not only can a bridge extend an Ethernet network to 2,500 meters (the maximum length using thick coaxial cable), but it can extend an Ethernet network to virtually limitless boundaries. This may seem unrealistic and in most cases it is. Ethernet bridges can optimally extend a network to 8 2,500-meter segments. Although there is no restriction to the number of bridges that a packet is allowed to traverse, most network software latencies will allow for seven or eight bridges. More than this is usually poor network design.

Bridges use the physical layer to transmit their data on the cable, but it is at the data link layer that their operation truly takes place. Specifically, it is at the MAC sublayer of the data link layer that this operation takes place; this is where physical addressing is placed on the packet that allows bridges to make their filter/forward decisions.

Bridges are not bound to any single protocol. This means that network software protocols such as TCP/IP, XNS, and AppleTalk can all traverse the same bridge. When bridges were introduced, routers were still single units that could be used to route only one protocol. If multiple protocols had to be routed, multiple routers would have to be used. Bridges allow for one unit to be used for all protocols.

The main advantage of bridges is their ability to segment traffic effortlessly. Their operation is rather simple. They operate completely transparent to any network stations on the Ethernet. This means a bridge could be placed on an Ethernet network and all stations attached would operate the way they always have. A transparent bridge is placed on a LAN without disrupting any other network station currently operating on the LAN. The original packet format of Ethernet does not change and when two stations communicate over a bridge, neither station knows that it is operating over the bridge. The bridge operates on the source and destination address of the packet, and only forwards those packets that are destined for another Ethernet segment.

Introduction to Transparent Bridges

- Interconnect multiple cable segments to allow for extension of a network.

- There is no restriction on the number of bridges; only design considerations
- Can be used to interconnect different access methods (Ethernet to Token Ring) and different physical layers.

- Operate at the data link layer.
  - Specifically, they operate at the MAC sublayer.

- They are protocol transparent.
  - They are designed to operate regardless of the upper-layer protocol.
  - They operate on the source and destination address in the MAC header.

- Bridges only forward traffic destined for other cable segments.

- They operate transparently to any stations that are active on the network.

- Ethernet packet formats and software drivers on the workstations remain the same.
  - This is called transparent operation.

LEARNING, FILTERING, AND FORWARDING

A bridge port may be in any of five states:

1. Learning

2. Filtering

3. Forwarding

4. Blocked—used with the spanning tree protocol, explained later

5. Disabled—by network management or a network administrator

When a bridge is initialized, it listens to the cable plant on all active ports. Transparent bridges operate in promiscuous mode, which means that they receive and process each packet that traverses the cable plant even though it is not destined for the bridge. This process is known as learning, and in it, the bridge is trying to build a forwarding table, which contains a list of MAC addresses and the number of its own port from which it learned the address (each port on the bridge is assigned a port number). As the bridge learns the MAC addresses on each of its attached LANs, it adds these entries into the table. A typical forwarding table can hold 8,192 MAC address entries on a per bridge port basis.

When a bridge receives a packet, it reads the packets source address and compares it to the forwarding table. If the received packet's address is not in this table, the bridge will add the address to the table. If the address is already in this table, it will not relearn the address, it simply exits this process.

Next, the bridge reads the destination MAC address of the packet. This address is compared to the forwarding table. If the received packet's destination address is in the forwarding table and its associ-ated port number is the port number on which the bridge received the packet (indicating the destination is on the same cable plant as the source) the packet is discarded or *filtered*. If the address is not associated with that port, the bridge finds the port number with which it is associated. The packet is forwarded out that port. When the packet is transmitted, it is regenerated as a new packet. This allows the packet to traverse 2,500 meters of cable segment.

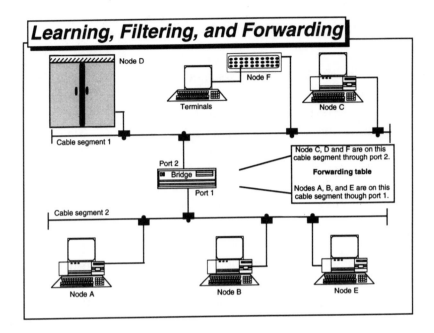

Learning, Filtering, and Forwarding

Node D

Node F

Terminals

Node C

Cable segment 1

Port 2

Bridge

Port 1

Node C, D and F are on this cable segment through port 2.

Forwarding table

Nodes A, B, and E are on this cable segment though port 1.

Cable segment 2

Node A

Node B

Node E

- There are five operational states to a bridge: learning, filtering, forwarding, blocking (using when a loop is detected, discussed later), and disabled – by network management or an administrator.

- Upon initialization, the bridge listens to each of its active ports.
  - It operates in promiscuous mode.
  - It receives all packets to learn their source addresses.
    - — It builds a table of addresses (called a forwarding table) and marks the port number on which the address was learned.
      - + A port number is simply a number that is assigned to the port that is attached to a cable segment.
  - The bridge bases its forwarding decision on the destination address of the received packet.

- When the packet arrives:
  - The bridge reads the source and destination address.
    - — It performs table lookup on both addresses.
    - — If the source address is not in the forwarding table, the bridge adds the address and its received on port number to the table (*learning*).
    - — If it finds the destination address, the bridge forwards the packet out the port associated with the destination address (*forwarding*).
    - — If the port associated with destination address is the same port number the packet was received on it will discard (*filter*) the packet.

LEARNING, FILTERING, AND FORWARDING (CONT.)

When the received packet's destination address in not in the forwarding table, the bridge must forward the packet to all active ports on the bridge. This is part of the forwarding process and is known as *flooding*. The bridge must do this for it has not yet learned the whereabouts of a particular address, which could be on any of the segments. This should occur only once, for when the destination responds, the bridge learns where that destination is and will add the address to its table. From that point on, the bridge forwards the packet only to the appropriate cable plant. Broadcast or multicast packets are the exception; they are destined for all stations on the network and the bridge will forward these packets to all of its active attached cable segments.

When a packet is transmitted on an Ethernet LAN and is received by a bridge, the bridge determines whether to forward the packet to another cable segment. The forwarding decisions are made only by the bridge. The communicating station assumes that the destination station is local. This allows for bridges to be implemented with no changes to the controller or software driver.

The bridge forwards the packet exactly as it was received. The source and destination MAC addresses of a received packet are those of the final source and destination of the two communicating stations. Bridges are not allowed to alter the packet in any way.

Learning Filtering, Forwarding (cont.)

- The exceptions for forwarding are unknown, broadcast or multicast addresses.

- Typical bridge tables can hold up to 8192 entries per port.
  - This is dependent on the vendor of the bridge.
  - Memory requirements may force smaller tables.

- Bridges are the only devices that make the forwarding decisions.
  - End stations on the Ethernet assume that all stations are local.
    » Bridges do not alter the received packet in any way.

  - End stations do not forward the packets directly (MAC) addressed to the bridge.
    » End stations have no idea that a bridge even exists.

  - Bridges operate in a special mode known as promiscuous mode.
    » This allows the bridge to receive and process all packets; even those not destined for it.

FILTERING—AN EXAMPLE

The following example assumes that all network stations' MAC addresses have been learned and have been placed in the forwarding table.

When node C transmits a packet to node D, the packet's source address field is C and the destination address field is D. The packet is seen by all stations on the network. All stations discard the packet except for the bridge and node D. The bridge receives and processes the packet because it is operating in promiscuous mode. The bridge checks to see whether the source address is in the forwarding table. Since it is, the bridge exits out of the learning process.

The bridge then checks to see if node D is in the forwarding table. The bridge sees this address in the table and also knows that the address of node D was learned from port 1. This indicates to the bridge that node C and node D are on the same cable plant and the bridge will discard the packet (not forward it to any other cable plant). However, just because the bridge receives and processes the packet does not mean that node D did not receive the packet. Ethernet is a broadcast medium, meaning that every packet on the LAN is seen by every station on that LAN. A packet is discarded when a station that cannot match its address to the destination address of the packet. There are no special indicators in the Ethernet packet to indicate that a network station has received and processed the packet. The packet is also received by and processed by node D just as if the bridge were not there. Nodes C and D have no idea that a bridge is currently operating on this LAN.

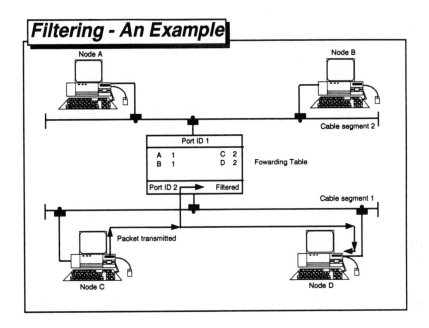

Filtering - An Example

- Node C transmits a packet to Node D.

- The bridge receives the packet.
    The bridge performs a forwarding table lookup on the source and destination address.
        — The source address already exists (previously learned).
        — The destination address exists, therefore, if the Port ID in the table matches the port ID of the port the packet was received on, discard the packet.

- The packet will still be received by Node D as if the bridge does not exist.
    Ethernet is a broadcast medium.
    The packet was not sent directly to the bridge.

FORWARDING—AN EXAMPLE

The following example assumes that the MAC addresses of all network stations have been learned and are in the forwarding table.

When node C transmits a packet to node A, the packet is seen by all stations on the cable plant. The bridge therefore receives this packet and checks to see whether node C's address is in the forwarding table. The bridge finds this address in the table and notices that the associated port number is the same as the port number it received the packet on. It does not relearn this address and exits the learning process.

The bridge then checks to see whether node A's address is in the forwarding table. The bridge finds a match in the forwarding table but its associated port number is not the same as the port number on which the bridge received the packet. The packet is forwarded to the port associated with node A's address.

The advantages to this method of extended networking is that when nodes C and D need to converse, the packets are never seen by nodes A and B. Each packet on each cable segment is filtered by the bridge. This greatly reduces the traffic load on each cable segment and allows for a more efficient network design and management. Response time between communicating devices should decrease, allowing more traffic to pass over each of the cable segments.

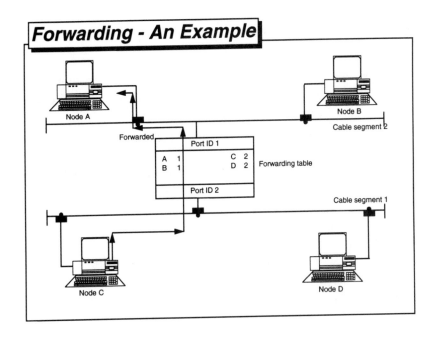

Forwarding - An Example

- Node C transmits a packet to node A.

- The bridge receives the packet.

- The bridge performs a forwarding table lookup on the source and destination address.
    The source address already exists (previously learned).
    The destination address exists and the port ID does not match the port ID of the received packet.
        — The bridge forwards the received packet to port ID 1.

FORWARDING BEYOND ONE BRIDGE

Bridges do not know where network stations actually reside. That is, as far as the bridge is concerned all network stations are located on one side or the other of the bridge. A bridge does not understand that network stations may be separated by more than one bridge. This is done to simplify the bridge.

Say, for example, that there are three bridges separating nodes A and D. If node A transmits a packet to node D, bridge 1 receives the packet and tries to learn the address of node A. Bridge 1 determines that the packet needs to be forwarded to cable segment Y. As far as bridge 1 is concerned, the destination station, node D, is on cable segment Y. But it is not.

Bridge 2 receives the packet on cable segment Y and tries to learn the address of node A. It determines that the packet needs to be forwarded to cable segment X. As far as bridge 2 is concerned, node A is on cable segment Y and node D is on cable segment X. But they are not.

Bridge 3 receives the packet and tries to learn the address of node A. It forwards the packet to cable segment V. Node D resides on cable segment V so it processes the packet and may transmit a response back to node A. The reverse of the above process then takes place.

It is important to note that bridges 1, 2, and 3 have identical forwarding tables. Bridge forwarding tables contain the MAC addresses not only of nodes on the segments to which they are directly attached but of nodes on segments that are separated by other bridges. In this case, all three bridges assume that the nodes A and D are directly connected to one of their segments, but only bridge 1 has a direct attachment with node A through cable segment Z and only bridge 3 has a direct connection with node D through cable segment V. It really is not important for the bridges to understand exactly where the nodes reside; packets are forwarded anyway.

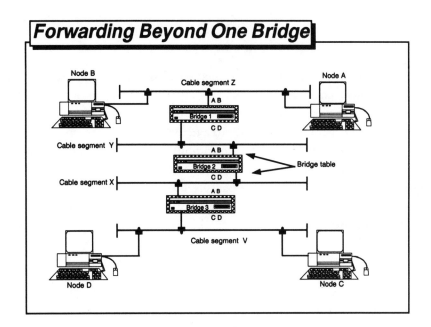

- Bridges assume that all stations are either on one side or the other of the bridge.
  They need not be burdened with the responsibility of knowing the exact location of all end station locations.

- The following example assumes that all bridges have seen packets from each of the stations.

- Node A transmits a packet to node D.
    Bridge 3 receives the packet.
      — Bridge 3 assumes node D is on cable segment Y and forwards packet to cable segment Y.
    Bridge 2 receives the packet.
      — Bridge 2 assumes that node D is on cable segment X and forwards packet to cable segment X.
    Bridge 1 receives the packet.
      — Bridge 1 assumes that node D is on cable segment V and node D does reside on cable segment Z.
        + It does not matter if it did or not.

LOOPS

The concept of forwarding a packet to another network based on the destination address is quite simple once it is explained. The complexity of bridging arises when two or more bridges are interconnecting the same two or more cable segments. This is called *redundancy* or providing a loop. This is a required design feature, because if one path to a network were to become disabled, how would any of the stations on that network communicate without the use of a secondary path?

This may seem like a simple concept but many problems arise when this design is implemented. These problems are associated with duplicate packets, broadcast packets, and unknown destination packets. Without control of this design, a bridged network can quickly become a down network.

The problems caused by a looped network can be avoided, however. We will look at solutions later in the book.

Loops

- Complexity of bridging arises when two or more bridges interconnect the same two cable segments.
- This is called providing redundancy or providing a loop.
- There are problems with this type of design including:
  - duplicate packets,
  - broadcast packets, and
  - unknown destination packets.

DUPLICATE PACKETS

One problem in loops is duplicate packets. A single packet is transmitted to a single destination. Node C transmits a packet to node A. Since the Ethernet is a broadcast media type, all stations on Node C's LAN receive the packet. This means that two bridges on the cable segment 1 will receive and process the packet. This is where the problem occurs. Neither bridge knows that the other bridge is operating on the same cable segment and therefore, they have identical address tables. Therefore, both bridges will transmit the packet to network 2. This is the problem. One packet was transmitted, but duplicate packets are received by node A. This scenario is not fatal and node A recovers—A's higher-layer software (software that operates at the network layer and above) notices that this packet has already been processed, and the duplicate is discarded. But another problem is that node B has had to receive the same packet twice and twice has had to discard it. What does this mean in practical terms? Any other station on cable segment 2 had to receive, process, and discard the same packet twice.

Another problem occurs when the bridge learns that the MAC address C is on two different ports. When the packet is forwarded by both bridge 1 bridge 2, each will receive the other's packet. Each bridge will try to learn the source address of the packet. This corrupts the bridge's forwarding table. Different bridge manufacturers implement different correction methods to avoid this dilemma, but the possibility still exists.

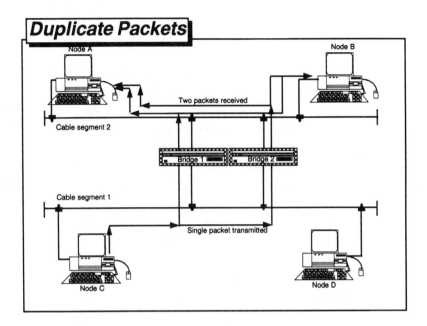

- Node C transmits a packet to node A.
  Both bridge 1 and bridge 2 receive the packet and determine that node A is on the other side of it.

- Neither bridge knows of the other and therefore each bridge will forward the packet to cable segment 2.

- Two packets (duplicated) are now transmitted on cable segment 2.
  Node A receives two of the same packets.
    — Node A should be "smart" enough to discard the duplicate.
    — Node B will discard anyway, but had to discard the same packet twice.
    — All other stations on cable segment 2 had to twice discard the packet.

- Duplicate packets can cause forwarding table corruption on each bridge.
  Both bridge 1 and 2 will forward the packet to cable segment 2
  Each bridge will try to learn nodes C and D (the source addresses) on cable segment 2.
  This allows the bridge to incorrectly learn that node C and D are on cable segment 2.

- This also adds unnecessary overhead to cable segment 2.

BROADCAST PACKETS

Remember that with a broadcast MAC address, all stations can receive and process the same packet. When a bridge receives this type of packet, it must forward the packet to all active ports on the bridge without performing any forwarding table lookups. The proper operation of some network protocols require the use of broadcast packets to be processed by any station on the LAN running that protocol.

This has special consequences in a looped bridge environment. If node C transmits a broadcast packet, both bridges that interconnect the same two cable segments receive and forward the packet to all active ports—in this case only to cable segment 2. Not only does this produce two broadcast packets on cable segment 2, but each bridge receives the other bridge's forwarded packet.

This means that bridge 1 receives bridge 2's transmission and forwards it back to cable segment 1. Bridge 2 receives bridge 1's transmission and forwards it to cable segment 1. The same process will then happen on network 1 when each bridge again receives each other's transmissions. This continues until one of the bridges becomes disabled. The packets will loop endlessly on each cable segment, and generally cause broadcast storms. This definitely causes network degradation, and it also corrupts the forwarding table.

Each broadcast packet transmitted on the cable segments loops indefinitely. Depending on the size of the network, literally hundreds of thousands of broadcast packets can be transmitted in one day. Each time, the packet loops endlessly until the problem is corrected by one of the bridges being taken out of the loop. This creates broadcast storms and eventually causes the network to crash.

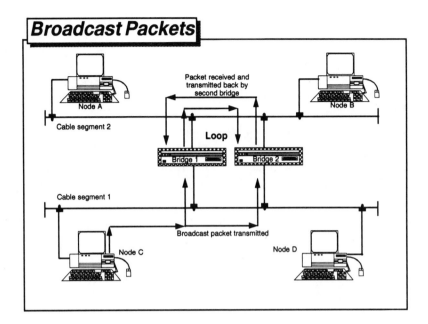

- A bridge automatically forwards a broadcast packet to all its active ports without a forwarding table lookup. The bridge does not forward it to the port it was received on.

- Broadcast packets have special consequences in a looped environment.

- Example:
    Node C transmits a broadcast packet on cable segment 1.
        — Both bridge 1 and 2 receive and process this packet.
    Each bridge forwards it to cable segment 2.
        — Since the packet is addressed to broadcast, each bridge forwards it without a table lookup.
    Each bridge receives each other's forwarded broadcast packet.
        — Bridge 1 forwards bridge 2's packet back to cable segment 1 and bridge 2 forwards bridge 1's packet back to cable segment 1.
        — This loop will continue until one of the bridges becomes disabled.

- Every broadcast packet will loop in this design.
    There is a potential of hundreds of thousands of broadcast packets transmitted in a single day on a network.

- Like the previous loop, this causes forwarding table corruption based on the fact the bridges think the source address is on both sides of the bridge.

UNKNOWN DESTINATION ADDRESS

It was stated before that bridges must forward a packet with an unknown destination address to all active ports since the bridge has not yet learned of the destination address. This creates another problem in a looped environment.

If node C transmits a packet to node Z, both bridges receive this packet. In turn, both bridges forward the packet to cable segment 2. In this case, a loop has been created, because bridge 1 receives bridge 2's packet and forwards it back to cable segment 1. Bridge 2 receives bridge 1's packet and forwards it back to cable segment 1. Not only does this corrupt the forwarding table for MAC address C, but the destination is still unknown and each bridge forwards the packet back to cable segment 1.

This creates two packets for each one transmitted and creates a looped environment in which each bridge continues to forward the other bridge's packet until one of the bridges becomes disabled. This could be a fatal error (depending on how the bridge can fix the forwarding table for MAC address C), but at the very least it causes network degradation and increased response time.

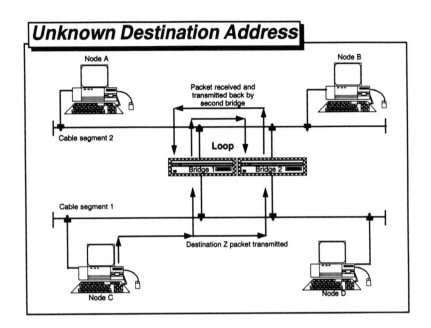

• A bridge must forward an unknown destination address to every active port except the port that it received the packet on.

• Node C transmits a packet to node E (Node E does not exist on this network).

• Each bridge receives the packet.
  Each bridge does not know of MAC address E.
  Each bridge forwards the packet to cable segment 2.

• Each bridge receives the other's forwarded unknown address packet.

• Since the address is still not known, each bridge again forwards the packet back to cable segment 1, and this continues until the address of E is learned or one of the bridges becomes disabled.

• This corrupts the forwarding tables, increases response time, and degrades the network.

THE SPANNING TREE ALGORITHM (STA)—AN OVERVIEW

Designing a bridge network requires forethought. A single path to any destination in the network is a proper design. But redundancy needs to be built in—a single link failure should not cause a section of the network to stop communicating. This is where the Spanning Tree Algorithm comes into play.

The Spanning Tree Algorithm, or STA, is built into almost all bridges and is an integral part of the bridge's software. It dynamically configures a loop-free active topology from the arbitrarily connected components of any bridged LAN. This means that a bridged network can be designed in any fashion and the STA will adapt to it. There are only a few special considerations for STA.

This protocol was first used on Ethernet networks with the transparent bridge protocol. STA should not be confused with transparent bridging. The STA is a protocol unto itself, though you will often hear a transparent bridge called a spanning tree bridge. The two terms should not be intermixed. STA simply provides a loop-free topology on any bridged LAN, so that there is only one path to any destination.

In a loop-free topology, packets are forwarded through some of the bridge ports in the bridged LAN and not through others, which are held in the blocking state. It is the STA that configures the bridges to put their ports in the forwarding state or blocking state. Bridges will receive and transmit packets on its ports that are placed in the forwarding state. Ports that are in the blocking state do not forward packets in either direction, but may be included in the spanning tree configuration. Blocked ports are in standby mode until the topology changes due to a fault in the bridged LAN, such as a link failure or a newly added bridge.

Placing bridges that do not run the standardized version (as published by the IEEE 802.1d) of STA or that do not run the STA at all will cause a network to crash. The STA is an algorithm that is coded to run as part of the bridge software by the bridge vendor.

STA Overview

Bridged networks must allow for redundancy.
  – Only one path should be enabled to any destination on the network.

- STA dynamically configures a loop-free active topology from the arbitrarily connected components of a bridged LAN.

- STA is a protocol unto itself.
  – It should not be confused with the transparent bridge protocol.
  – It has been adopted by the IEEE 802 committees to run on any LAN.

- In an active STA topology certain bridges are allowed to forward packets.
  – Other bridges will participate in the STA but do not forward packets.
  – These are backup bridges that dynamically become available.

- Bridges that participate in the active topology are known as forwarding bridges.

- Bridges that do not forward packets are placed in blocking mode.
  – These bridges still participate in the spanning tree protocol.

- The active topology will re-configure if there is a topology change.

STA TERMS

Bridge identifier: This is determined by combination of the bridge's physical (MAC) address and a network-administrator-defined 2-byte bridge priority field. A lower bridge identifier enables a bridge to assume the role of root bridge.

Designated bridge: This is the bridge attached to each LAN segment in the network with the lowest path cost to the root bridge. In the case where all bridges have the same root path cost, the bridge with the lowest bridge identifier becomes the designated bridge. The designated bridge conveys network topology information to all the other bridges that are connected to the same physical LAN via the designated port. The root bridge is the designated bridge for all LANs that are attached to it.

Designated port: This is the port on each designated bridge that is attached to the LAN segment for which that bridge is the designated bridge. The designated port conveys topology information received from the root bridge to all other bridges on the network. Similarly, the root port is the port on each bridge that has the lowest path cost to the root bridge.

Path cost: The path cost is the summation of the individual bridge port costs of a path to the root bridge. A port cost is a number that is inversely proportional to the speed of the port interface. For example, a bridge may be assigned a path cost of 100 with the port interface speed of 10 Mbps. A 4-Mbps network might be assigned a cost of 250. These values are usually settable by the network administrator. The faster the media speed, the lower the cost. Always allow for expansion. Media speeds are continually increasing every two years.

Port identifier: This is the identification for each port of the bridge. This identifier contains a settable priority field and a fixed port number. Each port in a bridge (no matter how many ports a bridge may contain) is assigned a bridge number by its operating system.

Port states: Blocking and forwarding are the two steady states that are possible on each port of a bridge. Forwarding means the bridge has the ability to forward packets out the port and blocking means any packet will be blocked from being forwarded out that port.

Root bridge: This is the bridge that is the "ruler" of the bridged network. All ports on the root bridge are in the forwarding state.

STA Terms

- Bridge Identifier

- Designated bridge

- Designated port

- Path cost

- Port Identifier

- Port states

- Root bridge

- Root port

STA Packet Format—Topology Messages

The STA protocol allows bridges to communicate with one another only for the purpose of creating and maintaining a loop-free bridged topology. Bridges do not exchange any other information, such as forwarding tables. STA bridges communicate with one another mainly to ensure that the bridge topology provides only one path to any destination in the network. To configure a loop-free extended network or should a loop-free network topology change, the bridges are notified through special configuration packets known as Bridge Protocol Data Units, or BPDUs. There are many names for these packets and they will be called *topology messages* throughout the course of this discussion.

This packet is self-contained. In other words, the topology message contains all the information that a bridge requires to determine the topology of the network. Bridges cannot "see" the network, and therefore rely on these messages to configure the network into a loop-free topology.

The packet format for these topology messages is shown on the following page. The definitions of these fields are on the preceding page.

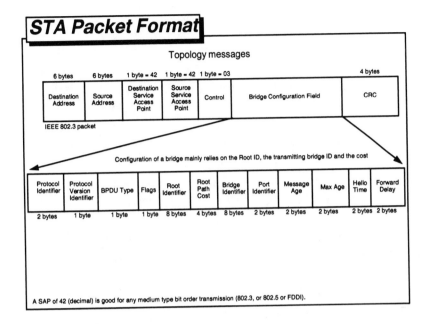

- A bridge communicates with another bridge through the use of topology messages.

- Topology messages contain a reserved multicast destination MAC address that can only be received and processed by bridges running STA.
  All other stations on the network will discard the message.
  This is the only message transmitted by an STA bridge.

- Bridges cannot "see" the network.
  Through the use of this message all bridges can determine the best topology for the network.
  This message is used to maintain a stable network.
  The message is used to configure or reconfigure the bridge network.

- Most fields were defined on the previous page.

How STA Works

On any extended LAN, there is one bridge that is dynamically elected as the *root bridge*. Once the root bridge is selected, all other bridges must then decide if they may participate in the active topology. Basically this means, should they forward packets or enter blocking mode?

To decide this, each bridge (except the root bridge) will find out if it provides the lowest path cost to the root bridge. Each port on a bridge is assigned a path cost. At this point, the bridges do not calculate the lowest cost to any destination; they simply determine the lowest cost to the elected root bridge. This cost is forwarded in topology messages sent to other bridges.

Since an *extended* LAN consists of many *individual* LANs connected through bridges, bridges on each single LAN elect a *designated bridge* for that LAN. There may be many bridges connected to a single LAN and only one is elected as the designated bridge. The designated bridge is the one that has the lowest path cost to the root bridge. The duty of the designated bridge is to forward topology (not data) packets to and from the root bridge. Do not confuse this with all packets (data) being forwarded to the root bridge. After the spanning tree configures, the bridges will still operate as stated previously.

Each designated bridge then determines which ports will participate in the active topology. It is common for bridges to contain more than two ports; some bridges contain up to fifty-two. The bridge designates one port as the root port and other ports will either belong as designated ports or blocked ports. There will be only one root port per bridge. Root topology messages should be received only on the root port, and the designated port forwards root topology messages recieved on the root port, away from the root port towards their designated LAN. In other words, root topology messages should not be received on a designated port. This indicates a loop in the network.

Once the extended network is stable (all bridges are either in the forwarding or blocking state), the root bridge must transmit root topology messages (one every two seconds by default). It transmits these messages out each of its active ports. In turn, designated bridges will receive these messages on their root ports and forward these packets to their LANs. All bridges should receive these packets whether they are in the blocking or forwarding state. If a bridge does not receive this packet, it will rerun the STA algorithm.

How STA Works

- One bridge, the bridge with the highest priority (lowest bridge ID), will become the root bridge.
  - All ports on the root bridge are placed in the forwarding state.
- Other bridges select a port with the lowest path cost to the root bridge.
  - This becomes the root port and is placed in the forwarding state.
  - There is only one root port per bridge, regardless of the number of ports on the bridge.
- The bridge that provides a LAN with the lowest path cost to the root is selected as the designated bridge for that individual cable segment.
- Certain ports are designated as the designated ports
  - These ports are placed in the forwarding state.
- Other bridges or ports not selected have their ports placed in the blocking state.
  - The blocking state prevents data packets from being forwarded on that port.
  - These ports still participate in the STA for future updates.

- On a stable STA topology:
  - The root bridge transmits configuration messages out all of its active ports.
  - Designated bridges should receive this messages on their root port and should propagate the information out all of its designated ports.

DETERMINING THE ROOT BRIDGE

If the network reconfigures, all bridges assume they are the root and will transmit root topology messages accordingly. The root topology message will contain the root ID, the transmitting bridge ID, and the path cost, among other things. The root ID is the MAC address that a bridge thinks the root bridge is, the transmitting bridge ID is the MAC address of the bridge that sent the topology message, and the path cost is the cost to the root bridge and will be 0 (for root topology messages only).

Each bridge continues to receive these root topology messages on each of its ports and saves the "best" information. Best information is a message with more accurate information than a preceding message. For example, if the root ID of a received message is lower than the previously saved message, then the bridge discards the previously saved message and keeps the new one. If the root IDs are equal, then the bridge will check the cost. If the cost is lower, the bridge discards the perviously saved message and keeps the new one. If the bridge IDs and the costs are equal, the bridge checks the transmitter ID. If the transmitter is lower, then the bridge will discard the previously saved message and keeps the new one.

The point here is that once a bridge receives better information, it stops transmitting its own root topology messages. This will allow only one bridge to continue sending a root topology message that will eventually propagate the entire extended LAN (each bridge forwards the root message). This enables only one bridge to become the root bridge. The above process shows only how the root bridge is selected. The next process determines whether a bridge is allowed to particpate in the active topology, that is, whether it is allowed to forward packets or place its ports into the blocking state.

Determining the Root Bridge

- Upon bridge initialization, each bridge assumes that it is the root bridge.

- Each bridge transmits topology messages indicating that it is the root bridge.
  - All bridges will receive this information and each will save the "best" information.
  - The "best" information is basically based on three items in the topology message:
    - » the Root ID field,
    - » the Transmitting bridge ID, and
    - » the cost field.

- For example, if a bridge receives a topology message from a root bridge, the best information is:
  - If the root ID of the received message is of a better priority than the previously saved message (including its own)
    - » discard the previously saved message and keep the new one.

  - If the root IDs are equal, check the cost.
    - » If the cost is lower, discard the previously saved message and keep the new one.

  - If the root IDs and costs are equal, compare the transmitter ID.
    - » If it is lower, discard the previously saved message and keep the new one.

CALCULATION OF THE ROOT BRIDGE

The following figure shows four Ethernet segments separated by five bridges. The top two LAN segments have two bridges interconnecting them, as do the bottom two segments. In the middle is one bridge that interconnects the top two segments and the bottom two segments.

Upon initialization, each bridge will assume that it is the root bridge and will start transmitting root topology messages out each of its ports. Bridge 1 has the best information to become the root bridge (bridge ID is 1), so it is bridge 1 that will win the right to be the root bridge. Eventually all the bridges will store this information; they will stop transmitting their root topology messages and propagate bridge 1 root topology messages. Eventually the network will stabilize with bridge 1 as the root.

The numbers shown by each bridge port indicate the root ID, cost, and transmitting bridge ID for each root topology message that is sent. It does not show the final message stored with bridge 1 as the root.

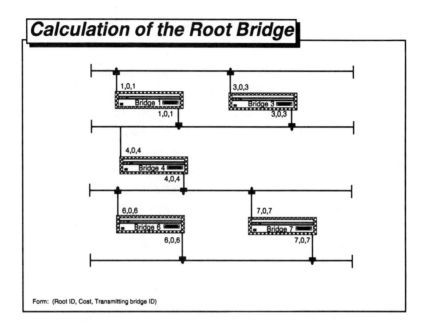

Calculation of the Root Bridge

Form: (Root ID, Cost, Transmitting bridge ID)

• Four Ethernet segments and five bridges are to configure a loop-free topology.

• The first rule in STA is that one bridge must become the root bridge.
   Upon initialization, each bridge will transmit a topology message indicating that it is the root bridge.
   Bridge 1 wins the right to become the root bridge.
   The bridge ID of bridge 1 is 1 and it is the lowest of all the bridges.
   Bridge 1 will transmit its topology message as shown in the form above.
      — All bridges receive bridge 1's topology message, save it , and propagate it to all other bridges.
      — Eventually all bridges will keep this message which identifies bridge 1 as the root.

• The numbers on each bridge show the root topology message each bridge transmits.

CALCULATION OF THE PARTICIPATING PORTS

To select bridges that will be included in the active topology requires each bridge to determine whether it should become the designated bridge for a LAN. The designated bridge is the one that determines which of the bridge's ports to place forwarding mode. Remember that bridges may have multiple ports, and each port must be told whether it will be included in the active topology. In the case just illustrated, each cable segment is a unique LAN that must have a designated bridge. Once bridge 1 is selected as the root bridge, all bridges will transmit the root ID as bridge 1 in all subsequent topology messages. Selection of participating ports is chosen on the basis of which bridge has the lowest path cost to the root. Each bridge will receive a topology message. Each message received will be forwarded by the bridge. Before the topology message is forwarded, it will have 1 added to the cost field of the message, before a bridge will forward it to its LANs (this illustration shows a cost of 1 on each port, but it may be in the range of 1–65,535).

Since the root bridge (here, bridge 1) is also the designated bridge for each of the LANs to which it is connected, bridge 3 will determine that it is on the same LAN segments as the root bridge and will put one of its ports in blocking mode. This is done on the basis of the port number. The port with the highest number will be placed in blocking mode. Bridge 4 will put both of its ports in the forwarding state, because it has no loops on its interconnected LANs. Bridge 4's second port will become the designated port for the LAN (working from the top down).

The interesting problem comes up on cable segments 1 and 2 with bridges 6 and 7 providing equal cost to the root. Normally, only the cost is used to determine designated ports—not the bridge ID or the transmitting bridge ID. Notice here, though, the path costs on bridge 6 and 7 are the same to reach the root.

Since the cost is the same on both ports (a cost of 2), bridge 6 will win the right to be in the active topology. This is because, when costs are equal, the transmitting bridge ID becomes the tie breaker. Bridge 6 has a lower ID than bridge 7. Bridge 7 will put one of its ports into blocking mode. Again, the port placed into blocking mode will be based on the port ID; the higher port ID for the two ports on bridge 7 will be placed in blocking mode.

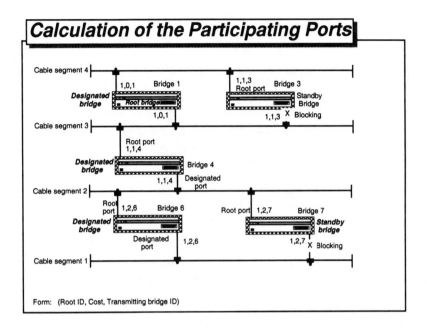

Calculation of the Participating Ports

Form: (Root ID, Cost, Transmitting bridge ID)

• Since the root is selected, each bridge must determine if it will become the designated bridge for any of the cable segments to which it is connected.

• The root bridge places its ports in the forwarding state.
    The root bridge is the designated bridge for cable segments 3 and 4.

• Bridge 3 places one of its ports in the blocking state
    It is on the same cable segments as the root bridge.
    Only one of its ports will be placed in the clocking state.
        — It is based on port ID.

• Bridge 4 becomes the designated bridge for cable segment 2.
    It selects its root port and its designated port.

• Bridges 6 and 7 have equal cost to the root.
    The tie breaker is based on the transmitting bridge ID.
    6 is lower than 7, so bridge 6 becomes the designated bridge for cable segment 1; it selects the root port.
    Bridge 7 places one of its ports in blocking mode.
        — It is based on the port ID.

• With a bridge that has more than two ports, it is possible for a single bridge to become designated on some cable segments to which it is connected and to place some of its other ports into blocking mode.

Spanning Tree Link Failure

There are two times when a spanning tree will reconfigure.

1. When a link breaks. If a spanning tree topology is stable, data will flow in a normal (no loop) bridge environment. A problem will occur if a link in the network breaks. This will cause the network to recalculate the spanning tree. A link breaking could occur if port on the bridge becomes disabled.

Each bridge contains an internal timer called *max age*. Upon receipt of the root topology message, the bridge will reset this timer to 0. If the max age timer expires (default set to 20 seconds), a bridge will assume that a link has failed and will attempt to find another one of its ports to assume the role of the root port. If it cannot find another port, it will assume itself to be the root and transmit root topology messages stating this. This will force the active topology to reconfigure.

2. When a bridge receives better information. With better information, the bridge will reconfigure with a new root ID, root cost, and root port. This could happen when a new bridge is placed on the network. All bridges will do this.

When a bridge initializes, it assumes that it is the root bridge and transmits information stating so. Other bridges on the same LAN segments as the new bridge will receive this information and determine whether to change the topology (if the new bridge has a lower bridge ID than the current root bridge) or disregard the new information and pass a topology message to the new bridge. Based on this information, the new bridge may then decide that it has a better cost to the root bridge, and the topology will change to reflect this.

Spanning Tree Link Failure

- Every two seconds the root bridge will transmit a root bridge topology message on all its active ports.

- Every bridge (designated or not) should receive this message on its root port only.
  - Bridges that are not part of the active topology still participate in the STA.
  - Upon receipt of the packet, each designated bridge will retransmit this packet with the message age field set to zero
    » As the message is propagated, the cost field is incremented by the cost associated with the port the message is forwarded on.
  - Each bridge contains a max age timer.
    » When a bridge receives a root topology message, the timer is set to zero.
    » If the timer reaches a maximum value (default is 20 seconds) the bridge assumes the root or the path to the root has failed.
      • The bridge attempts to find another port (if it has more than two ports) to become the root port.
      • If no other port, assumes itself as the root bridge and reconfigures the topology

- The active topology will also reconfigure if a bridge receives a topology packet that contains better information than what is currently stored.
  - This information will be propagated to other bridges and the topology reconfigures.

BRIDGE DESIGNS

Bridges can be placed anywhere on a LAN, but usually certain designs are used. The three common designs are:

1. Cascaded, which locates one bridge next to another in a pillar fashion.

2. Backbone, which is used with a backbone cable to connect LANs on different floors of a building to a common cable. The speed capacity of the backbone should be five to ten times faster than the fastest interconnected LAN.

3. The hub and spoke, in which one central location accepts connections from many remote locations.

Of the three designs, the hub and spoke configuration has become the most popular.

Bridge Designs

- COMMON BRIDGE DESIGNS

    - Cascaded

        » Locates one bridge next to another in a pillar fashion.

    - Backbone

        » This is used for interconnection of many LANs.
        » Backbone cable is run vertically in a building's riser with LAN "ribs" run on each floor.
        » The backbone cable capacity should be 5 - 10 times its slowest interconnection.

    - Star

        » Used in wide area networks or remote bridged networks. This design can be taken further to enable a central hub in one site with all other sites connected to it.

CASCADED

To build a cascaded network, the first bridge interconnects two LANs. The second bridge also has two connections: one to the second LAN and one to a third LAN. The third bridge will also connect two more LANs, and so on. This creates a pillar configuration.

This network design is limited in that no two communicating stations should pass through more than seven bridges. Although this is not part of the IEEE 802.1 standard, it is generally accepted. When crossing more than seven bridges, the bridge design could introduce delays that will cause network time-outs between the two stations. Network time-outs cause retransmission of original packets and may cause session disconnects.

This type of design is limited to connecting multiple segments of a LAN together in one building.

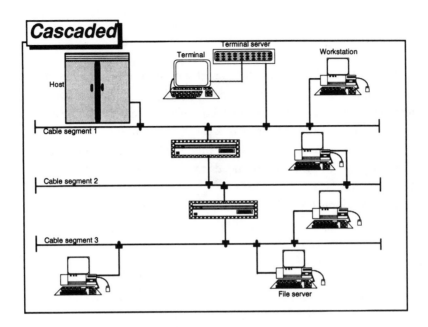

• Common network design that is used for small to medium sized office networks.

• Cannot cascade through more than seven bridges (network delays).
    This is not a recognized standard but usually leads to better design.

• Generally, when more than three bridges are to be cascaded, a backbone should be installed.

BACKBONE

When Ethernet networks were first installed, the most common building design was the backbone design. With the advent of wiring concentrators and very powerful multiprotocol routers, it is not the most popular network. A single cable of thick coaxial cable runs up a riser (or vertical open space, in the building, such as an elevator shaft or a trunk cable of telephone wire).

On each floor a bridge interconnects with the building backbone. Thus, every floor would contain its own traffic; when a network station needs to access another network station on a different floor, the bridge allows it.

The backbone cable should be five to ten times faster than its fastest connection medium or LAN cable.

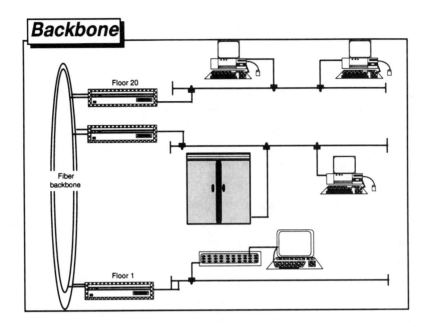

• Commonly used in building configurations to interconnect many cable segments.

• Backbone cable plant runs up the riser of a building.

• The speed capacity of the access method should be five to ten times faster than its fastest interconnection link.

• Bridges from each floor are attached to this backbone.

HUB AND SPOKE

With hub and spoke topology there is one location hosting connections from many remote locations. It is for remote locations that need access to other remote locations. This provides a very efficient connection. The hub site has the responsibility of providing a connection to any other remote site. Each site could have an independent connection with each of the remote locations or a ring topology could be implemented. But both of these topologies are expensive and inefficient.

Hub and spoke is an efficient design for almost any topology. It is also cost-effective. It the shortest data path for an "any location to any location" type of connection.

The one disadvantage to this topology is that if the hub site becomes disabled, all connections would become disabled and the remote stations cannot communicate with one another. Fault-resiliency is usually built into the bridge that is located at the hub site, so that this should not occur.

Remote locations may be connected through telephone lines or they may be connected through another LAN medium. Telephone lines are also known as serial lines. These types of lines are specially conditioned to handle digital data. The connection from a remote site to the hub site is a point-to-point link that is set up by the telephone company. The connection may be thought of as a straight piece of copper wire from the remote to the hub site.

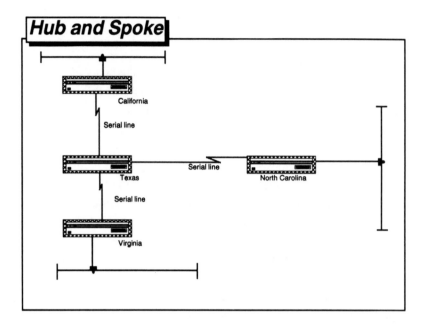

- This can be used for local and remote configurations, but it is usually found in remote (serial line interconnection) configurations.

- Usually has one site that acts as a hub for all the other sites.

- Allows redundancy between sites by providing the shortest path to any location.
    This reduces the amount of bridges through which network stations communicate.

- Contains a single point of failure; if the hub site become disabled, all other sites lose communication.
    Most bridges and routers are fault-resilient in that they contain redundancy options in the event of a
        failure.

STATIC FILTERS

Forwarding devices such as a bridge have an important feature called *static filters*. Filters provide security and more efficient use of the bridge. The bridge has a natural ability to filter packets. If the destination address of a received packet is on the cable segment from which the bridge received the packet, the bridge filters the packet and does not forward it onto any other LAN segment. This is the dynamic filtering capability of a bridge.

The basic operation of bridges allows for the isolation of data traffic to a particular LAN. The expansion of LANs in recent years brings many problems. Data can now be accessed by anyone who is on a LAN, and hackers have caused problems for many organizations. Furthermore, not all data that naturally traverses LANs needs to. To provide for some security and more efficient use of a network, a network administrator may add static filters to a LAN bridge.

Remember, packets contain much information—the source and destination MAC address, a type field, and other network information. A filter can be set up so that if the bridge finds a pattern match to a received packet, it can take certain actions. For example, a bridge filter may not allow a particular MAC address to cross the bridge. Another filter could be set up so that only certain packet types cross the bridge, such as a filter that allows only Novell NetWare traffic to cross the bridge. All other packet types are discarded. There are literally thousands of reasons to set up filters.

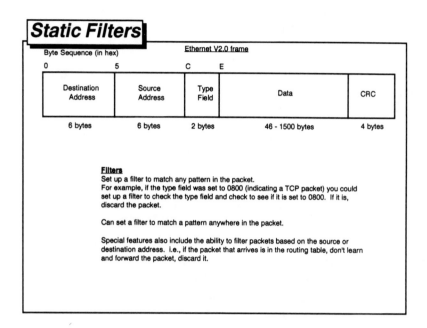

Static Filters

Byte Sequence (in hex)   Ethernet V2.0 frame

Destination Address	Source Address	Type Field	Data	CRC
6 bytes	6 bytes	2 bytes	46 - 1500 bytes	4 bytes

Filters

Set up a filter to match any pattern in the packet.
For example, if the type field was set to 0800 (indicating a TCP packet) you could set up a filter to check the type field and check to see if it is set to 0800. If it is, discard the packet.

Can set a filter to match a pattern anywhere in the packet.

Special features also include the ability to filter packets based on the source or destination address. i.e., if the packet that arrives is in the routing table, don't learn and forward the packet, discard it.

• Since the bridges are the only devices that will allow data to traverse other LANs, they can be set up to secure a network.

• A data-forwarding device can be manually configured to allow or disallow data to traverse it.

• Each bridge can be configured to allow certain packets to traverse the bridge.
  The filter could be set up to trigger on the MAC addresses, user names, or packet protocol type.
  — Virtually any pattern in a packet.

• Very similar to the way a business phone system can be set up for calls.
  Some phones are allowed to make local calls.
  Other phones are allowed to make long distance calls.
  The internal controller of the phone system for a company can be set up to allow these different phone functions.

STATIC FILTERS—AN EXAMPLE

A typical corporate headquarters has many divisions—human resources, accounting, engineering, sales, and marketing, for example. All these different divisions will have their computing devices attached to a LAN which enables all the computing devices to see one another throughout the entire network.

Anyone on the corporate network with enough information will be able to find addresses, user IDs, and passwords, which enables them to log in to any other computer attached to the LAN.

A bridge can be set up with static filters that allow only certain devices to traverse specific portions of a network. If each of the divisions in this corporate office were segmented by its own bridge, each of the bridges could have a set of filters essentially telling the bridge which packets are allowed to traverse the bridge and which ones are not.

For example, if the engineering department stated that only marketing devices can have access to its network, a network administator may set up the engineering bridge with all the MAC addresses of the marketing department allowing only people having marketing department MAC addresses to traverse the bridge. All other MAC addresses would be filtered.

There are many different types of filters that may be set up and all bridge vendors implement filters differently. Their main purpose is to provide additional filtering capabilities for network management or security purposes.

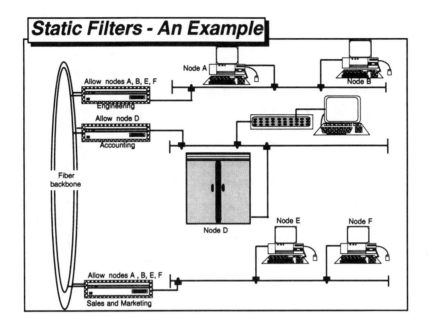

Static Filters - An Example

- In the above example, there are three departments:
  Sales and marketing, which has nodes E and F, accounting has Node D, and engineering has nodes A and B.

- The bridges have been set up with filters based on MAC addresses
  Accounting allows only node D to traverse its bridge.
  Sales and marketing allows only nodes A, B, E, and F to traverse its bridge.
  Engineering allows only nodes A, B, E, and F to traverse its bridge.

- These static filters have been set up so that only those MAC addresses specified will be able to cross the bridge.
  If the source address in the packet matches the filtered MAC address, the packet is forwarded.
  Filters are set on a port basis.
  All other addresses will be filtered.

- The filters allow sales and marketing and engineering to talk to each other.

- The filters also allow no one but accounting's node D to cross its bridge.

- This is only an example, and there are literally thousands of ways to set up filters.

TRANSPARENT BRIDGING SUMMARY

Available in local (directly interconnecting two LANs) and remote (interconnecting two LANs but with an intermediate serial line in–between) configurations, with transparent bridging, all intelligence is carried in the bridge. There are no responsibilities for the end stations. End stations on the Ethernet do not know that the bridges exist. The forwarding table, on which forwarding decisions are based, is carried in the bridges. Ethernet was designed with a special feature known as promiscuous mode. This enables an Ethernet controller to receive and process all packets that traverse the Ethernet cable. It also enables a transparent bridge to build a forwarding table without having to query any of the end stations on the Ethernet. This is one reason why Token Ring cannot operate as a transparent bridge; most Token Ring controllers cannot operate in promiscuous mode without some modification. Promiscuous mode is part of the Ethernet design specification. Though there are special versions of Token Ring firmware that now allow promiscuous mode, they are not widely used.

The packet that an end station transmits and receives did not change. Ethernet end stations transmit the same frame whether they are on a bridged network or not.

Transparent bridges are very fast. Today, most transparent bridges on the market can transmit at wire speed. For Ethernet, this means that the bridges can decide whether or not to forward a packet at the fastest packet rate for Ethernet, 14,880 pps.

The spanning tree algorithm allows a network administrator to place two bridges between the same two LANs for redundancy. STA dynamically removes the loops in a network and offers the capability of a stand-by bridge. The algorithm also operates with very little network administration. A network administrator basically turns it on and leaves it alone to provide a loop-free spanning tree topology. There are a few parameters that may be changed, but the defaults are usually used. STA offers dynamic reconfiguration: should a primary path fail, a secondary path will automatically be brought up (usually within thirty to thirty-five seconds). The redundant (secondary) paths do not forward traffic until a primary path is disabled. Therefore, there will be only one path to any destination on a spanning tree network.

Spanning tree topology messages are MAC multicast (I/G bit set).

Transparent Bridges and Spanning Tree Benefits

- All intelligence is contained in the bridge (not in the end-node).

- No end node responsibilities.
    - Even the packet format stays the same.

- Centralized forwarding tables.

- No active loops in the network.

- Local and remote capabilities.

- Redundant path(s) are disabled (dormant).

- Bridge reconfigurations are accomplished via multicast addresses, not broadcast addresses.

- Spanning tree algorithm works independently of the bridge.
    - Dynamically configures a loop-free network.

Token Ring Bridges

IBM and the IEEE 802.5 committee introduced a different type of bridging for Token Ring called source routing. It has been adopted only by the IEEE 802.5 working group and not by any of the other IEEE 802.x working groups. Therefore, source routing is not used on Ethernet/IEEE 802.3 LANs.

Source routing incorporates some of the routing features found in true routing protocols. But it is still a bridge layer protocol. Source routing gained popularity due to IBM's support of it. Transparent bridging was not feasible on Token Ring because Token Ring controllers could not operate in promiscous mode. Although there are modified Token Ring chipsets out today that allow this operation, the first Token Ring chip sets did not allow for promiscuous mode.

IBM intended two protocols to run over their Token Ring: SNA and NetBIOS. Neither can be routed in the conventional means. Therefore, in order to provide some LAN routing features to their non-routing protocols, source routing was invented.

There are some advantages to the source routing protocol. Troubleshooting a source-routed network with a protocol analyzer (a device that can receive and translate all packets into human readable form) will show ring numbers and bridge numbers inside of a packet. In this way, a network administrator may ascertain the path taken by a packet. This also allows the network administrator to determine which MAC addresses reside on which rings.

Source routing is the way the IBM Token Ring network routes frames through a multiple-ring LAN. A *route* is the path that a frame travels through a network from an originating station to a destination station. Unlike transparent bridging, source routing does not build forwarding tables. In fact there is very little intelligence in the bridge; it only reads certain information in the packet and determines whether to add information to it and to forward the packet based on information in the packet. Each frame carries information about the route it is to follow.

Token Ring Bridges

- Developed as a bridge protocol for Token Ring LANs.
  - Only adopted by the IEEE 802.5 working group.

- Source routing gained popularity due to IBM's support of it.
  - It is easy to install a source route network.
  - It is not easy to grow a source route network into a large network.

- Invented due to technical limitations of the source route chip set.
  - Early source route chip sets could not be set for promiscuous mode.

- Source routing was also invented to allow two non-routing protocols to be placed on a LAN: NetBIOS and SNA.
- Troubleshooting source route networks with a protocol analyzer provides many benefits due to a packet being able to show the path that it is taken.
  - MAC addresses can be associated to certain ring numbers.
- Source Routing does not build forwarding tables based on MAC addresses.

- Most of the intelligence for this algorithm is found in the network stations.

- Each packet carries complete route information with it.

SOURCE ROUTING OVERVIEW

With source routing, each ring separated by a bridge is assigned a unique ring number, which is assigned to the bridge port when the bridge is configured. Each bridge is also assigned a bridge number pertaining to all ports on the bridge. Each port of a single bridge is not assigned a different bridge number. Futhermore, the bridge numbers of all the bridges in a source route network may be the same number. Only the ring number needs to be different.

With source routing, when a network station wishes to communicate with another station, it issues a special packet to discover the location of the destination station. When a bridge receives this packet (a bit in the source address of a Token Ring packet indicates whether the packet contains source route information or not), it adds information into a field in the packet called the *Routing Information Field (RIF)*. Generically, it adds a ring number and bridge number and then forwards the packet.

Each bridge adds this information until the packet reaches the destination. When the destination receives the packet it may return the packet with the original RIF field (to be read in reverse order by a bridge), or the destination station may build a response discovery packet to which the bridges again add information until this response packet reaches the source station. The source station may receive multiple response packets and upon receipt of a response packet, it will choose the route it will take to reach the destination station.

In source routing there is a hard and fast rule that a packet may not traverse more than seven bridges (or *hops*). The eighth bridge must discard the packet. This is the IBM-imposed limitation on how large the RIF field may be.

A packet indicates that it contains source route information by setting the U bit in the source address field. This is bit 0 (the first bit) of the first byte of the source address. If it is set to a binary 1 the packet contains source route information; if it is set to a 0, it does not.

Source Routing Overview

- Each separate ring is assigned a unique ring number.
  - Assigned on the source route bridge port and not on the ring station.

- Each bridge is assigned a bridge number.
  - There is a single number for the whole bridge, no matter how many ports it has.

- End stations try to find destination ring stations by broadcasting special discovery frames.
  - The requesting ring station should receive a response, which will indicate the path to the destination.
  - This information is placed into a field in the frame by bridges that the discovery frame traversed on the way to the destination.

- A frame will contain source route information based on one bit in the source address
  - The I/G bit (the U bit in the source address).
    » If it set to a 1 (binary) the frame contains source route information.
    » It is called the Routing Information Indicator (RII).

- A source route frame may not cross more than seven bridges.
  - At the eighth bridge, the frame is discarded.

SOURCE ROUTING EXAMPLE

If node 1 wanted to connect to node 2, node 1 would first attempt to find this station on the local ring. This is true for SNA and IBM NetBIOS protocols. Other protocols may skip this step. It would transmit a frame to try to find node 2 on the local ring. If there is not a response to this packet, node 1 will determine that node 2 may not be located on this ring. To find node 2 off-ring, node 1 will have to transmit a dynamic route discovery packet.

A dynamic route discovery packet is a packet that is meant to find a station that is not on the same ring as the source station. This type of packet has special meaning to a bridge for it must receive the packet, check it for possible errors, then forward the packet to one of all of its ports. Before forwarding this packet, it will place information in the RIF indicating the ring number of the port it received the packet on, its bridge number and the ring number of the port that the bridge forwarded the packet on.

There are many different types of dynamic route discovery packets; wherever possible, they will be called by their unique names from this point on.

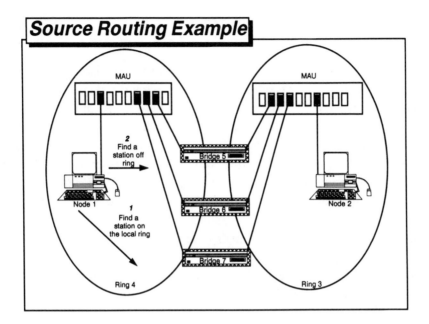

- For most source route implementations to find a destination station, the local station follows the following procedure:

    The local station sends a request frame addressed as if the station were on the local ring.

    — This frame will not contain source route information.

    If there is no response, the local station resends the frame with the source route bit (RII) set.

    — The RII indicates an off-ring frame.

    — This enables source route bridges to receive and possibly forward the frame to other rings.

TOKEN RING SOURCE ROUTING AND THE RIF FIELD

A packet that is to be transmitted off the local ring needs information placed into the packet so that a bridge may determine its route. Let's take a look at the Token Ring packet, especially the RIF field.

The first thing to notice is bit 0 of the source address. This is the Routing Information Indicator (RII) bit. It usually indicates whether the address is an individually or group assigned address. Since the source address can never be set as a group address, this bit is used to indicate to a Token Ring controller the presence of source route information. If bit 0 of byte 0 is set (binary 1), then the packet contains source route information. If it is not set (binary 0) then the packet does not contain source route information. A packet does not contain an RIF for those stations that are communicating on the same ring.

The Routing Information Field (RIF) contains two entities:

1. The Routing Control (RC) field. There is only one 16-bit Routing Control field in the RIF and it is further divided into four fields:

- Broadcast indicator bits indicate the type of source route broadcast.

- RIF field length bits indicate the length of the RIF field. This field will always be set to an even number equal to or less than 18 excluding 4 (explained later).

- Direction bit indicates to the bridge to read the RIF field from left to right (forward direction) or from right to left (reverse direction).

- Largest Frame Size Supported bits are placed into the RIF header by a bridge. It indicates the largest frame size the bridge can forward.

- rrrr bits are reserved by IBM but are being used as an extension to the Largest Frame Size bits. This allows more definitive largest frame sizes.

2. The Routing Designator (RD) field, which is explained next.

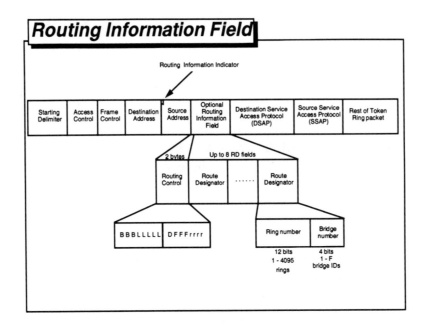

- B=Broadcast indicators   Ring number – indicates a traversed ring number.
- L=Length bits
- D=Direction bit   Bridge number – indicates a traversed bridge number.
- F=Largest frame bits
- r=reserved bits   Length bits – indicates the length of the RIF.

- Broadcast indicators
  - 000 – Non broadcast or specifically routed frame
  - 100 – All routes broadcast with a specific route return
  - 110 – Single route broadcast with an all routes return
  - 111 – Single route broadcast with a single route return

- Largest frame bits
  - 000 – up to 516 bytes
  - 001 – up to 1500 bytes (maximum Ethernet frame size)
  - 010 – up to 2052 bytes
  - 011 – up to 4472 bytes (maximum FDDI and 4-Mb Token Ring frame size)
  - 100 – up to 8144 bytes
  - 101 – up to 11,407
  - 110 – up to 17,800 bytes (maximum frame size for 16-Mbit Token Ring)
  - 111 – Used in an all routes broadcast

- Direction bit – indicates which way to the read the RIF
  - 0 – read RIF left to right (forward direction)
  - 1 – read RIF right to left (backward direction)

THE ROUTE DESIGNATOR

The Route Designator (RD) is also two bytes long and there can be eight of these 16-bit fields in one RIF. IBM allows only eight due to the mandatory seven-hop limit of source routing. A hop is when a packet traverses a bridge to another ring.

Each RD contains two fields, a 12-bit ring number and a 4-bit bridge number. Twelve bits allows for 4,095 ring numbers to be assigned. The last 4 bits are for the bridge number. This allows for fifteen bridge numbers (0 is reserved). Each ring number must be unique on a Token Ring LAN. The bridge number may be the same on every bridge unless there are two or more bridges interconnecting the same two LANs.

When a station submits a dynamic route discovery packet (after it has determined that the destination station may not be located on the same ring), it is usually sent as a MAC destination addressed broadcast packet. But the source route (RII) bit in the source address of the packet is set to indicate the presence of source route information.

A bridge located on the ring receives the packet and determines that the packet is a dynamic route discovery packet by looking at the broadcast indicators in the received packet's RC field. The following example is generic to the source routing algorithm; more detailed examples will follow:

1. If the bridge is the first bridge to receive the packet (there is a 2 is the RL field), it adds the ring number and the internal bridge number of the ring from which it received the packet to the first RD field. It then adds another RD with the ring number of the ring to which it will forward the packet and sets the bridge number in this second RD to a zero. The bridge must set it to a zero for it has no idea if there are any other bridges out on the forwarded ring, and the field must always end on a 16-bit boundary. As the packet traverses more bridges, they continue to add RDs. Other bridges do not add two RDs but will replace the bridge field of the last RD (set to 0) with their bridge numbers and add the ring number of the port to which they forwarded the packet.

2. Before forwarding a frame, a bridge always adjusts the RC field. It sets the RIF length and may set the largest frames size field only if it cannot transmit a frame as large as the one already indicated in this field. If it can transmit a larger frame, it does not touch this field. It also recomputes the CRC field before it forwards the frame.

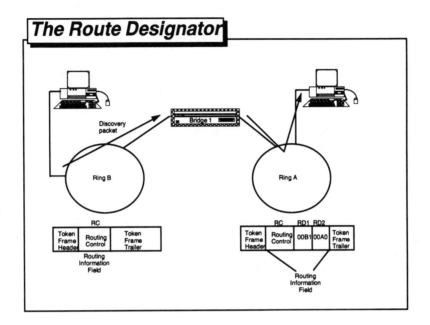

- A route designator is 2 bytes long and it contains 2 fields:
    - a 12 bit ring number - allows for 4095 rings.
    - a 4 bit bridge number - allows for 15 bridge numbers, 0 is reserved.

- Each time an *explorer* frame crosses a bridge, the following procedure occurs:
    - If it is the first bridge to receive the explorer frame (RC length field is a two), the bridge:
        — adds the ring number of the receive port to the first RD,
        — adds its bridge number to the first RD,
        — adds the ring number of the ring to which it will forward the frame, to the second RD, and
        — places a 0 in the last 4 bits of the second RD.
            + The frame must be on a 16-bit boundary.
        — The bridge adjusts the RC field to indicate the new length and sets the maximum size indicator for the maximum size frame it can send.
        — The bridge calculates a new CRC.
        — The bridge then forwards the frame to the next ring.

    - If it is not the first bridge (RC length field is 6 or higher), the bridge:
        — changes the bridge field of the last RD of 0 to its bridge number,
        — places the ring number of the port on which the frame will be forwarded in a new RD and fills out the remaining 4 bits of the new RD with zeros.
        — It adjusts the RC, calculates a new CRC, and forwards the frame to the next ring.

SOURCE ROUTE PACKET TYPES

Source Routing Packet types are indicated by the broadcast indicators in the RC field. There are four types:

1. Single Route Explorers (SRE, but also known as Spanning Tree Explorers, STE). The response to this request packet is an all routes response.

2. Single Route Explorer (SRE) with a Single Route Return. Allows a single route explorer frame to be returned by using the acquired RIF field.

3. All Routes Explorers (ARE). The response to this is a single route response.

4. Specifically Routed Frame (SRF). This is a frame that already has the RIF built and it will be forwarded only by those bridges that are in the RIF.

Source Route Packet Types

- Four types of Source Route frames:

    - Single Route Explorer (SRE)
        - » Also known as Spanning Tree Explorers (STE)
            - So named by the IEEE 802.5 working group

    - All Routes Explorer (ARE)

    - Specifically Routed Frame (SRF)

    - Single Route Explorer with a specific route return

SINGLE ROUTE EXPLORERS (OR SPANNING TREE EXPLORERS, STE)

A single route explorer packet will be forwarded throughout a multiring network so that only one copy of the frame appears on any ring in the source-routed network. It uses the spanning tree protocol (with a few modifications) to know if it may transmit to ensure that only one copy appears on any ring.

The spanning tree protocol, as explained before, is an independent protocol that finds loops and disables them so that there is only one path to any destination on the network. The protocol is also used on Token Ring source route networks to determine where loops exist and to disable them for SRE packet forwarding only. (ARE packets will still be forwarded by the blocked SRE port.)

When a station broadcasts an SRE packet, it is received by any bridge on that ring. The best example is: Two bridges interconnect the same two rings, which provides a loop. When node Y transmits an SRE packet, both bridges A and B will receive the packet. But the spanning tree protocol has blocked bridge A's interface from forwarding SRE packets but placed both of bridge B's ports in the forwarding state. Therefore, when bridge B receives the packet, it forwards the packet to ring 2.

The destination station receives this packet and in response, does not flip the direction bit so that the packet will follow the return path but issues a response packet in the form of a new All Routes Explorer (ARE). The important thing to note is that a bridge that has a port in blocking state will still forward ARE packets; it just does not forward SRE packets.

In this case, the response packet is forwarded by both bridges A and B. Two copies of the response packet (one from each bridge) are placed on ring 1. Source station Y will then determine which path to use (it usually chooses the path of the first response packet received in good condition). After the path is chosen, any further communication between the stations is accomplished using the SRF frame.

Node Y could choose bridge A as the source route path. This is okay because bridge A can forward SRF frames, though it cannot forward SRE frames.

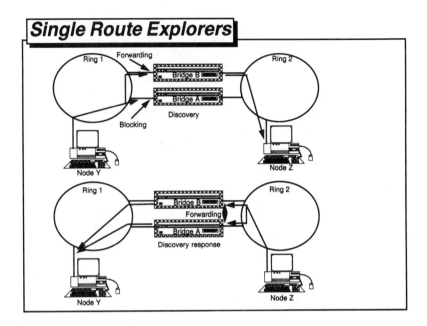

- SREs are used so that only one copy of the explorer appears on any ring in the network.

- Bridges use the STA to force ports into the blocking mode for SRE frames only.
    These ports still forward ARE and SRF frames.

- **Example:**

- Node Y transmits an explorer for destination Z.
    Bridge A receives the SRE frame and drops it.
        — STA puts that port in the blocking state.
    Bridge B receives the frame and forwards it to ring 2.
        — STA puts that port in the forwarding state.

- By source routing rules, node Z responds with an ARE explorer response frame.
    Bridge B receives the frame and forwards it to Ring 1.
    Bridge A receives the frame and forwards it to Ring 1.
    Node Y receives both of these response frames.
    Usually, node Y chooses the route indicated in the first frame it receives and discards all other responses.

- When node Y chooses a route, any further communication between node Y and Z will change to an SRF frame.

- Should Node Y choose bridge A's route, this would be okay, for bridge A is still able to forward a SRF.

SOURCE ROUTE FLOWCHART FOR SINGLE ROUTE EXPLORERS—
PACKET DISCARD

The following is a flowchart describing source route packet flow for a bridge that receives an SRE packet on one of its ports. When a bridge receives a single route explorer (SRE) packet, it examines the RIF field.

Bridges running the spanning tree protocol for single route discovery packet forwarding will only forward packets received on ports that are in the forwarding state.

The ring in (R/I) port is described as the port that the bridge received the packet on. Likewise, the ring out (R/O) port is the port that the bridge will forward the packet to. If the bridge's R/I port and R/O port (not the same as the R/I and R/O ports of a Token Ring MAU) are in the forwarding state, the bridge will discard the packet for the following reasons:

- The ring number to which the bridge will forward the packet is already in the RIF field— a loop may exist in the bridged network.

- The number of route descriptors in the RIF field is equal to or exceeds the largest allowable RIF field for the bridge—too many bridges have already been crossed.

- The RIF length field is equal to a 4—this field should always be a 2, or 6 to 28. A source station submits a source route packet with the RIF length equal to a 2 for only the RC field is in the RIF. The first bridge to receive this packet will always add 2 RDs to the RIF. This makes the RIF length field jump to a 6 from 2.

If the R/I port is in the forwarding state and if the last ring number in the RIF field does not match the ring number of the port on which the bridge received the frame, the bridge will discard the packet based on the ring number mismatch.

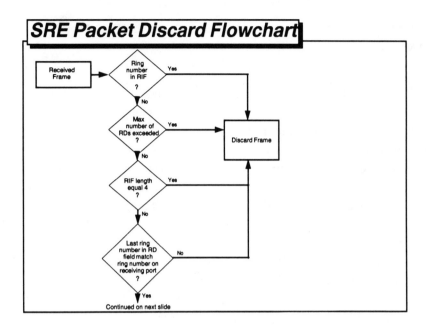

• The above flowchart shows why a source route bridge would discard a received SRE frame.

SOURCE ROUTE FLOWCHART FOR SINGLE ROUTE EXPLORERS—
DATA FORWARDING

If the R/I port and the R/O port are in the forwarding state, the length field is set to 2, and the bridge's RD limit is greater than 1, this bridge is the first bridge to receive the packet. The bridge will add two RDs to the RIF field since it is the first bridge. The first RD it will add will contain the 12-bit ring number of the port on which it received the frame and its 4-bit bridge number. The second RD field will contain the 12-bit ring number of the port to which it will forward the frame. The last four bits of the second RD will be set to a zero. This is the bridge number field for the ring to which the frame is forwarded. The bridge has no idea whether there are any more bridges on the forwarded ring, and the field must be rounded to a 16-bit boundary. All subsequent bridges will modify this RD and add one RD.

Before forwarding a packet, the bridge will also modify the RC field by setting the length field to a 6, and it will set the largest frame field to the lowest number that it can transmit between the minimum number in the received frame and the minimum frame size. In other words, if the largest frame size the bridge can send is 1518 bytes but the minimum size set in the received frame is set to 512, it will leave this field alone. The bridge will then recalculate the CRC field of the Token Ring packet and transmit the packet onto the forwarded ring.

The bridge will also forward the frame if: (1) the R/I port is in the forwarding state, (2) the port to be forwarded to is in the forwarding state, (3) the RIF length field is between 6 and 18 (inclusive, even numbers only), and (4) the number of RDs in the RIF field does not exceed the limit of RDs for that bridge. Before forwarding the frame, however, the bridge will modify the frame by setting the last four bits of the last RD in the RIF to its bridge number. It will add another RD on which it places the ring number of the port to which the packet will be forwarded, setting the last four bits to a zero.

The bridge will increment the length field by two and set the largest frame field to the largest frame that it can transmit, if it is not greater than the received packet's largest frame size.

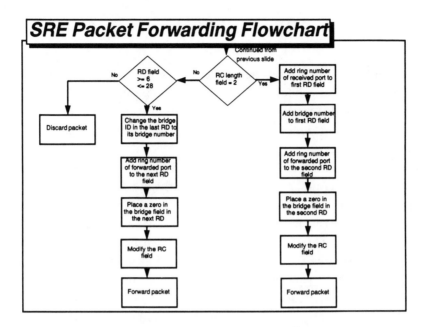

• The above flowchart shows how a bridge forwards an SRE frame.

• Although the bridge will check for a 28-byte RIF length field, the RIF length is still not supposed to be larger than 18 bytes.
    Newer revisions of source route bridges are allowing for the 28-byte RD fields.

• The above flowchart was created using the IEEE 802.5m specification.

ALL ROUTES EXPLORER (ARE)

All Routes Explorers (ARE) are packets transmitted by a source station so that every bridge in the path to the destination station will forward the packet. This means that the ARE discovery packet may be copied by every bridge on the path to the destination even if there are loops in the network. The bridge is smart enough to know whether the packet has already traversed its bridge and discards it, preventing a looped packet.

For example, when source station Y transmits an ARE to find destination station Z, there are two bridges interconnecting two rings, ring 1 and ring 2. For the one ARE transmitted by station A two packets will appear on ring 2. Bridges A and B each will forward the packet to ring 2. Each of the packets would have the same ring numbers in the RIF field but separating those ring numbers would be different bridge numbers. This is the only time that a bridge must contain a different bridge number. If there were more rings in this example and more bridges connecting those rings, as long as those bridges do not present a parallel path, as shown above, these bridges may contain the same bridge number. They may even contain the same bridge number as bridge A or B.

When the destination station receives the packet, it will not respond with an ARE response packet. In this case, the destination station simply flips the direction bit (from the binary 0 to a binary 1), which instructs the bridges that a preconfigured RIF field exists but to read the RIF field from right to left. (The RIF field is built from the left to the right and therefore the reverse direction would be right to left.) This is known as a *specifically routed response frame*.

Once a path is found between two communicating stations, the RIF field does not change. The source and destination station simply change the direction bit to indicate the direction in which the bridge should read the RIF field.

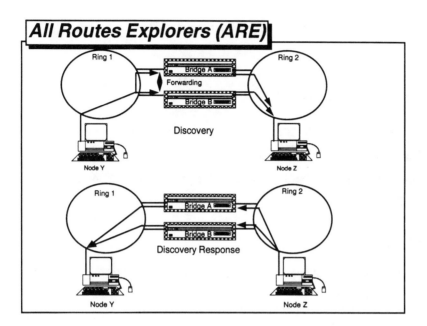

- ARE frames are sent so that every bridge will forward the ARE frame to all of its active ports.
  Depending on the topology, the frame could be replicated many times before reaching the destination.
  According to source routing rules, the destination station responds with an SRF frame.
    — The destination will flip the direction bit of each frame it receives and transmit the response frame back to the source.
      + The route that was collected along the way is reused in the response frame.
    — Each bridge forwards only the frame in which it is indicated, otherwise the bridge will drop the frame.
      + For a bridge to determine whether it should forward a frame, it uses the combination of ring number in, bridge number and ring number out.

- The source station may get many responses back from its single request.
  Usually, the source station chooses the first response frame it receives.
    — To communicate with the destination station, it will change the direction bit and transmit the frame as an SRF.

- Example:
  Node Y transmits an ARE to Node Z.
    — Bridges A and B forward the frame to ring 2.
  Node Z responds to each forwarded frame by changing the frame to an SRF and flipping the direction bit.
  Bridge A forwards one response frame and bridge B forwards the other response frame.
  Node Y will choose the route in the first response frame it receives.

ALL ROUTES EXPLORER (ARE) FLOWCHART—PACKET DISCARD

The following assumes that the packets received are ARE packets. The bridge will discard a received ARE frame for the following conditions:

- The last ring number in the RIF field does not agree with the ring number of the port on which the bridge received the frame.

- The number of RDs in the RIF field is equal to or exceeds the number of RDs allowed by the bridge.

- The RIF length field is a 0, a 4, or an odd number. It must be an even number, and be at least 2 or 6 to 28.

- The direction bit is a not a 0—AREs are always originated by a station. They are used to find a station and to respond to an SRE. In either case an ARE acts like it is an original packet, and therefore, the direction bit must be set to a 0.

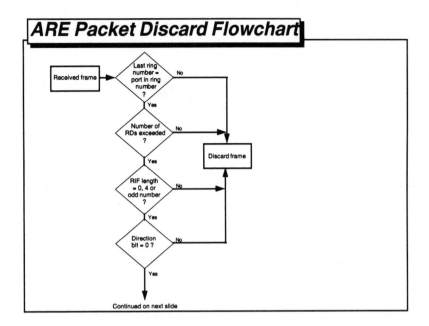

• This flowchart shows why a bridge would discard an ARE frame.

• The direction bit should always equal a 0 for an ARE frame.
    This is true if the frame is generated by a station looking for a destination station or by a destination station responding to an SRE request.
    An ARE frame does not contain any RIF information when first generated.

ALL ROUTES EXPLORER FLOWCHART—PACKET FORWARDING

If the bridge receives a frame and the length field is 2 and the bridge's RD limit is greater than 1, this bridge is the first bridge to receive the ARE discovery packet. The bridge will add 2 RDs to the RIF field (which is why the RIF length field in the RC should never be a 4) since it is the first bridge. The first RD it will add will contain the 12-bit ring number of the port on which it received the frame and the bridge's 4-bit bridge number. The second RD field will contain the 12-bit ring number of the port to which the bridge will forward the frame. The last four bits will be set to zeros. This is the bridge number field for the ring to which the frame is forwarded. The bridge has no idea whether there are any more bridges on the forwarded ring, and the field must be rounded to a 16-bit boundary. All subsequent bridges will modify the previous RD (the four bits of 0) and add one RD.

This bridge will also modify the RC field by setting the length field to a 6 and it will set the largest frame field to the min(k,n), where k is the minimum number in the received frame and n is the minimum frame size that it can transmit. It will then recalculate the CRC field of the Token Ring packet and transmit the packet onto the forwarded ring.

If the bridge receives a frame with the RIF length field between 6 and 28 (inclusive, even numbers only), and the number of RDs in the RIF field does not exceed the limit of RD for that bridge, the bridge will forward the frame, but first it will modify the frame by setting the last 4 bits of the last RD in the RIF to its bridge number. Next it will add a new RD to which it will add the ring number of the port to which the packet will be forwarded as the first 12 bits of the new RD and setting the last 4 bits to zero. It will increment the length field by 2, and set the largest frame field to either its largest frame forwarding size or, if this exceeds the largest frame size already in the RIF, it will leave it alone.

If the bridge receives a frame and the ring number of the port to which the bridge will forward the packet is already in the RIF field, the bridge will not forward the frame to the port indicated by the ring number in the RIF field. The packet has already traversed that ring. Forwarding the packet to that ring would create a loop. The packet, however, will be forwarded to all other ports on the bridge for which the ring number is different.

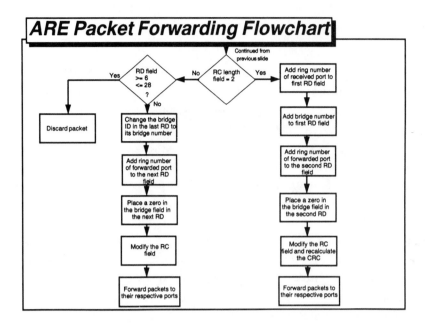

- This flowchart shows the forwarding process of a bridge receiving an ARE frame.

- Although the flowchart reads that the bridge should find the RIF length between 6 and 28, most RIF's are not allowed to exceed 18 bytes.
    This allows for a frame to traverse 7 bridges.
    The RIF length includes a 2-byte RC field.

SPECIFICALLY ROUTED FRAME (SRF)

A specifically routed frame is used when a source route path has been established between the source and destination station. In other words, an explorer packet was transmitted by the source station and it was responded to by the destination station. After the source station chooses the route it wants all future data packets are then specifically routed between the source and destination station as indicated by the RIF.

When a bridge receives an SRF (indicated by a 000 in the broadcast indicators of the RC field), it will read the RIF. Depending on the direction bit, it may read the RDs right to left or left to right. In either case, if a combination of its bridge number and ring in and ring out numbers is not in the RIF, the bridge will discard the packet. In other words, the RIF did not indicate that this bridge should forward the packet. In this way, only one specific path is used by an SRF.

This RIF field will not change throughout the course of the communication between the source and destination end stations. This type of packet gives us the best look into the direction bit. In the RC field is a bit known as the direction bit. This bit is used by the bridge to indicate in which direction to read the RD fields of the RIF. If it is set to a zero, the RIF is read left to right and the path to the destination is being indicated. This is known as the forward direction; the packet is being sent by the source station on its way to the destination. If this bit is set to a 1, the RDs in the RIF should be read right to left. This means the bridge should find the last RD in the RIF field and start reading to the left, looking for the combination of ring in–bridge number–ring out. This means that the packet has been sent by the destination station and is en route to the source station.

The only time that the RIF field may change between two established communicating stations, is when the original path is no longer valid. This could happen if a Token Ring bridge removed itself from the ring. In this case, the source station must find another path. All communication between the source and destination is stopped and the source station will attempt to find another path to the station. This is accomplished using the explorer methods decribed earlier. Once the new path is found, the communication will start again.

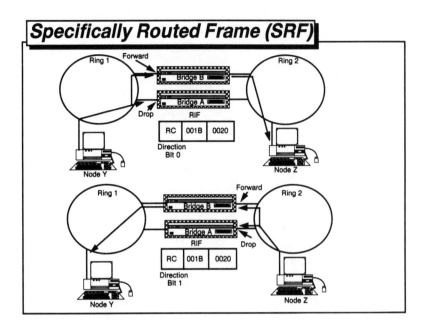

- This frame is used when a source route path has been chosen.

- The RIF field was previously built and the source and destination station simply flip the direction bit to send frames to each other.
  - If the direction bit = 1, the bridge reads the RIF from right to left (backward direction); this indicates a destination to source frame.
  - If the direction bit = 0, the bridge reads the RIF field from left to right (forward direction); this indicates a source to destination frame.

- When the bridge receives an SRF frame (Broadcast Indicator = 000), it must find the following combination in the RIF in order for it to forward the frame out one of its ports:
  - the ring in number, bridge number, and the ring out number in the frame that it can match to its own ports and bridge number.

- Example:
  Node Y transmits a frame to node Z.
  The RIF field is 001B 0020 and the direction bit is a 0 (read the RIF left to right).
  - Bridge A drops the frame.
    + The three-part combination is not found in the RIF.
  - Bridge B forwards the frame.
    + The three-part combination of: received on ring 1, it is bridge B, and it can forward it to ring 2.
  When Node Z responds, the direction bit will be a 1 and the bridges will read the RIF from right to left.

SPECIFICALLY ROUTED FRAME FLOWCHART

In order for a bridge to forward a frame to another ring, if must find a combination of three things:

1. The ring number of the port on which the bridge received the packet.

2. Its bridge number

3. The ring number of the port to which the bridge will forward the packet.

If a bridge receives a frame and it cannot find this combination, it will discard the packet.

If a bridge receives a frame and it finds this combination, but the RIF length field is 0, 4, or an odd number, the frame will be discarded with an invalid RIF field indication.

If a bridge receives a frame and it can find this combination, but there are multiple occurrences of this combination in the RIF field, it will discard the packet (since there may be a loop in the network).

If in the received frame the bridge finds a match to the following combination: ring number of the port on which it received the frame, its bridge number, and the ring number of the port on which it will forward the frame out and if the RIF length field is even and no multiple occurrences of this combination exist in the RIF (indicating a loop), the frame is forwarded out on the port indicated in the RIF field.

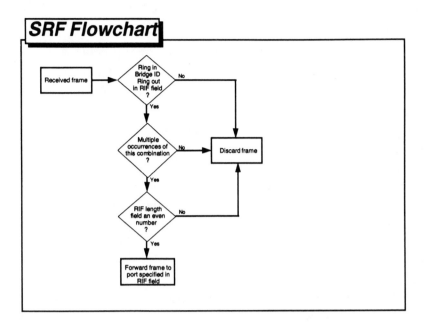

SRF Flowchart

- This is an SRF flowchart showing the process of discarding a frame.

- The bridge will discard the frame if it cannot find this exact combination, in the order shown, somewhere in the RIF before it will forward the frame:
    Ring in
        — The ring number of the port that the bridge received the frame on.
    The bridge ID
        — The bridge number.
    The forward to ring number (ring out)
        — The ring number of the port that the frame will be forwarded out on.

SOURCE ROUTING SUMMARY AND BENEFITS

One of the original problems with Token Ring is that the Token Ring controllers didn't support promiscuous mode. This made it impossible for it to support the transparent bridge protocol. The transparent bridge protocol makes a bridge receive all packets on its attached LANs before making a forwarding decision. Since the early Token Ring chip sets did not support this, source routing became the standard for Token Rings. Today, there is new firmware that does allow Token Ring bridges to operate in promiscuous mode.

Source routing is the Token Ring alternative to transparent bridging. It is a bridging protocol, but there are many differences between source routing and transparent bridging. Source Routing was originally produced for NetBIOS and Token Ring SNA traffic. It originated as a LAN protocol and was never intended to become a major contender for routing traffic. It was built for protocols that could not be routed. The protocol of NetBIOS is a good example. NetBIOS is a session layer protocol used in work group file server networks, and it does not have a network layer implemented in the protocol. It cannot be routed in the true sense of the routing protocol. To provide some routing benefits to these types of protocols, source routing was implemented.

Source routing forces the end station to carry the intelligence of route path discovery and selection. The Token Ring frame was modified so that routing information could be placed in the packet. While this does cause more overhead (discovery packets are placed on the LAN), there are designs in place so that this overhead is kept to a minimum.

A discovery packet (ARE or SRE) is transmitted to the desired destination station by a source station to ensure that the path is available and to ensure that the destination is willing to accept a connection. Source routing leaves all paths open even for redundancy. Specific route descriptors (RD) are placed in the RIF field starting after the RC field that indicate the specific path to take to a destination. These are the ring numbers and bridge numbers of the route used by a packet. These RD are helpful when troubleshooting a source routed network. When a protocol analyzer is placed on the network, you will be able to see what packets are transmitted from any ring and the paths they are trying to take. It enables a network administrator to uniquely indentify stations on any ring.

Source Routing Features

- Source routing requires split intelligence to be carried in the node and the bridge.

- All packets contain routing information, which does produce more overhead.

- Uses STA to configure which bridges will forward single route broadcast packets.

- All paths are active which legally allows loops to be designed.

- Provided a routing solution for those protocols that could not be routed (NetBIOS).

- Easy to follow ring/MAC address for troubleshooting.

SOURCE ROUTING—SUMMARY AND BENEFITS (CONT.)

A single route explorer will be transmitted so that source route bridges using the spanning tree algorithm (STA) will forward the packet to the next LAN only if STA has left their ports in the forwarding state. Remember, STA is an independent protocol that works on source routing as well as transparent bridge networks. It is only transparent bridging that does not work well on Token Ring; source routing that does not work at all on Ethernet.

When two source routing bridges are placed between the same two rings, the STA may be running on these bridges so that only one has the forwarding capability for SRE packets. This significantly reduces the amount of overhead on the LANs for source routing. The twist to this is that even if a bridge has its port blocked for single route explorers, it may still forward all routes explorers.

During the discovery process, AREs may be used to find all paths to a destination, whether it be the source or destination station. When a packet is transmitted in this manner, an end station will receive multiple packets from a single transmitted one (one from each redundant path). The purpose of this is to allow a fairness in the multiple paths between stations. The theory is that, if a path is not busy, then that discovery packet will make it to the desired end station first. If the path was busy, that packet will make it to the desired end station last. Therefore, the fastest path will be chosen, reducing the chance of more load being placed on the slow path.

Source Routing Benefits (cont.)

- Source Routing originated as an alternative to transparent bridging

- Originally, Token Ring could not be placed in promiscuous mode (requirement for transparent bridging) and therefore an alternative model was created

- Allowed for SNA and NetBIOS traffic an attempt to enjoy the benefits of routing
  - As a data link layer implementation

TRANSLATION BRIDGING

To deal with the incompatibilities of communicating between Ethernet and Token Ring networks (only with bridging and not routing), a translational bridge can used. Token Ring and Ethernet packets are formatted differently, and without the use of a translational bridge, stations on either type of LAN cannot communicate with each other. Primarily, this translation only applies to the data link headers of the packet. Remember that Token Ring makes bit 0 the leftmost bit of the byte and Ethernet makes it the rightmost. Refer to those sections for a more detailed explanation.

A translational bridge provides for conversion between different access protocols (token passing and CSMA/CD) and frame format conversion for data transmission between two LAN segments. The following are the frame format conversions provided by tranlation bridging:

- Token Ring to Ethernet MAC layer conversion

- Ethernet to Token Ring MAC layer conversion

- Token Ring to IEEE 802.3 MAC layer conversion

- IEEE 802.3 to Token Ring MAC layer conversion

- Address Resolution Protocol (ARP) translation used for TCP/IP protocols

- Reverse Address Resolution Protocol (RARP) translation used for TCP/IP protocols

- Token Ring to Ethernet for LLC-based protocols

- Ethernet to Token Ring for LLC-based protocols

The Ethernet port of the translational bridge should support:

- Ten Mbps Ethernet V2.0 or IEEE 802.3 and support both of these frame types at the same time

- The Spanning Tree protocol on the Ethernet segment

- The transfer of packets between Token Ring and Ethernet V2.0 or IEEE 802.3 segments. with the appropriate access method and data format conversion

- Isolation and not increase contention problems for either of the two LANs that it interconnects

Translation Bridging

- Due to the incompatibilities of Token Ring and Ethernet (at the MAC layer) a special device is used to convert Token Ring packets to Ethernet packet and visa versa.
- Provides translation for those protocols that cannot be routed as well as those that can be routed.
    - All protocols will be bridged by the 8209.
- Provides for the following conversions between the different access methods and packet formats:
    - Token Ring to Ethernet.
    - Ethernet to Token Ring.
    - Token Ring to IEEE 802.3.
    - IEEE 802.3 to Token Ring.
    - Some network protocol translation.
    - Token Ring to Ethernet for LLC-based protocols.
    - Ethernet to Token Ring for LLC-based protocols.
- Supports:
    - 10 Mbps Ethernet V2.0 or IEEE 802.3 simultaneously.
    - Incorporates STA on the Ethernet segment.
    - Provides for the transfer of packets between Token Ring and Ethernet or IEEE 802.3 segments with the appropriate access method and data format conversion.

THE IBM 8209 BRIDGE

The 8209 provides translation bridging for Ethernet and Token Ring networks. There are many deficiencies with the 8209, no WAN support, but it does provide a good introduction to the translation bridge functions. The 8209 is not standardized by any authority but it does provide the basic translation functions needed. The 8209 is emulated by most bridge vendors and is the accepted method to provide translation bridging for Ethernet and Token Ring networks. The 8209 builds two separate database tables. On the Ethernet port, it operates in promiscuous mode, watching all traffic on the Ethernet segment. While doing this, it builds an *adapter forwarding table*. This is similar to the transparent bridge operation. Included in this table will be the frame format of the Ethernet station (Ethernet V2.0 or IEEE 802.3 frame format). This table allows the 8209 to convert a Token Ring packet to a properly formatted Ethernet packet. Remember that Ethernet V2.0 and IEEE 802.3 frames are formatted differently.

On the Token Ring port of the 8209, the 8209 caches the source address of a received discovery packet into the Token Ring database table. Mated with this source address is the received RIF associated with the source MAC address. Therefore, when the 8209 receives a source route discovery packet (an explorer packet) it reads the source address and the RIF field of the received packet. The 8209 places the source address and its RIF into a table, translates and forwards the packet to the Ethernet port.

The 8209 treats the Ethernet port as a ring in that it is assigned a ring number. When a packet is received on the Ethernet port destined for some ring station for which the 8209 has a table entry, it places the Ethernet's ring number in the RIF before transmitting it to the ring indicated in the RIF database table. This will be illustrated in the following pages. A full example is shown at the end of this section.

A problem arises when the 8209 does not know the Ethernet frame format. It can be either Ethernet or the IEEE 802.3 format. This can happen when a ring station sends an explorer packet to an unknown destination address or to a group address (a multicast or broadcast). The 8209 has a switch selection that forces the 8209 to choose one packet format or another. If the 8209 receives an explorer packet with a group address, for example, it will check a manual switch set at installation time. The switch has two positions. Set in one position, an unknown Token Ring destination frame is forwarded to the Ethernet port with an Ethernet V2.0 frame format. If the switch is set in the alternate position, the unknown destination station frame is forwarded in the IEEE 802.3 frame format to the Ethernet port.

The IBM 8209 Bridge

- The 8209 builds two separate database tables:
  - One for the Ethernet port
    - » which contains the source addresses learned from the Ethernet and their encapsulation types (similar to transparent bridging).
  - One for the Token Ring port
    - » which contains the source address and an associated RIF.
- When the Token Ring port receives an explorer frame:
  - It records to the Token Ring database table:
    - » the source address and the RIF of the frame, and
    - » then converts the frame and forwards the frame to the Ethernet cable segment.
- When the Ethernet port receives a frame:
  - Records the source address and the encapsulation type to the Ethernet table.
    - » Converts the frame and forwards it to the Token Ring.
- The 8209 treats the Ethernet as a Token Ring.
  - A ring number is assigned to it on the 8209.
  - When it receives a frame on the Ethernet port that is destined for the a station on the Token Ring port, it will add the Ethernet's ring number to the RIF before forwarding the frame onto the Token Ring.
- Problems arise when the 8209 does not know the Ethernet encapsulation type.

8209 INTRODUCTION

Using a switch selection to determine the format of the Ethernet packet is constraining. An alternative to this would be to transmit one packet of each type to the Ethernet segment. This would be valid only for certain protocols. Novell NetWare, for example, can use any of four packet types. When the response packet was received, the 8209 could record the packet format of the received packet and any further transmissions would be of that packet type. This introduces more traffic onto the Ethernet segment, but the amount should be negligible since very few of these packets would be transmitted and none would be transmitted once the address was learned on the Ethernet port.

Alternatively, the 8209 could guess, but this is very risky. DECnet and the TCP/IP protocol generally use the Ethernet frame format, but not always. There are implementations that use the IEEE 802.3 format. AppleTalk V2.0, a network protocol used with Apple computers, uses the IEEE 802.3 with SNAP frame format. AppleTalk V1.0 uses the Ethernet V2.0 frame format (most companies have switched to AppleTalk V2.0). There really is no easy answer.

Novell NetWare uses a protocol called Internet Packet Exchange (IPX) to transfer its information across a LAN. As of April 1991, the 8209 provided an enhancement for supporting this protocol. For Ethernet transmission, IPX can use any of four frame formats. In some instances, Novell NetWare must use certain frame types to support certain types of protocols. For example, it must use the IEEE 802.3 SNAP format to support the AppleTalk protocols. What this all boils down to is that the network administrator must be sure that when installing an 8209 bridge, the packet format for all stations that will be communicating through the 8209 should be known.

Please note that the 8209 is not standardized. The IEEE 802 committee is reviewing a standard but has not yet adopted it. Every implementation of this conversion is considered proprietary. A much simpler method of providing Token Ring to Ethernet connectivity is to use a router. Granted there are some protocols that cannot be routed and must be bridged (SNA, NetBIOS, LAT). But most protocols today can be used in a routed environment. A router is smart enough to know how to convert the packets between the media types and which packet type to use in each case.

8209 Introduction (cont.)

- Constraints are placed on a non-standard product.
  - The 8209 is not approved by any standards committee.

- There is a switch setting to determine unknown Ethernet encapsulation types.
  - If the encapsulation type is unknown for an Ethernet bound frame
    - » The 8209 checks a switch setting to forward the frame in either 802.3 or Ethernet encapsulation format.
    - » Alternative would be to forward multiple copies of the frame each with its own encapsulation type and wait for a response.
      - • After receiving a response frame, the 8209 could then mark the encapsulation type and all future frames would use it.
    - » Another alternative would be to make the best guess at the expected encapsulation type, and if it didn't work, use another encapsulation type.

- Novell LAN administrators must be careful when installing this type of bridge.
  - On Ethernet Novell supports up to four encapsulation types.
  - Novell support started in April, 1991.
- If at all possible, use a router to provide connectivity between Ethernet and Token Ring.
  - Routers know of the encapsulation types (Ethernet to Token Ring) and are more efficient when routing the frame.

8209 TOKEN RING (SNAP) TO ETHERNET CONVERSION

This conversion process is fairly simple. For any Token Ring packet received a new packet will be built (translated from the received Token Ring packet) that is forwarded to the Ethernet port. The received Token Ring packet is assumed to have a SubNetwork Access Protocol (SNAP) header and this type of packet is converted to Ethernet by stripping out the RIF, DSAP, SSAP, and control field from the datalink header and protocol ID field from the SNAP header of the Token Ring packet.

Next, the destination and source addresses are copied to the new frame that will be forwarded to the Ethernet port. During this copy procedure, the bytes are bit-reversed. For example, if byte 0 of the destination address contained a 10000010 (binary), the bit conversion process would place a 01000001 (binary) into byte 0 of the destination address of the new Ethernet packet; a 20 (hex) becomes a 40 (hex). Bit-swapping means take each byte and reverse the bit pattern.

Next, the type field portion of the received SNAP header is placed into the type field of the new Ethernet frame. The packet is then forwarded to the Ethernet port.

The bit reversal process can lead to problems such as duplicate and malformed addresses. Ethernet reserves only 1 bit in the destination address (the multicast bit) allowing for 47 bits to be used for addressing (IEEE 802.3 reserves 2 bits just like IEEE 802.5). Therefore, consider an 02 in the first byte of an Ethernet destination address. When it is converted to an IEEE 802.5 MAC address, it becomes a 40. This indicates a Locally Administered Address (LAA). This is okay, but the address might not actually be an LAA or the Ethernet station's address, when translated, may form an LAA that is already used on the Token Ring network. This will cause a duplicate address on the Token Ring network. Having a duplicate address is not fatal, but unknown errors may occur due to this. This is just one example of the kind of problems associated with this conversion.

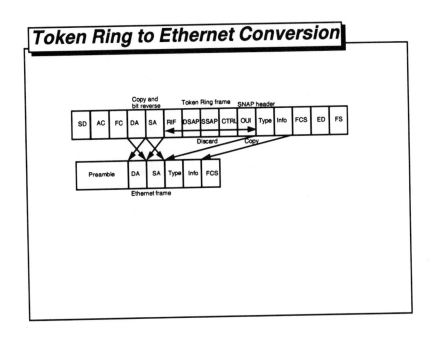

- The received Token Ring frame is assumed to have a SNAP header.

- The frame is converted to Ethernet by stripping the RIF, DSAP, SSAP, control, and SNAP header fields.

- The 8209 places the type field (2 bytes following the OUI) into an Ethernet type field. It does not copy the OUI.

- Copies the destination and source address providing the bit reversal during copy.
  This is for the MAC header only (the physical addresses).
  The bit reversal can lead to address problems.

- The 8209 bridge calculates a new CRC field and transmits the packet to the Ethernet port.

ETHERNET TO TOKEN RING (SNAP) CONVERSION

This conversion is basically the reverse of the Token Ring to Ethernet conversion. The destination and the source address are copied to the new frame (bit reversal takes place during this copy). The 8209 then takes the Type and information fields and copies them over to the new Ethernet packet, to be placed in the SNAP header.

After this, the 8209 retrieves the source route information (the RIF) for this packet. This information is stored in a table in which the 8209 performs a lookup for the destination address of the received packet. This RIF found is inserted directly after the source address field. The 8209 places a SNAP header into the packet with the DSAP and SSAP fields set to AA (hex) and the control field set to 03 (hex). The protocol ID field of the SNAP header will be set to three bytes of zeros (00-00-00), which indicates an encapsulated Ethernet frame.

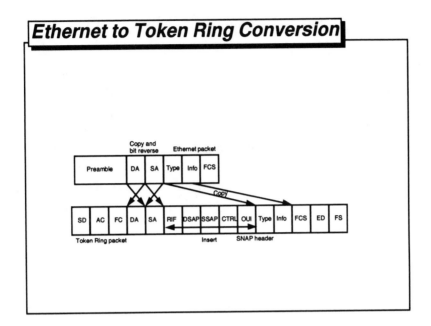

- This is the reverse of the Token Ring to Ethernet conversion.

- The destination and source addresses are copied to the new Token Ring frame
  A bit reversal takes place during the copy.

- The 8209 bridge retrieves the cached RIF from the Token Ring table for the destination address.

- The 8209 bridge places a SNAP header after the DSAP, SSAP, and control fields.

- The OUI has a 00-00-00 header indicating an encapsulated Ethernet frame.

- The type field of the SNAP header will have the type field copied from the received Ethernet frame.

- The 8209 bridge calculates a new FCS field.

- The converted packet is forwarded out the Token Ring port.

TOKEN RING TO IEEE 802.3 CONVERSION

Since the IEEE 802.3 frame is constructed differently than the Ethernet frame, a conversion process is needed for Token Ring to IEEE 802.3. With this type of conversion, only the RIF is extracted from the Token Ring frame and discarded (remember, the 8209 should already have a database table entry for this packet; therefore it can discard the RIF). The destination and source address are copied into the IEEE 802.3 frame and bit-swapped during the copy. The DSAP, SSAP, control, and information fields are then copied to the IEEE 802.3 frame. The 8209 calculates a length field and transmits the frame as an IEEE 802.3 frame to the IEEE 802.3 network. There is not a SNAP header associated with either packet.

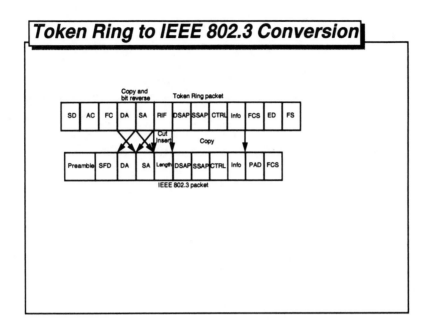

- Only the RIF field is extracted and discarded from the received Token Ring frame.
    The RIF should already be cached in the Token Ring table.

- Destination and source address are copied to the new frame.
    A bit reversal takes place during the copy.

- DSAP, SSAP, and control fields are directly copied into the new frame.

- The 8209 bridge calculates a length field and a new CRC and forwards the IEEE 802.3 frame to the Ethernet port.

IEEE 802.3 TO TOKEN RING CONVERSION

This conversion is basically the reverse of the Token Ring to IEEE 802.3 conversion. The destination address, source address, and the IEEE 802.3 information fields are copied to the Token Ring frame (the addresses are bit-swapped during the copy). The length field is discarded. The 8209 retrieves the RIF for the associated Token Ring destination address and inserts this field after the source address. The frame is then forwarded to the Token Ring port.

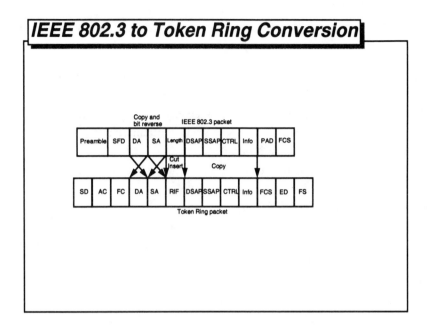

- This conversion is the reverse of the Token Ring to IEEE 802.3 frame conversion.

- The destination and source addresses are copied to the new frame.
    A bit reversal takes place during the copy.

- The bridge copies the DSAP, SSAP, control, and information fields to the new frame.

- The length field is discarded.

- The bridge retrieves the RIF for the destination address from a Token Ring table.
    The bridge inserts the RIF after the source address field.
    The bridge sets the RII bit.

- The 8209 bridge calculates a new FCS and forwards the frame to the Token Ring port.

TOKEN RING TO ETHERNET CONVERSION FOR LLC-BASED PROTOCOLS

Two final conversions will be shown. Although these are not common conversions, the equipment that supports them may still be in use and therefore an example is needed. To support these conversions, the 8209 contains another table, called a Service Access Protocol (SAP) table. If the received Token Ring packet contains a SAP that matches any entry contained in the table, the packet must be formatted according to the following conversion.

When a Token Ring packet receives a packet that it knows is destined for an Ethernet V2.0 station, the 8209 checks its internal SAP table. If the DSAP of the Token Ring packet is 00, 04, 08, or F0 (these are IBM registered SAPs), the conversion process will take place as follows:

The RIF is extracted from the received Token Ring packet and discarded. The destination address, source address, and the DSAP, SSAP, control, and information fields (the datalink headers and the data field of the IEEE 802.2 header), are copied to the Ethernet frame.

The LLC type field (80D5 hex), a length field, and a pad field are then inserted into the Ethernet packet, and the packet is transmitted to the Ethernet segment.

This packet should look peculiar. A type field along with a length and pad field on an Ethernet packet? This is a special conversion for support of an older IBM personal computer known as the IBM PC-RT and the older software operating system of OS/2 EE (extended edition). This also supports Token Ring to Ethernet conversion for the NetBIOS protocol running with the IBM LAN Server program.

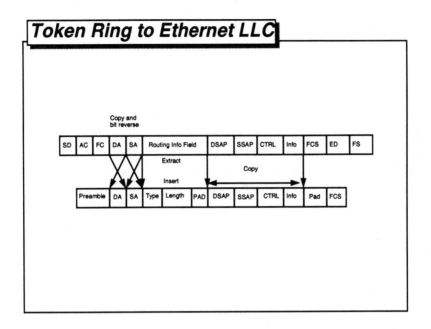

- A special conversion to support certain IBM equipment and protocols.
   These are the IBM PC-RT protocol, OS/2 EE, native NetBIOS, and SNA.

- The 8209 bridge has an internal SAP table.
   These registered SAPs are defined for SNA and NetBIOS.

- If the received frame has a DSAP of 00, 04, 08, FO, F4, or FC, a special conversion takes place.

- The RIF is extracted and discarded.

- The destination and source addresses are copied over to the new packet.
   A bit reversal takes place during the copy.

- The DSAP, SSAP, and control fields are copied to the Ethernet frame.

- A special Type field of 80D5 is used in the Ethernet Type Field.

- A length and pad field are generated and placed in the Ethernet frame.

- A new CRC is calculated and the packet is forwarded out the Ethernet port.

- Obviously, this is a special type of Ethernet packet because the length and pad fields are in the same packet as an Ethernet type field.

ETHERNET TO TOKEN RING CONVERSION FOR LLC-BASED PROTOCOLS

This conversion is the reverse of the previous LLC-based protocol conversion. Upon the Ethernet port receiving this type of packet (indicated by the 80D5 [hex] in the type field), the type, length, and pad fields are extracted and discarded. The source and destination fields are copied into the Token Ring frame (a bit swap process is performed during the copy). The DSAP, SSAP, control, and information fields are copied to the new Token Ring frame.

The 8209 then looks up the RIF entry in the Token Ring database table and inserts it into the Token Ring frame. The 8209 then forwards this frame onto the Token Ring.

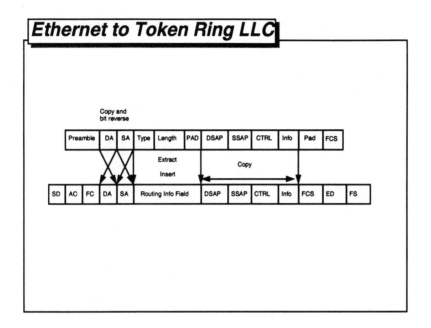

- Basically, this is the reverse process of the Token Ring to Ethernet LLC conversion.

- The 8029 receives the frame with an 80D5 Ethernet Type field.

- The type, length, and pad fields are extracted and discarded.

- Destination and source addresses are copied.
    A bit reversal takes place during the copy.

- The 8209 bridge obtains a RIF field from the Token Ring table associated with the destination address.

- A new FCS is calculated, and the frame is forwarded to the Token Ring port.

CONSIDERATION OF THE ADDRESS RESOLUTION PROTOCOL

It is not the point of this book to explain the TCP/IP protocol, but there will be readers who are familiar with it, and these readers need to know about the ARP packet traversing the 8209 bridge. Those readers who are not familar with the protocol may skip this topic and continue with FDDI bridging topic.

TCP/IP addresses are based on a four-octet, 32-bit address. This is known as a *protocol address*. The TCP/IP protocol was not originally developed to run on high-speed LANs. When this protocol was developed, it primarily ran on host computers that were tied together with a synchronous communications medium. This was a point-to-point topology, meaning that the only hosts on the medium were the two communicating hosts. Therefore, the TCP/IP address was sufficient to identify these machines.

TCP/IP eventually migrated to high-speed LANs, but high-speed LANs were developed to run as protocol-independent. A controller attached to a high-speed LAN had its own unique (usually 48-bit) address. This address had to be mapped to the 32-bit TCP/IP protocol address. The Address Resolution Protocol (ARP) accomplished this.

On an extended LAN, in order to find a destination station's 48-bit MAC address, the ARP protocol will send a query packet known as an ARP request. The destination MAC address of this ARP request is set to broadcast. Also inside the packet, beyond the data link headers, is a field set to the desired destination station's IP address and an empty field for the desired destination station's MAC address. When the destination station receives this *ARP request*, it responds with an ARP reply. In this reply, the destination station places its MAC address in an empty field and sends the packet back to the source.

Consideration of the ARP Frame

- Other problems will surface beyond the address duplication problem (bit swap).

- Certain protocols were written with the routing concept built in.

    - Bridges were not existent when the network protocols were written.

- An example is TCP/IP.
    - IP host addresses are based on a 32-bit (four-octet) address.
    - Address is not associated with a MAC address.
    - IP address must be mapped to a station's MAC address.
    - IP process to find a MAC address is known as Address Resolution Protocol, or ARP.
    - ARP is not part of any protocol layer in TCP/IP.
    - Inside the ARP request/response frame are MAC addresses (beyond the MAC header).
    - Internal MAC addresses must be bit-swapped just as the MAC address headers are.

THE 8209 AND THE ARP PACKET

Now there are two places that need to be bit-swapped: the MAC address inside the packet and the source and destination address on the MAC header of the packet. The 8209 usually only bit-swaps the MAC headers of a packet. The 8209 needs to be programmed so that is knows where else in a packet the MAC addresses may reside.

The 8209 bridge is acutely aware of this type of packet and is able to handle it. TCP/IP usually communicates on an Ethernet LAN using the Ethernet frame format. Therefore, when an 8209 bridge receives this type of broadcast packet on its Token Ring or Ethernet port, it must broadcast to its Ethernet or Token Ring port. It shows only the ARP packet and assumes that the reader knows how an Ethernet/Token Ring packet conversion takes place.

The hardware field is converted to indicate either Token Ring or Ethernet. The protocol, header length, protocol length, operation code, senders, and target (destination) IP address are copied to the new frame (either Token Ring or Ethernet). The source hardware address and the destination hardware address (do not confuse these with the physical or MAC addresses) are bit-converted before they are put into the new frame. The target hardware address is usually filled with zeros, though not always (dependent on the programmer, trash bytes could be in this field).

The ARP request/reply frame has an Ethernet type field of 0806 (hex). An ARP request/response packet is not part of the IP header. In fact, it does not contain an IP header and therefore it cannot traverse any routers (it shouldn't need to anyway). This is a standalone packet. For more information on the TCP/IP protocol please refer to *The Protocol Handbook,* published by McGraw-Hill, Inc., 1993.

It will simply be stated here that this conversion process must also take place for the RARP (Reverse Address Resolution Protocol). Basically, this is when a TCP/IP workstation starts up knowing its MAC address but not its IP address. The workstation will send a RARP request packet out for this information directed to a single station on the LAN known as the RARP server. The RARP server should be able to answer and give the requesting workstation its IP address. Diskless workstations are the best example for this protocol need. The RARP protocol uses the same packet format as the ARP protocol and the conversion process is the same. Its Ethernet type is 8035, and the 8209 will recognize this.

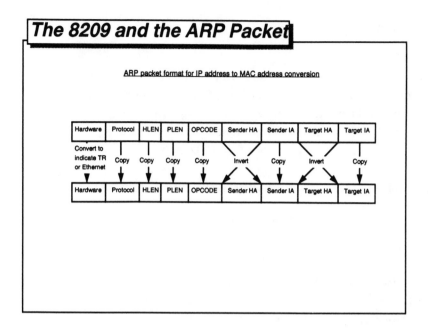

- The IBM 8209 is aware of the TCP/IP ARP packet.

  An ARP packet is indicated by an 0806 in the Ethernet Type field.

  It is indicated by a 0806 in the Type field of a SNAP header of a Token Ring frame.

- ARP requests are sent as MAC-addressed broadcast packets.

  The 8209 must forward this packet in either direction.

- The bit swap must be performed not only on the MAC header but also inside the packet in the field of the Sender HA (hardware address, or MAC address) and the Target HA.

An 8209 Example

A Token Ring source station A would like to talk to an Ethernet destination station Z. Between station A and station Z is one ring. Station A will send out an explorer packet (assuming it has not found the source on the local ring) for station Z. Token Ring bridge 1 will receive this packet and insert two RDs into the RIF (I have skipped the RC field for simplicity here):

001E 0020

The 8209 will receive this explorer packet and place in its Token Ring database table the following entry:

Station A - 001E 002F 0030

This means that the 8209 inserted its bridge number (2) and the outgoing ring number (3) into its table. The 8209 treats the Ethernet port as a ring number. Ring 3 is the Ethernet port.

Since the packet is a broadcast packet, the 8209 will use the switch setting to determine the frame format when it forwards the frame to the Ethernet port.

When the frame returns, the 8209 will note the frame format, convert the Ethernet frame to a Token Ring Frame, insert the cached RIF entry into the RIF, and transmit the SNAP packet onto the Token Ring. Station A would receive this frame and believe that the destination station's path is:

ring 1 to bridge E, ring 2 to bridge F, ring 3.

This means that the destination station is on ring 3. When assigning ring numbers to the 8209 it is helpful to assign the Ethernet port's ring number so that it is uniquely identified as an 8209 Ethernet port.

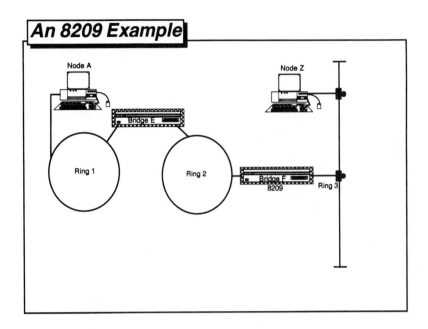

An 8209 Example

• Stations A and Z are separated by two Token Rings and one Ethernet.

• Station A sends an explorer frame looking for station Z.
  Bridge 1 receives the explorer frame and places entries in the RIF field.
  The RIF now reads: RC 001E 0020 (RC is the routing control field).

• The 8209 receives this frame and caches the source address and RIF entry as:
  station address A - 001E 002F 0030, and the direction bit is set to a 1.
      — Ring 3 was added as the third RD because the 8209 treats the Ethernet as a ring
  Frame will be converted and forwarded in some format to the Ethernet, using the beforementioned
      process, appearing as an Ethernet packet.

• Upon receipt of the response frame (on the Ethernet port of the 8209), the 8209 will convert the Ethernet
  frame into a Token Ring frame.

• The MAC addresses are copied (bit-swapped), and the RIF is retrieved from the cache.
  It is inserted into the Token Ring frame.
  A SNAP header is placed in the frame.
  Included in the RIF field will be ring 3 in the final RD.

• The frame is then sent back to the originator on the Token Ring (station A).

FDDI BRIDGING

The IEEE 802.1h specification standardizes how Ethernet and IEEE 802 LANs can communicate. This specification does not specify how to translate between source route Token Ring LANs and FDDI. It pertains only to Ethernet or IEEE 802.3 translation to and from FDDI. Remember, it is best to route packets between different media types, because the expected results are easier to attain than with bridging. But for those who require a bridge for the translation of media and MAC types, the following recommended practice is shown.

There is a standard that will bridge any protocol between Ethernet and FDDI. There is not a standard (as of this writing) for Token Ring to FDDI bridging. Even though the FDDI standard allows for source route packets, it is not practically used. This does not mean that Token Ring data may not traverse an FDDI network. FDDI bridges do provide a way to encapsulate Token Ring data in order for it to traverse an FDDI ring.

Therefore there are two ways to bridge different access methods (Ethernet or Token Ring) through FDDI networks: translation and encapsulation. Translation will take a received packet and translate to a native medium format for the forwarded LAN. In this case, it will enable any Ethernet station to communicate directly with an FDDI station. The only access method that supports this is Ethernet. Therefore, Ethernet stations can communicate directly with FDDI stations through FDDI translation bridges. On the other hand, encapsulation means that the FDDI network will be used only as a transport. A packet that has been encapsulated for transport on the FDDI network cannot be received by any station on the FDDI network. The FDDI network will be used for transport only. An example of this is Token Ring to FDDI. For example, if an FDDI network separates two Token Ring networks, and one of the Token Ring networks wants to talk to the other Token Ring, the bridges that separate the two Token Rings will encapsulate the packets between the Token Ring networks. The problem is, only the two Token Rings will communicate. If either Token Ring needs to communicate to any station on the FDDI, it cannot. There is not a standard that provides the bridge translation between the two.

There are four concerns with FDDI bridging:

1. Forwarding from Ethernet or IEEE 802.3 to FDDI

2. Forwarding from FDDI to Ethernet or IEEE 802.3

3. Encapsulating packets

4. Protocols that require tunneling (only one is defined here—Phase 2 AppleTalk Address Resolution Protocol [AARP])

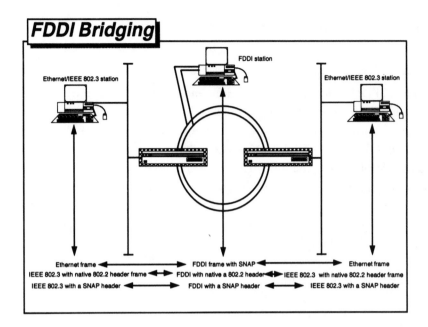

- The above picture depicts the interaction of FDDI and Ethernet/IEEE 802.3 frames.

- The FDDI LAN can send and receive frames to and from the Ethernet/IEEE 802.3 stations.
    In other words, stations on the Ethernet/IEEE 802.3 LANs can communicate directly with the FDDI stations.
        — This is not possible with Token Ring to FDDI communication except through proprietary methods.
    This is an example of the translating function.

- Encapsulating bridges simply use the FDDI as a tunnel.
    Stations on the IEEE 802.3/Ethernet cannot communicate directly with any station on the FDDI.
    An example of this would be Token Ring to FDDI bridging.
        — Token Ring can only use the FDDI LAN as a transport.
        — This also would require two bridges from the same vendor's bridges.

- Encapsulating bridges can only talk to the same vendor's bridges.

ETHERNET TO FDDI (SNAP) BRIDGING

For received Ethernet frames, the destination and source addresses will be copied to the FDDI frame. Since Ethernet and FDDI transmit their bytes differently (bit 0 is the leftmost bit of a byte on FDDI and bit 0 is the rightmost bit of a byte on Ethernet), a bit conversion will take place during the conversion (for more information on this process see the IBM 8209 section). A SNAP header will be placed on the FDDI frame. The DSAP and SSAP will be set to AA. The control field will be set to 03. The organizationally unique identifier (OUI, the first three bytes of the SNAP header) will be set to 00-00-00 (to indicate an encapsulated Ethernet frame) and the type field will be copied from the Ethernet frame to the type field of the SNAP header. The data field from the Ethernet frame will simply be copied to the FDDI frame. A new FCS (CRC-32) will be calculated and then the frame will be transmitted onto the FDDI.

Stations on the FDDI can receive and process this packet if it is broadcast or multicast or if it is uniquely identified to that FDDI station.

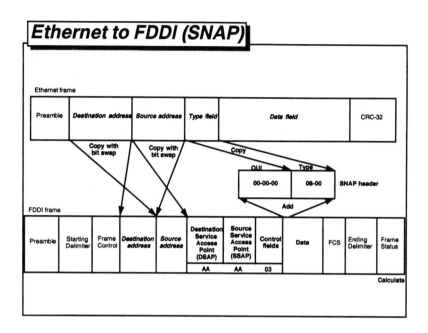

- The above illustration shows how an Ethernet packet is converted to an FDDI frame.

- The text in italic indicates the fields that are affected.
    The source and destination addresses are copied over.
    A SNAP header is added to the FDDI frame.
    The DSAP and SSAP fields are set to AA (hex).
    The control field is set to 03 (HEX).
    The OUI header will be filled with 00-00-00.
        — This indicates an encapsulated Ethernet frame.
    The type field is copied over.
    A new FCS is calculated, and the frame is then transmitted to the FDDI LAN.

- Please note that the 80-00 used in the Type field is an example only.

IEEE 802.3 WITH A NATIVE IEEE 802.2 HEADER

For IEEE 802.3 packets that are received with true LLC 802.2 headers (the DSAP and SSAP are filled with registered SAPs; E0 for Novell NetWare, for example), the frame will be translated to FDDI without SNAP headers. The destination and source addresses are copied to the FDDI frame. A bit conversion takes place during this copy. After this the 802.2 header will be directly copied to the FDDI. The data field is copied and a new FCS is calculated. The frame is then transmitted on the FDDI network as a native FDDI packet.

Stations on the FDDI can receive and process this packet if it is a broadcast or multicast, or if it is uniquely identified to that FDDI station.

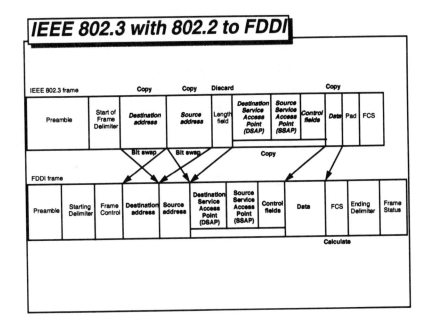

- The above picture shows how an IEEE 802.3 frame with a native 802.2 header is converted to FDDI.

- The text in italic indicates the fields that are affected.

- The source and destination addresses are copied to the FDDI frame.
    A bit conversion takes place during this copy.

- The length field is discarded.

- The 802.2 headers are copied to the FDDI frame.

- The data field is copied to the FDDI frame.

- A new FCS is calculated and the frame is then transmitted on the FDDI LAN.

IEEE 802.3 WITH SNAP TO FDDI WITH SNAP

If the bridge receives an IEEE 802.3 frame with a SNAP header, the frame will be translated to the FDDI with a SNAP header. The destination and source addresses will be copied to the FDDI frame. A bit conversion takes place during this conversion. The length field will be discarded. The IEEE 802.3 SNAP header is then placed into the SNAP fields of the FDDI frame which will contain the OUI assigned by the particular company. It will be set to a number other than 00-00-00, that uniquely identifies the vendor (08-00-07 to indicate Apple Computer, for example). This will indicate an IEEE 802.3 frame when it is translated from FDDI back to the Ethernet. After the OUI, the Ethernet type field will be copied. The data field will be copied and a new FCS will be calculated. The FDDI frame is then transmitted on the FDDI.

Stations on the FDDI can receive and process this packet if it is a broadcast or multicast, or if it is uniquely identified to that FDDI station.

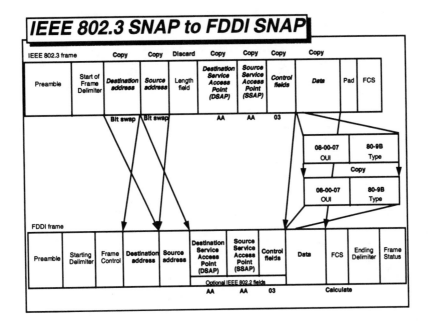

- The above diagram shows the process of converting a received IEEE 802.3 packet with a SNAP header to an FDDI frame.

- The text that is in italic indicates the fields that are affected.

- The source and destination addresses are copied (bit-swapped) to the FDDI frame.

- The length field is discarded.

- The DSAP, SSAP, and control fields are copied over.

- The SNAP header is copied over.

- The data field is copied over.

- A new FCS is calculated and the frame is transmitted on the FDDI LAN.

- The values used in the OUI and Type fields are examples only.

FDDI TO ETHERNET OR IEEE 802.3

Basically this is the reverse of the Ethernet to IEEE 802.3 translation.

FDDI to Ethernet or IEEE 802.3

- This process is the reverse of the beforementioned conversion.
- Reverse the process to convert a frame received on the FDDI port of the translation bridge and forwarded to the Ethernet port.

FDDI Translation Bridging Gotcha

There is one case that a translation bridge has to be aware of. This is when the received packet is an AppleTalk Phase 2 AARP packet. Basically, AppleTalk uses its own set of addresses to uniquely identify AppleTalk stations, called an *AppleTalk protocol address*. It uses these addresses because AppleTalk originally ran on (and still supports) an access method known as LocalTalk, which is built into every Apple Computer device. This was developed by Apple Computer as an inexpensive method of hooking together Apple devices. To translate between the AppleTalk addresses and the 6-byte MAC addresses used on LANs, AppleTalk uses the AppleTalk Address Resolution Protocol (actually borrowed from the TCP/IP protocol's ARP).

To operate on an IEEE 802 LAN, AppleTalk Phase 2 uses the IEEE 802.3 or IEEE 802.5 packet format with a SNAP header. Usually the SNAP header OUI is set to 08-00-07 and the Type field is set to 80-9B to indicate AppleTalk protocols running on an IEEE 802 LAN. But Phase 2 AARP's SNAP header uses 00-00-00 as the OUI. Even though it is being used with IEEE 802 headers, this OUI indicates an Ethernet encapsulated packet format (via a de facto standard known as RFC 1042.) Reception of this type of packet by a translating bridge requires the original packet to be tunneled, not translated, using a SNAP header on the tunneled packet with the OUI set to 00-00-F8. This keeps the bridge from incorrectly determining the forwarded frame format.

In tunneling the *whole* received packet is encapsulated. The original packet is simply surrounded by FDDI headers and trailers and placed on the FDDI. Other bridges will de-encapsulate this packet and place the original packet back onto an Ethernet segment.

It is recommended to upgrade to AppleTalk Phase 2, which provides many more capabilities than Phase 1. Also, most routing vendors do not support Phase 1, requiring that Phase 1 protocols be bridged.

FDDI Translation Gotcha

- AppleTalk uses the Ethernet Type field of 80F3 for the AppleTalk Address Resolution Protocol (AARP).
    - Converts AppleTalk addresses to MAC addresses.
    - Similar to the TCP/IP ARP protocol.

- AppleTalk uses this for Ethernet or IEEE 802.3 encapsulated frames.
    - For IEEE 802.3 frames, AppleTalk uses a SNAP header
        » Normally the OUI is set to 08-00-07 to indicate Appletalk phase 2 protocols.
        » The problem is that AppleTalk uses 00-00-00 as the OUI for AARP.
        » This will cause a translation bridge to misinterpret it as an encapsulated Ethernet frame
            • A translation bridge will receive this and put it back out on the Ethernet as an Ethernet format frame instead of an IEEE 802.3 frame with SNAP.

    - If a translation bridge receives this frame it should automatically use SNAP on the FDDI frame.
        » Exception here in that the OUI field will be set to 00-00-F8.
        » The type field will be set to 80F3 to indicate tunneling for FDDI.
            • The whole original frame (no translation) will be tunneled through the FDDI LAN.
            • The bridge will tunnel the whole Ethernet frame.
            • The bridge will tunnel the whole IEEE 802.3 frame.

FDDI Bridge Encapsulation

Encapsulating bridges were the first type available for FDDI. When FDDI was first introduced it was used primarily in backbone networks. Other, lower-speed networks were interconnected through FDDI. To provide for this, FDDI encapsulation bridges were used.

There is not a standard for encapsulation so each vendor provides a different method. This means that if there are four encapsulating bridges on an FDDI LAN, two manufactured by vendor X and two manufactured by vendor Y, a packet encapsulated by vendor X's bridge can not be seen by vendor Y's bridge. Encapsulating bridges that receive packets that are destined for another station on the other side of an FDDI LAN are encapsulated in an FDDI packet. During the encapsulation, the whole received packet, with the exception of the CRC field (MAC headers and data field, but not the CRC field), are encapsulated in an FDDI packet, which can be seen only by other bridges from the same vendor.

The IEEE 802.1h specification is a standard used for translating Ethernet/ EEE 802.3 bridges to FDDI. Token Ring to FDDI is not yet standardized and therefore each implementation is proprietary, and encapsulation is the preferred method.

Note that FDDI will act as a source route hop with Token Ring encapsulation. The RIF will be changed to indicate this in the Token Ring packet. The many proprietary methods used lead to non-compatible bridges.

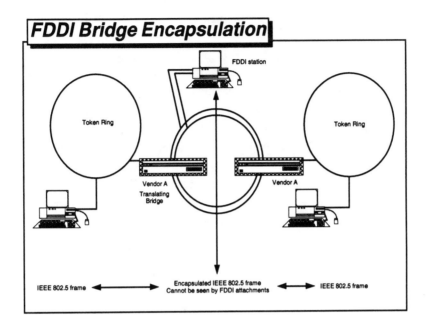

- Encapsulating bridges take received frames and place FDDI headers and trailers around the original frame.
    The original frame includes the original MAC header and original data.
        — A new FCS is calculated after the FDDI MAC headers and trailers are added.
    Encapsulated frames use the FDDI only as a transit system.
    This topology can be found in backbone topologies for Token Ring.
        — There is no standard for Token Ring to FDDI bridging.
        — Stations on the FDDI ring will not be able to receive and process the encapsulated frame.
        — Requires that two bridges be from the same vendor on the FDDI.
    For source route bridging , the FDDI LAN acts as a one source route hop.
    The encapsulating bridges will place a ring number and bridge ID in the RIF field of the received and forwarded frames.

AN INTRODUCTION TO ROUTERS

Routers also forward packets to their appropriate destinations but operate completely differently than the way a bridge operates. Routers separate networks into regions. Network stations are grouped together into a specific region. Each of the regions is assigned a unique number called a *network number*. This is not the same as a MAC address. It is more like the area code in the telephone system. Routers forward packets to the specific network number, operating at the OSI network layer. Packet forwarding is based on network IDs, not on the MAC addresses.

A router routes packets based on the protocol that runs on its LAN. Most routers are multiprotocol; one unit may perform routing functions with many different types of protocols.

Like bridges, routers can interconnect both local and remote sites. To connect remote sites, routers use serial (telephone) lines.

Introduction to Routers

- Routers are data forwarding devices but operate differently than a transparent or source route bridge.

- Routers separate networks into regions.
  - Each region is assigned a unique network number.

- These network numbers are unique for each network they are assigned to.
  - They are not the MAC address.

- Packet forwarding is based on these network IDs.

- Routers route packets based on a protocol as well as a network ID.

- Most routers today are multiprotocol in that one box can forward different protocol packets.

- Routers, like bridges, can be used locally or remotely.

ROUTING

True network-layer routing offers many different capabilities from bridging. Most LAN protocols were built with a network layer, thereby enabling them to be routed. Routing is a technique that forwards packets to their destinations based on a unique network number, which is similar to the area code of the phone system. The benefits of routing over bridging are so tremendous that a saying goes: "Route if you can, bridge if you can't!"

This is stretching it, but an analogy can be drawn to the telephone system. When making a local phone call, you simply dial the seven-digit number of the desired destination phone. The phone company's local switch receives the call and routes it locally to its destination. But if the destination you want is in a different state, for example calling from New York to California, you must dial the area code for California before the call can be routed to there. The local switches determine that the call is not local and route it to other switches, which route it to the remote destination. At the remote destination, the phone company's local switches will forward the call to the final destination. The concept is similar for routing data packets.

Routing offers a more elegant method of moving packets to their final destination. Like area codes, individual network stations are assembled under one umbrella called a *network number*. Any number of network stations can be grouped to one network number (within the limitations of the specific LAN and network protocol specification). This is accomplished so that packets destined to a network station may be routed based on a network number and not on an individual end station address. Most routing protocols do not keep track of individual end stations, only of network numbers. That is, routers have no idea where network stations are really positioned on the network, but they do know where all the network numbers are on the network and route based on the destination network number located inside the packet. This reduces the routing table size and allows routers to become faster and more efficient.

Networks combined together form an internet.

Routing

- Most network protocols were designed with network-layer routing.

- Routers base forwarding decisions on an embedded network number in the network layer header of the packet.

- Network numbers can be thought of as area codes in the phone system.
    - Must use the area code to call different areas.

- Any number of end stations may be assigned to one network number.
    - Most routers do not keep track of individual end stations' addresses.

- Network numbers group network stations into one or more network numbers.

- Taken as a whole, routers combine networks and form internets.

ROUTER INFORMATION IN THE PACKET

Network layer information is placed in a packet after the data link headers; an Ethernet packet remains in the range of 64 bytes (minimum) to 1,518 bytes (maximum). Up to the data link level there are specific areas of the packet that are reserved fields. The source and destination MAC address and the type field are reserved at the beginning of the packet. The four-byte CRC field at the end of the packet is also reserved. This leaves 1,500 bytes for data. It can be any kind of data, whether it is user data or network control information. It is in this area that the network layer places its specific information.

The network layer header information contains much more than simple network numbers. Each protocol is different with the type of network layer information that is added to the packet. The important point is that the network number is placed in the beginning of the data portion of the packet as part of the network layer header.

Each upper layer in the OSI model has specific information to add to the packet that will be used by the receiving station. This information is used by each respective OSI layer in the receiving station and includes the connection IDs, sequence numbers, acknowledgments, session numbers, and so on. This is all network control information that is used by the network stations to understand how to process a packet. End-user data is also placed in this field after all the OSI layer-information headers.

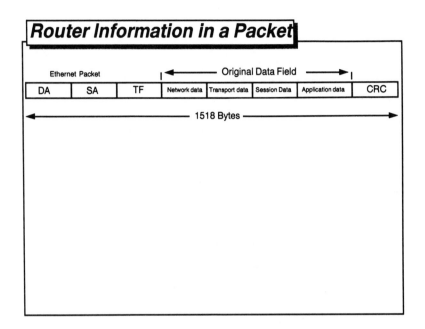

- Each OSI layer implementation in the hardware and software of a LAN controller will be placed in the packet.

- Network layer information is placed in the data field of a packet.
    Contained in this header will be network numbers.
    The network layer header contains more than just network numbers.

- Source and destination MAC address fields are reserved at the beginning of the packet.

- Whatever bytes in the packet the hardware and software headers do not consume are left for user data or control information.

ROUTERS—OPERATION

Each protocol used on a network is different. The text in this section discusses a protocol called Xerox Network System (XNS) Internet Datagram Protocol (IDP), a network layer implementation developed by Xerox Corporation. Other protocols are similar to those discussed in the following text—Novell NetWare, for instance—but there are great differences between the protocols on routing. The following will strictly explain XNS.

Routers forward packets based on network numbers. These special network identifiers are usually assigned to a router's ports when the router is first configured. Routers determine the network number for each LAN. Each separate network is assigned a unique network number. The individual network that contains a network number can be made up of multiple bridges and repeaters to extend the LAN. But the same network number will apply to all network attachments. Only when a router is traversed will the network number change.

In the case of XNS, end stations only know the number of the network to which they are directly attached. The router holds the numbers of all the networks that it knows about, and distributes these network numbers to the end stations upon request.

When a source station would like to transmit a packet to a destination station, the source station will compare the destination network number to its own local network number. If the two match, the destination is on the local network (like a local phone call). If the network numbers do not match, the source station must use a router to forward the packet to its final destination.

The source station may already have a router's MAC address in a local table, or it may have to transmit a special packet on the network requesting for that information from a router (*an all-routers broadcast packet*). The source station places in this packet, the desired destination network number and transmits it to the network in the hope that a router will respond. A router should respond indicating to the source station that it knows about the desired network number and it can route the packet there. The source station gives the packet to that router for it to forward to the final network.

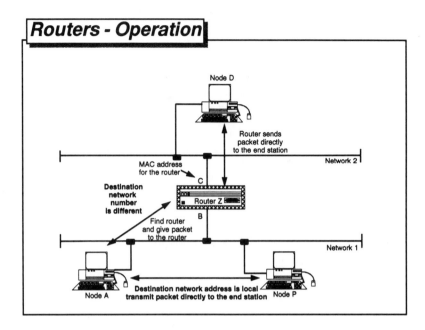

- Routers forward packets based not on the MAC address of the packet but on the network number inside the packet.

- Each network separated by a route is assigned a unique network number.

- End stations know only of the network number of the network to which they are attached.

- Before an end station transmits a packet, it compares the network number of the destination to its network number.

>   If the network numbers are the same, the packet is simply transmitted on the cable, addressed to the destination station.
>
>   — The destination station is local.
>
>   If the network numbers do not match, the end station must find a router that it can send the packet to, so that it can be forwarded to the proper network.
>
>   The requesting station will submit a special type of packet to the network requesting information from the routers.
>
>   — The requesting station acquires the router address by some means specific to the protocol.

ROUTERS—DIRECTLY ATTACHED NETWORKS

The source station builds a packet to send to the router. The destination MAC address of the packet is addressed to the router and not to the final destination station. The packet is MAC addressed to the router so that the router can receive and process it. The final destination station's MAC address is held in the network header portion of the packet to be used by the final router in the path. The final router extracts this MAC address from the network header and routes the packet directly to the destination station.

After the router receives this packet, it determines how to forward the packet. The router contains a table of network numbers in which the router looks up the destination network number. If the router finds the destination network number, it then determines whether it is directly attached to the destination network or if another router is needed to get the packet to its final destination.

If the destination network number is directly attached to the router, the router extracts the destination MAC address out of the network header and places it in the destination MAC address. It places its own MAC address in the source MAC address header, then forwards the packet to the network.

The destination station receives this packet and if necessary responds to the source station using the same method.

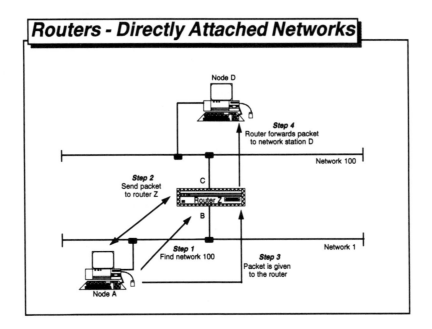

Routers - Directly Attached Networks

• A router receives the request and, if it can find the network number, it sends a response back to the requesting station.

• Node A picks the path that has the lowest cost to the final destination.
     There is only one router response in this example.

• Node A sends the packet to router Z.
     The source MAC address is A and the destination MAC address is B.

• The destination network is located on the other side of the router.
     Packet is forwarded by the router directly to the end station.
     Packet is addressed with source address as the router's address C.
     Destination address will be the destination end station D.

• If the destination network is not on the other side of the router, the router should have the next router's address to get to the destination in its routing table and the packet is forwarded to the next router.

• Different network protocols operate differently.
     This example pertains to XNS.

ROUTERS—NON-DIRECTLY ATTACHED NETWORKS

If the destination network number is not directly attached to the router, the router has to forward the packet to another router. The routing table includes the MAC address of the next router to receive the packet for the target destination network number. The router builds a new packet that sets the MAC destination address to the next router and the source MAC address will be its own. The rest of the packet will contain the original contents of the received packet. In other words, the router rebuild only the data link header portion of the packet. It then transmits the packet out the port indicated by the routing table. Now the MAC addresses of the packet are of the two routers. Remember, the original source and final destination MAC addresses are placed in the network header.

When the new router receives the packet, it processes the packet as previously stated. If the destination network number is directly attached, the new router will deliver the packet to the destination end station. If the destination network number is not directly attached, it finds the next router to forward the packet to, and that router will then determine the next fowarding of the packet.

Every router in the path between a source and destination station processes the packet in this manner. The router whose destination network number is directly attached to it delivers the packet to the destination station. It will set the destination MAC address to the MAC address that is embedded in the network header. It uses its own MAC address for the source MAC address.

Routers -- Non-Directly Attached Networks

- If the destination network is not directly attached to the router, the router will forward the packet to another router in the forwarding path of the destination network.
- Router-to-router communication is directly MAC addressed.

- All routers in the path will perform the same decisions as the previous router.

- The last router in the path to the destination will forward the packet directly to the destination.

- Important to note that the data link MAC headers will constantly change while the packet is being forwarded.
  - Very little information in the network header will change.
    - » The network layer header in the packet will contain the originator's full address and final destination address of the packet.
    - » The full address of a network station is the combination of the network ID and its MAC address.
      - This uniquely identifies any station on the internet.

Routing Diagram

In the following diagram, the source and destination networks are separated by three routers. Each of the four LANs has a separate and unique network number. For simplicity, the networks have been assigned a network number of 1 to 4. In reality, XNS employs a 32-bit mechanism for network numbers.

Next, notice that each attachment to the network has a unique MAC address. The source station—a PC in this case—is assigned a MAC address of A and the destination station is assigned a MAC address of H.

The source station wants to transmit a packet to the destination station. It has to use the router in order to deliver the packet. If source station A does not have the MAC address of a router to deliver the packet to, it sends a request packet out to the network. This request packet contains the destination network number (network 4). Upon receipt of this packet Router Z knows that it can deliver the packet to network 4, and responds to source station A.

Source station A builds a packet and sets the destination MAC address to B (the router's MAC address) and the source MAC address to A. This is placed in the data link header of the packet. Station A then places the MAC address of the destination host, H, and its own MAC address in the network header. Also in the network header are the final source and destination network numbers, which will be 1 and 4 respectively. Other things are placed in the network header, but they are beyond the scope of this book.

When router A receives this packet, it looks in a table of network numbers for the destination network number that it extracted from the network header. It notices that it is not directly attached and therefore, it also looks up the address of the next router in line to the destination—in this case, router Y. Router Z sets the destination MAC address to D (router Y's MAC address) and the source MAC address to its own. The network header information is not touched.

Router Y forwards the packet to router X, which determines that the destination network is directly attached. Router X extracts the destination MAC address out of the network header and forwards the packet to host H. The source MAC address is G (router X's MAC address).

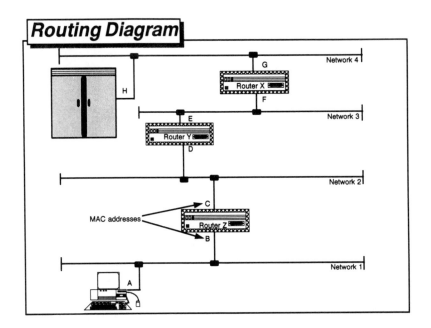

• Each of the four above LANs have unique network numbers 1 through 4.

• Each station has its own unique MAC address.

• Example:
  Station A wants to transmit a packet to station H.
  — Those stations reside on different networks.
  Station A requests information about network 4.
  — Router Z responds with that information.
  Station A transmits the packet to router Z.
  — The MAC source address is A and the MAC destination address is B.
  Router Z receives the packet.
  — The destination network is not local so router Z transmits the packet to router Y with the MAC source address C and MAC destination address D.
  The destination network is not local to router Y, and router Y gives it to router X.
  The destination network number is local to router X.
  — Router X extracts the destination end station's MAC address from the network header.
  — Router X transmits the packet to end station H with a source address of G (router X's MAC address).
  — Router X transmits the packet to station H.

NETWORK NUMBERS

It should now be understood how end stations and routers interoperate to deliver packets. With routers added to the networking scenario, there are now two types of identification on the network. The first is the MAC (or physical layer) address of every network attachment. This identifies a network attachment only at the physical level. All these addresses must be unique even when they are separated by a router.

The second identification level is the network address. The network address groups network stations into one common number. This is used for routing purposes. Network stations not separated by a router all have the same network number, but their MAC addresses are different.

For XNS, network numbers are 32 bits (4 bytes) long. This represents the possibility of 4,294,967,294 network numbers—more than is conceivable for any single XNS internet. MAC layer addresses are 48 bits long, but remember that the first 3 bytes are reserved to be assigned by the IEEE to indicate the vendor.

Therefore, with XNS, to route a packet to its final destination we must know the network and MAC addresses of the destination. How are these addresses found? An end stations can determine its network number by listening to the network. Routers periodically broadcast their tables out to the network; when an end station receives this packet it can determine the local network ID. Other methods include assigning a network number to the end station, allowing end stations to act as passive routers (able to contain a routing table but not allowed to route packets), or allowing end stations to request their network numbers from a local router. In more complex networks, end stations can query *name servers* that reside on the network for a name/address translation.

A routers is assigned network numbers to the ports that directly attach to its networks. It basically has no other way to determine its local address. A network administrator must assign these network numbers when the routers are initialized. How routers determine all the network numbers on the entire network is the topic of the next discussion.

Network Numbers

- With the addition of routers, there are now two types of addresses on the network:
  - network numbers, and
  - MAC addresses.

- XNS network numbers are 32 bits long, allowing for 4,294,967,294 unique network numbers.

- Multiple methods for acquiring a network number:
  - Routers are assigned their network numbers, usually one per port.
  - End stations can listen to the network (router updates).
  - It can be assigned to an end station.
  - End stations can build passive tables based on router updates.
  - An end station can request it from a router.

- An end station can acquire a remote stations network address from a name server.

ROUTING TABLES

Routers perform the following functions:

- Respond to end stations for network reachability.

- Respond to network stations for network number identification.

- Route packets to a destination network.

- Update other routers on the internet with reachability information.

Routers keep track of all network numbers on an internet by creating and maintaining routing tables. A routing table is nothing more than a section of memory in the router that contains a network number and some specific information about the network number. These tables are maintained in the router's internal memory, and are dynamic. This means that if a route to a destination network changes, the router changes the reachability information about that network.

In order to respond to the above responsibilities a routing table must contain five fields:

- A known network number,

- The metric (hop count) for that network number,

- The MAC address of where to forward the packet,

- The amount of time since the router heard about the network, and

- The port number on the router to which a packet may be forwarded.

Routing Table

Network	Hops	Next Hop	Age	Port ID
1	1	B	30	1
2	1	C	45	2
3	2	D	20	1
4	3	D	5	2

• Router functions:
  Respond to end stations for network reachability information.
  Respond to network stations for network number identification.
  Router packets to a destination network.
  Update other routers on the internet with reachability information.

• Routing tables contain:
  A known network number on the internet.
  A cost (hop count) for that network number.
  The MAC address of where to forward the packet.
  — This could be the MAC address of the local port, indicating the network number is local.
  — It could also be the MAC address of the next hop router, indicating the network number is not local.
  The amount of time elapsed since the router has heard about that network.
  The port number on the router on their network number.

• Routers update other routers on their network only.
  In other words, routers that are directly attached to the same cable segment as itself.

• First entries in the table are those networks that are directly attached to the router.

ROUTING TABLE FIELDS

The first field in the table is the network number. When a router is initialized it places into its table the network addresses of the networks that are directly attached to it. These network addresses are assigned to it by the network administrator that intialized the router.

Next, the router (depending on the router or specific network protocol implementation) informs other routers on its directly attached LANs about its directly attached networks by transmitting a packet (usually called a *response packet*) on all of its active ports. This update packet contains two entries from its routing table: the network numbers of its ports and the cost (hop count, explained later) of each.

Other routers that are attached to the same cable segments to which the router is attached will receive this information and update their tables with the network numbers of the new router. It is important to note that the original update packet by this router is not propagated throughout the whole internet. Only those routers that are directly attached to the same LANs as the router that sent the update packet receive and process the packet. When those routers update their tables, they send out their updated tables on all their active ports. This way, the network reachability information is propagated throughout the internet.

The new router then transmits a request packet asking other routers on the network for information about other network numbers that are on the internet. This request packet is transmitted on all active ports on the new router. This packet is not propagated throughout the internet; only the routers that are attached to the same LANs as the new router receive and process this packet.

When other routers receive this request they send their routing tables to the requesting router. When the requesting router receives this information, it updates its table. All this is accomplished dynamically; routers periodically inform other routers on the network with reachability information about networks on the internet.

Routing Table Fields

- The first entries in the routing table will be the directly attached network numbers.

- An XNS router should then broadcast its table to its directly attached networks.

- Other routers on that router's network will receive and process this information.
  - They update their tables and broadcast their tables to their attached networks.

  - The original packet is not propagated throughout the entire internet.
    » It is consumed, processed, and then propagated by the routers that are attached to the broadcasting router.

- The newly initialized router then requests network information from the other routers.

- Other routers should respond to this request by sending their tables to the requesting router.
  - Only those routers that are attached to the same network as the requesting router will send their tables.
  - Other routers do not receive the request.

ROUTING INFORMATION PROTOCOL (RIP)

Routers informing other routers about network number that they know about is known as a *routing update protocol*. A routing update protocol operates independent of any specific network protocol. The most common routing update protocol used is known as the Routing Information Protocol (RIP). It was developed by Xerox Corporation to be used on its network protocol known as XNS IDP. Since RIP is an independent update protocol, other protocols (TCP/IP, AppleTalk, and so forth) have adapted RIP for use on those individual protocols. Once RIP is adapted to run with a various network protocol, it becomes specific to that protocol. One RIP implementation cannot update another RIP implementation; that is, AppleTalk RIP cannot update a network that is running XNS RIP (though they may run on the same internet).

RIP is known as a *distance vector protocol*. The vector is the network number and the distance is the cost associated to the network number. RIP identifies network reachability based on cost. For RIP, this cost is called the *hop count*. One hop is considered to be one router traversed. Networks that are directly attached to the router automatically have a hop count of one in the routing table (this can be set to any number 1 through 15, but it is usually set to a 1). A hop count of sixteen means the network is considered unreachable; meaning the highest cost between any two networks can be fifteen hops, or fifteen routers.

RIP was devised for small to medium sized networks that are stable in that the topology does not change that often. These changes could be new networks being added, links that become disabled, etc. RIP is very slow to converge a network. (Convergence is the ability of an internetwork to reconfigure itself in the event of a topology change. The shorter the convergence time, the better the ability to control loops and lost packets.)

Routing Information Protocol (RIP)

- Known as a routing table update protocol.

- Most commonly found router update protocol is called Routing Information Protocol (RIP).

- Developed by Xerox and gained widespread acceptance by the proliferation of TCP/IP's implementation of it in UNIX.

- Other protocols (AppleTalk, NetWare) adopted RIP as their standard routing update protocol.
  - Different protocol implementations of RIP cannot update each other.

- Known as a distance vector protocol.
  - Vector is the network number and the distance is how far away (hops) the network is.
  - One hop is considered one router traversed.

- Devised for very stable, small-to-medium size networks (less than a few hundred nodes).

A COMPLETED TABLE

The following illustration shows a network that has four Ethernet segments; network numbers 1 and 2 are assigned to router A, network numbers 2 and 3 are assigned to router B, and network numbers 3 and 4 are assigned to router C. The routing table in router A has a hop count of one for networks 1 and 2, since they are directly connected to router A. Router A's entry for network 3 has a hop count of two, since there are two routers separating network 1 and 3. The entry for network 4 would have a hop count of three, since there are three routers separating network 1 and network 4. This may seem odd but a router always includes itself in the hop count calculation.

Router B would have a hop count of one for networks 2 and 3, since they are directly attached to it. The hop count for network 1 would be two, and the hop count for network 4 would also be two.

Router C would have a hop count of one for networks 3 and 4, two for network 2, and three for network 1. A router must include itself in the total hop count for a network number.

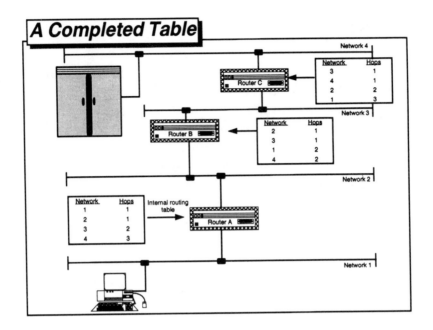

A Completed Table

• Router A's table shows:

    Networks 1 and 2 are directly attached with a hop count of one.

    Network 3 is two hops away.

       — Even though it is only 1 router away, a router must include itself in the cost.

    Network 4 is three hops away.

• Router B's table shows:

    Networks 2 and 3 are directly attached with a hop count of one.

    Network 1 is two hops away.

    Network 4 is two hops away.

• Router C's table shows:

    Networks 3 and 4 are directly attached with a hop count of one.

    Network 2 is two hops away.

    Network 1 is three hops away.

CALCULATING THE COST

How do routers calculate hop counts? As stated earlier, when a router is initialized, each port is pre-configured by the network administrator to have a hop count of 1. This number can be set to any number from 1 to 15; usually it is set to 1. When router A transmits its table to the network, it sends the table out its ports to networks 1 and 2 (this does not include a protocol known as split horizon, which is explained later). Router B receives this information and adds 1 to each of the hop count entries in the received table. It adds 1 because the hop count cost assigned to the received port is 1. Router B then compares the received table to its internal table. When router B compares the first entry, network 1 with a hop count of 2, it will notice that it does not have this entry in its table and will make an entry. Router B then compares the next entry in the received table, network 2 with a hop count of 2. Router B will notice that it already has an entry in its table for network 2 and that it has a lower hop count. Router B will then discard that entry.

Router B then transmits its table to networks 2 and 3. Router C receives this table and it adds 1 to each of the hop count fields in the received table. Router C then compares the received table to its table. It adds the network 1 entry to its table with a hop count of 3. It adds the entry for network 2 with a hop count of 2. It discards the entry for network 3 because it has an entry for network 3 with a lower hop count.

Router A then receives router B's table and adds the entry for network 3 with a hop count of 2. The other entries are discarded, because router A has a lower hop count to those networks.

When a table is updated, the router does not usually transmit it back out immediately. There is a periodic timer (every thirty seconds with XNS) that will expire in the router, and the router will then transmit its table out. Therefore, depending on the size of the internet, it may take a while to propagate this information to the whole internet.

Router C receives Router B's table and updates its table about networks 1 and 2 and discards the information about network 3.

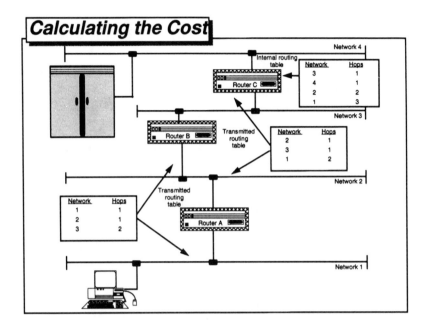

- The above slide does not include split horizon, which is explained later.

- Router A initializes and transmits its table out its directly connected ports.
    Router B receives this table and adds 1 to each entry in the received table.
        — This is the cost of the port the table was received on.
    Router B compares the received table with its internal table.
        — It does not have an entry for network 1 so it adds network 1 with a hop count of 2.
        — It has an entry for network 2 and it does not change that entry.

- Router B transmits its table out its directly connected ports.
    Router B does not yet know about network 4.

- Router A receives this table and adds one to each entry in the received table and it compares the received table to its internal table.
    It does not have an entry for network 3, so it adds network 3 with a hop count of 2.
    It has entries for networks 1 and 2 with a lower cost, so it does not change those entries.

- Router C receives B's routing table and adds 1 to each entry in the table and adds networks 1 and 2, and does not change the rest of its table.

CALCULATING THE COST (CONT.)

When router C transmits its table to networks 3 and 4, router B adds 1 to each of the entries in the received table. The only entry added is for network 4. It will add this entry with a hop count of two. The other entries will be discarded, for router B already has entries for networks 1, 2, and 3. Router B transmits its table again to networks 2 and 3. Router A updates its table because there is a new network that was not in router B's previous update. Network 4 is entered into router A's table with a hop count of three. The other entries are discarded.

All known and active networks have now been propagated throughout the internet. All routers know about all networks and how to route packets to those networks. The previous discussion shows one way that routers update each other. This update procedure could happen in any sequence. If all the routers were powered on at the same time, each would place the directly attached network numbers in their tables and each would transmit their tables out the ports. Each router, in turn, would update their tables based on the received tables. After this initial table update, the routers transmit their tables at thirty-second intervals. This will happen even when there have been no changes in the network. The whole table is transmitted. The transmitted table is medium-independent. Routing updates happen at the same rate on a slow-speed serial line as on a high-speed LAN. In other words, the periodic timer is the same regardless of the speed of the medium.

You should be able to see how network numbers are propagated throughout the network. It is the responsibility of the routers to propagate this reachability information to other routers.

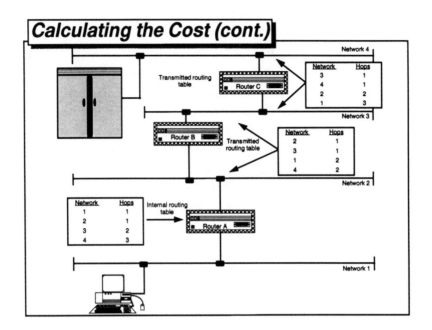

Calculating the Cost (cont.)

- Router C transmits its table out all of its active ports.
    Router B updates its table by adding network 4 with a hop count of two.
    It does not change the rest of the entries in its table.
    Router B transmits its tables.
    Router A receives B's table and adds network 4 with a hop count of three.
    Router A does not change the rest of the entries in its table.

- All routers are now updated with all the active network numbers.

- The routing tables from each router will be broadcast periodically.
    Each protocol implementation is different.
    Broadcast times are not synchronized, allowing each router to broadcast its table on its own time.

- When a routing table is updated, the updated table is not necessarily transmitted out immediately.
    When using the RIP protocol, this is true.
    Other protocols are different.

RIP DISADVANTAGES

RIP offered a great relief in the routing world. It allowed for dynamic routing updates and dynamic convergence (the ability of the internet to find alternate routes in the event of a failure). But it does have certain disadvantages. These disadvantages are slow convergence, and the possiblity of forming loops while converging. The previous two disadvantages are best explained through an example.

Networks 1, 2, and 3 are separated by routers A and B. Router A connects network 1 and 2 and router B connects networks 2 and 3. The routers have been initialized and the router tables of each routing contains complete information about the internet. Router A contains networks 1 and 2 with a hop count of 1 and network 3 with a hop count of 3. Router B contains networks 2 and 3 with a hop count of 1 and network 1 with a hop count of 2.

Now suppose that router A loses its connection with network 1. In other words, network 1 becomes disabled. Router A will change the entry in its table for network 1 so that the hop count is set to 16 (a hop count of 16 means that the network is not reachable). Before router A can update any other routers on the network, router B transmits its table to networks 2 and 3. Notice that with RIP, the table updates are not synchronized. A router broadcasts its table every thirty seconds, which may be at different times than another router transmits its table. One should notice that the only entries in a broadcast table are the network number and a hop count.

Router A receives this update and notices that router B can get to network 1 with a hop count of 2. Router A updates its table for network 1 because router B's path contains a lower hop count. The next hop entry in router A's table indicates router B as the next hop in the path to network 1.

Router A now routes packets destined for network 1 back to router B. In turn, router B sends them back to router A (according to its table, router A still has the path to network 1. Router A never got the chance to update router B). All packets destined for network 1 will loop between router's A and B, because RIP was unable to converge the internet quickly, which resulted in a loop. Future routing table updates will close this loop but it may take a few minutes to close it. This is called a slow convergence time.

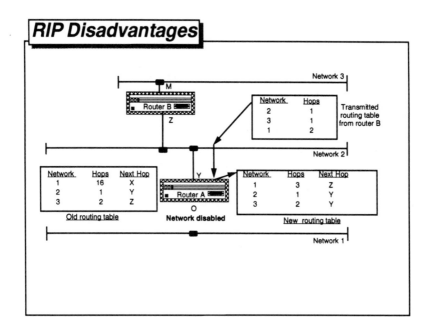

- When RIP was implemented, existing routers were being manually configured.

- This is a very tedious task and it does not work well in large and changing environments.

- RIP allows dynamic building of tables and dynamic convergence of the network in the event of a failure.

- Disadvantage example:
    Router A has a direct connection to networks 1 and 2.
    Router B has a direct connection to networks 2 and 3.
        — Router B also knows that to get to network 1; it must send the packet to router A.
    If router A loses its link to network 1:
        — It puts an entry in its table for network 1 with a hop count of 16, indicating that it is unreachable.
    Before router A has a chance to update any other routers, router B sends out its table indicating that network 1 is two hops away.
        — Router A receives this and updates its table (3 is less than 16) for network 1 with a hop count of 3, and indicates router B is the next hop to network 1.
        — Now all packets for network 1 received by router A are sent to router B.
        + Router B sends them to router A, and a loop is formed.

SPLIT HORIZON

Generally, inside the network layer header there is a safeguard to check for looping packets. For XNS it is called the Transport Control field. Each time the packet traverses a router, this field is incremented by 1. If this field reaches 16, the packet is dropped. Eventually, future routing table updates between the two routers will disable this loop, because each update will increase the hop count in each router's table by 1. Eventually, the tables will have an entries of 16. It will take many updates (every thirty seconds) before the loop is disabled. To eliminate this particular problem, another protocol called *split horizon* was added to the RIP protocol. Almost all implementations of the RIP protocol use split horizon.

Split horizon is a protocol that prevents the beforementioned condition from happening. Split horizon states that after a router receives an update on a network interface, after updating its table, it will not submit those same updates back out the port that it received the update from.

For example, when Router A updates transmits its routing table to network 2, Router B receives it and updates its table for network 1 with a hop count of 2. When router B transmits its table to network 2, it will not contain the entry for network 1; it will contain the entries for network 2 (hop count of 1) and network 3 (hop count of 1). Network 2 is in the update table because it is directly attached to router B. Split horizon does not keep network 2 from being included in the table, just network 1. In other words, Router B received an update from Router A about network 1. Router B, in turn, will not include this entry when it transmits its table out the port where it learned network 1.

This way, if Router A's interface to network 1 were to become disabled, it could update its table for network 1 with a hop count of 16 (indicating network 1 is not reachable). If Router B transmits its table to network 2 before Router A does and Router A receives Router B's table, Router A will not update its entry for network 1. Router B's update did not contain an entry for network 1. When Router A eventually transmits its table to network 2, Router B will receive the information about network 1 being disabled. It will place a 16 for the hop count associated with network 1 in its table (a hop count of 16 overrides any other hop count entry). Therefore, if there were any routers beyond Router B, they would eventually be updated with the information about network 1 by Router B. If Router B were to receive any packets destined for network 1, it would not route these packets.

There are many other additions that have been made to the RIP protocol to make it more viable. Please check the Bibliography for more information on routing protocols.

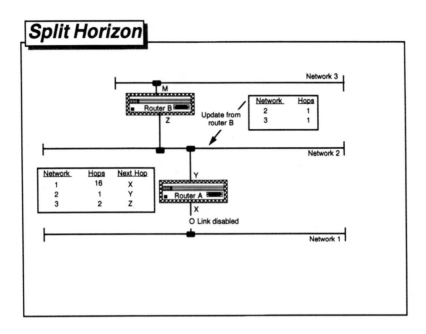

- Spilt horizon solves the convergence problem that may lead to loops being formed when a network link becomes disabled.

- It states that when a router learns about a network it will not broadcast the information about that network back out the same port on where it learned the information.

- Example:
    Router A loses a connection with network 1 and places an entry for network 1 in its table with a hop count of 16.
    Router B sends out its table, but this time there is no entry for network 1, for it learned about network 1 from the same port to which it is transmitting.
    Router A eventually sends out its table, and router B will then be informed that network 1 is disabled (hop count is 16).

- Split horizon only works between two routers.
    All routers in the network must be set up for split horizon for it to be effective.

MULTIPROTOCOL ROUTERS OR BRIDGE/ROUTERS

Most LANs operate with many different protocols on the same cable plant. LANs were developed to be protocol-transparent but also to allow for any type of network station attachment. There are not separate cable plants for each type of network attachment. IBM PCs, Apple Macintoshes, Sun Microsytems UNIX workstations, terminal servers, or any other type of host computer may be attached to the same LAN. Each attachment will probably have its own protocol. There may be AppleTalk for Apple computers, Novell NetWare for PCs, TCP/IP for UNIX workstations, Local Area Transport (LAT) for DEC terminal servers, etc. All of these network attachments and their protocols can operate on the same LAN; furthermore, one network station may use multiple protocols. In order for the protocols to operate efficiently, the use of a multiprotocol router should be used.

To require one router for each protocol would be ludicrous. Furthermore, placing independent bridges on a network with separate routers could be very dangerous. With so many protocols, an endless stream of routers and bridges would be needed.

Around 1986, multiprotocol routers entered the commercial marketplace. These devices allow multiple protocols—AppleTalk, DECnet, TCP/IP, and LAT protocols, for instance—to operate over the same box, which greatly simplifies the internetwork. The multiprotocol router is a complex device, but its functional operation is quite simple. Inside every packet, no matter what type, there are identifiers that indicate the type of packet it is. The multiprotocol router receives that packet and determines what packet type (the protocol type) it is. From here, it passes the packet to the appropriate packet router (known as a redirector) in the multiprotocol router. In other words, there are multiple routers running independently in the same box. The multiprotocol router receives a packet and routes it if it can. If it can't it tries to bridge it. If neither operation is available for the packet, the router will drop the packet. Each redirector in the multiprotocol router operates independently. Their operation will be covered in more detail later in this section.

Multiprotocol Routers

- LANs currently operate with many different types of protocols.
  - Apple Computers can use AppleTalk.
  - UNIX workstations use TCP/IP.
  - Client/Server applications could use Novell NetWare.

- To require one router for each protocol on the LAN is not efficient.

- Multiprotocol routers were invented to handle this.
  - Arrived around 1986.
  - Routes not only based on the network IDs but are able to pass the packet to the correct protocol processor by examining the Type of packet.

MULTIPROTOCOL ROUTERS AND BLOCK DIAGRAM

The multiprotocol router is an extremely complicated device. It must be able to operate simultaneously with any number of different hardware interfaces—Token Ring, Ethernet, Synchronous, FDDI, for instance—as well as up to twenty different protocols (this includes all the subsets of each protocol). The multiprotocol router allows for AppleTalk, XNS, IPX (Novell NetWare), TCP/IP, as well as both types of bridging and other protocols to run simultaneously in the same physical box.

It operates based on certain information in the packet. All packets contain some identifier as to what protocol owns the packet. With Ethernet, it is the type field. With Token Ring, it is the DSAP or SSAP field. For protocols using SNAP, its header also contains the Ethernet type field. It is based on information in these fields that the multiprotocol router will make its decision.

When the multiprotocol router that supports transparent bridging receives a packet, it will first add the MAC address to the bridge forwarding table (if bridging is enabled). After this, it will check to see if the packet is destined for itself. If it is, the multiprotocol router will process the packet and respond to the requester if necessary. If it is not necessary to respond, the multiprotocol router will determine the protocol "owner" of the packet. It will then check to see whether it can route this packet. If the packet can be routed, it will be given to that individual redirector (based on the protocol identifier in the packet) in the multiprotocol router for it to process. If the packet protocol type is not running, it will determine whether it can bridge the packet. If it can bridge the packet, it will do so using the normal bridge protocol. Otherwise, it will discard the packet.

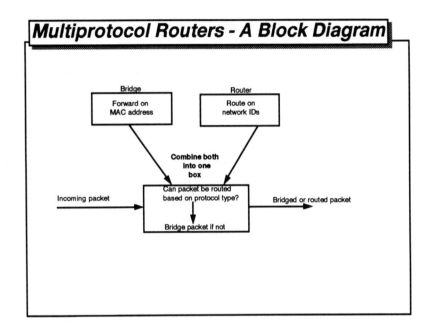

Multiprotocol Routers - A Block Diagram

• In modern LANs there are multiple protocols running on any single internet.

• The multiprotocol router is a device that allows simultaneous routing of different protocols and bridging throughout the same box.

• A multiprotocol router is an extremely complicated device.

• The multiprotocol router operates based on certain identifiers in the packet.
  This could be the Ethernet type field of the Ethernet packet.
  This could be the SAP fields of IEEE 802.x packets.

• When a multiprotocol router receives a packet:
  If transparent bridging is enabled, it tries to learn the packet's MAC address.
  Next, it reads the protocol identifier in the packet.
  Should the multiprotocol router route the packet?
      — If yes, then give the packet to the process that can route its packet type.
  Is the packet to be bridged?
      — If yes, give the packet to the task that can bridge the packet.
      — If no, discard the packet and go on to the next packet.

MULTIPROTOCOL ROUTER FLOWCHART

Every packet received will be processed in the manner shown in the illustration at right. In theory, the multiprotocol router is a relatively simple node; but in reality, it is very complex. The operation is simple: route the packet if the appropriate router software is enabled, if not, bridge or discard it.

The following shows a flowchart diagram of the multiprotocol router. The flowchart assumes transparent bridging is enabled.

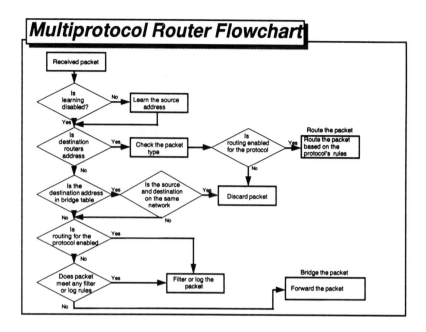

- The above flowchart shows the flow for a received packet on a multiprotocol router.

- Logging is the capability of a bridge or a router to write to a log file about an event that it was set up to look for.
    Similar to a static filter entry except that if the condition occurs, the multiprotocol router writes the condition to a log file.

GATEWAYS

Gateways are complex devices that provide protocol translation of some type. For example, the conversion of a synchronous SNA frame to an asynchronous stream is an example of a gateway. Coverting between X.25 and SNA is another example of a gateway.

Gateways differ from routers and bridges in that they perform protocol translation of some type. This is more than simple medium translation (for example, converting from a Token Ring packet to an Ethernet packet). A gateway converts one protocol type to another.

The theory of operation of a gateway is beyond the scope of this book. It is mentioned for simple comparison.

Gateways

- Complex devices that provide for a protocol translation during data forwarding.

- Examples are:
  - X.25 to SNA
  - asynchronous to synchronous serial stream

- Gateways differ from bridges and routers in that they perform protocol translation of the incoming packet to match the outgoing stream.

BIBLIOGRAPHY

3Com Corporation, NetBuilder Bridge/Router Operation Guide, manual number 09-0251-000, April (1991).

ANSI Std 802.2–1985 ISO/DIS 8802/2 Local Area Networks Logical Link Control, 1984 Fourth Printing, July (1986).

ANSI X3.166-1990 also ISO 9314-3: 1990, Physical Layer, Medium Dependent (PMD).

ANSI X3.148-1988 also ISO 9314-1: 1989, Physical Layer Protocol (PHY).

Black, Uyless, *Computer Networks Protocols, Standards and Interfaces* (New York: Prentice-Hall 1987).

Black Uyless, *OSI—A Model for Computer Communications Standards* (New York: Prentice-Hall, Inc. 1991).

Dalal, Yogen K. and Printis, Robert S., *48-bit Absolute Internet and Ethernet Host Numbers,* (available from Xerox Corporation Office Systems Division) (1981).

Digital, Intel, and Xerox Corporations, *The Ethernet: A Local Area Network, Data Link Layer and Physical Layer Specifications,* Version 2.0 November (1982).

FDDI Station Management, Revision 6.2.

IBM *Token Ring Network Architecture Reference,* 3rd ed., order number SC30-3374-02, September (1989).

IEEE Std 802.5-1989, "Local Area Networks 802.5 Token Ring Access Method," published by The Institute of Electrical and Electronic Engineers, first printing 1989.

IEEE Document Standard P802.5M-D6, "Unapproved Draft of Media Access Control (MAC) Bridges" P802.1D, (1991).

IEEE Document Standard 802.1d, May 2, October (1991).

IEEE Document Standard 802.1H, "MAC Layer Bridging of Ethernet in IEEE 802 LANs".

IEEE "Supplements to Carrier Sense Multiple Access with Collision Detection (CSMA/CD) Access Method and Physical Layer Specifications", The Institute of Electrical and Electronics Engineers, Inc., (1989).

IEEE Standards for Local Area Networks "Token Ring Access Method and Physical Layer Specifications", The Institute of Electrical and Electronics Engineers, Inc., September (1989).

Medium Access Control. ANSI X3.139-1987 also ISO 9314-2 (1989).

Naugle, Matthew G., *Local Area Networking* (New York: McGraw-Hill, 1991).

Naugle, Matthew G., *Network Protocol Handbook* (New York: McGraw-Hill, 1994).

Perlman, Radia, *Interconnections Bridges and Routers* (Addison-Wesley Publishing Company, Inc., 1992).

Stallings, William. *Handbook of Computer Communications Standards, The Open Systems Interconnection (OSI) Model and OSI Related Standards* (New York: Prentice-Hall, 1988), Vol. 1, 1st ed.

Tanenbaum, Andrew S., *Computer Networks,* 2nd ed. (New York: Prentice-Hall, Inc., 1989).

INDEX